Navigating the English Language Arts Common Core State Standards

BOOK TWO

Navigating the English Language Arts Common Core State Standards

Angela Peery | Maryann D. Wiggs
Thomasina D. Piercy | Cathy J. Lassiter
Lisa Cebelak

ENGLEWOOD, COLORADO

The Leadership and Learning Center
317 Inverness Way South, Suite 150
Englewood, Colorado 80112
Phone 1.866.399.6019 | Fax 303.504.9417
www.LeadandLearn.com

Published by Lead + Learn Press, a division of Houghton Mifflin Harcourt.

Library of Congress Cataloging-in-Publication Data

Navigating the English language arts common core state standards /
Angela Peery ... [et al.].
p. cm. — (Getting ready for the common core handbook series ; bk. Two)
Includes bibliographical references and index.
ISBN 978-1-935588-15-3 (alk. paper)
1. Language arts—United States. 2. Education—Standards—United States. I. Peery, Angela B., 1964-
LB1576.N338 2011
372.6—dc23

2011040559

ISBN 978-1-935588-15-3

Printed in the United States of America

16 15 14 13 12 03 04 05 06 07 08

Contents

List of Exhibits

About the Authors

Angela Peery is a Senior Professional Development Associate with The Leadership and Learning Center. Her extensive experience includes more than 10 years of classroom teaching, four years as a high school assistant principal, and various leadership positions at the building, district, and state levels. She has taught undergraduate and graduate courses in both education and English, and has been a codirector of a National Writing Project site. She has published five books, including *Writing Matters in Every Classroom* (2009) and *The Data Teams Experience: A Guide for Effective Meetings* (2011). Angela also generated several professional development seminars and accompanying materials, including the *Writing to Learn* series and *Power Strategies for Effective Teaching.*

With more than four decades of experience in education, **Maryann D. Wiggs** brings an abundance of expertise and wisdom to her presentations, ensuring that teachers and administrators gain practical strategies for enhancing instructional performance. As the former Assistant Superintendent of Curriculum and Instruction and Executive Director of Learning Services in two Colorado school districts, Maryann has been instrumental in orchestrating the alignment of all aspects of the leaders' and teachers' work to improve the quality of instruction in the classroom, including alignment of standards, assessment, curriculum, instruction, interventions, supervision, and evaluation. Maryann is a former speech pathologist, special and general education teacher, behavior consultant, and teacher leader, having served learners at the elementary, middle, high school, and college levels.

Thomasina D. Piercy is a Professional Development Associate with The Leadership and Learning Center. She earned her Ph.D. in curriculum and instruction with a focus on reading from the University of Maryland. As a pre-K–12 district literacy leader, principal, and teacher, she taught graduate writing and reading courses to educators from various states in the East Coast region. Thommie's research received the Reading Research Award from the State of Maryland International Reading Association Council. She was honored with the Joseph R. Bailer Award from McDaniel College in Maryland for her distinguished career in education, and she was the recipient of the Court Appointed Special Advocates for Children Hero Award. As a teacher, she was named one of five expert teachers by the Maryland State Department of Education.

Cathy J. Lassiter is a Professional Development Associate with The Leadership and Learning Center. She brings a sense of passion and energy to her work on school leadership, data, curriculum, instruction, and the Common Core State Standards. She has worked with superintendents, state departments of education, school boards, principals, and teachers to improve leadership and instructional practices across the United States, Canada, and Bermuda. Over the course of her 28 years in public urban education, she was a middle and high school teacher, middle school principal, and central office administrator. While serving her district as the Senior Director of Curriculum, Instruction and Staff Development, the district won the prestigious Broad Prize in Urban Education in 2005. Cathy also supervised middle schools in her role as the Executive Director. Cathy earned her doctorate in administration and policy studies from The George Washington University, and has also taught courses there in educational leadership.

Lisa Cebelak is a Professional Development Associate with The Leadership and Learning Center. For the past nine years she worked for the Thornapple Kellogg School District in Middleville, Michigan, where she was a secondary literacy coach and English language arts teacher. Lisa previously taught English at the American International School of Costa Rica. She has presented literacy strategies and workshops at the state and national levels, and has worked on projects such as partnering with The Ball Foundation and the National Council of Teachers of English (NCTE) in support of teachers using data to drive their instruction.

Introduction

Embodied within the English Language Arts Common Core State Standards (ELA CCSS) is the hope for literacy offered by this new era. But hope alone cannot carry the weight of change to fruition. Trust is needed for these new standards, wrought with high expectations, to succeed. How is the fiber of trust woven into the entire CCSS document? Considering all the good intentions of past initiatives, how can we trust that the new collective approach states are taking to provide excellent educational practices will produce the results today's students demand?

This handbook, the second in The Leadership and Learning Center's *Getting Ready for the Common Core* series, is a unique, rich resource that succinctly summarizes the extensive key components in the ELA CCSS, uncovers the deep connections between the four literacy strands, explains the base of research, and provides immediately transferable resources. The chapters within this handbook provide deep understanding and a strong foundation for educators by placing a laser focus on specific elements within the ELA CCSS. The powerful connections within the chapters fasten the CCSS to trust, a vital component of change.

Chapter One, "The Powerful Influence of the Learning Progressions in Planning for Instruction and Assessment," provides a unique, visually comprehensive view of the learning pathways students follow throughout the CCSS. These indispensible guidelines along the path to application, combined with an overview of the potential of the Common Core, including formative assessment connections, are succinctly conveyed through the expertise of author Maryann Wiggs.

How do you begin developing an encompassing understanding of the entire ELA Common Core State Standards document? In Chapter Two, author Angela Peery provides a comprehensive overview of the expectations based on the four prominent features of the reading strand. Clearly differentiating the Common Core standards for reading from past expectations, she uses the features of rigor, range, reasoning, and relationships to describe embedded characteristics. Including a detailed summary of the key features, this chapter, "The 'New' Reading—Rigor, Range, Reasoning, and Relationships," is a rich resource for developing a thorough foundational understanding of the ELA Common Core standards.

Chapter Three, "The 'New' Writing—Sharing, Shifting, and Sustaining Student Writing," provides a meticulous look at the writing strand of the Common Core. Providing a focused overview, author Lisa Cebelak integrates the key writing components to provide a deep understanding of both the broad college and career readiness anchor standards and the grade-specific standards, including the dramatic shifts in emphasis of expectations for shared responsibility, increased argument and informational/explanatory writing, and extended writing that allows for multiple drafts, research, and revision.

In Chapter Four, "The 'New' Speaking and Listening—The Need for Rich Conversations and Showcasing Knowledge," Lisa Cebelak again provides a succinct summary of a CCSS strand that has distinctive "new" expectations. This chapter highlights why the speaking and listening strand cannot be dismissed as a lightweight part of the standards by explaining its significant contributions. Composed of six anchor standards divided into two areas—comprehension and collaboration, and presentation of knowledge and ideas—the author's suggestions for implementation complement the robust potential of this strand.

Focusing on the language strand of the CCSS, Chapter Five highlights distinct shifts from current standards-based expectations. Author Angela Peery's expertise in this chapter, "So Much More than Grammar—How the Language Strand of the Common Core Supports and Strengthens the Other Strands," focuses attention on the demands of the six college and career readiness anchor standards for language by toggling the key differences between current standards and the new CCSS demands. Explicit examples direct attention to the depth of the new expectations.

In Chapter Six, "Preparing for Common Core Implementation of Literacy Expectations," I provide the context that guided the creation of the ELA CCSS demands, which dramatically raised text complexity expectations to strengthen the literacy core in major disciplines. Specific suggestions for teachers, principals, and district leaders to support transitioning instruction aligned with the CCSS are included. This chapter provides information about how to approach literacy leadership with guiding questions, analyze district curricular crosswalks, overcome digital reading barriers, establish goals for "invisible excellence" growth, and align the cognitive demand for core literacy instruction.

In Chapter Seven, I focus on text complexity, the hallmark of the ELA Common Core, and how it prepares students to meet future challenges. Included in "Text Complexity Structures: Comprehending Increased Levels of Complex Text" are a variety of resources to structure teacher judgment and confidence in determining levels of text complexity. Together with the increased cognitive demand of the CCSS and assessments, the detailed teacher resources align instruction for increased comprehension.

In Chapter Eight, I provide a Disciplinary Literacy instructional model for complex texts. This chapter, "Increasing Students' Deeper Understanding of Complex Texts with Disciplinary Literacy Instruction," supports alignment of CCSS curricular crosswalks where they are most narrow. Disciplinary Literacy instruction with text-specific questions guides students to read like historians, scientists, mathematicians, or literary critics. Specific steps support students' deep understanding of complex texts in major content areas.

Chapter Nine, "Teaching Strategies for Reading for Information in the English Language Arts Common Core," provides research-based support for instruction of informational texts. With extensive detail, author Cathy Lassiter delineates learning progressions aligned with specific skills and strategies while providing multiple examples for explicit instruction that supports informational text. A wealth of resources to enhance comprehension and instruction are provided.

The first handbook in the *Getting Ready for the Common Core* series, *Navigating Implementation of the Common Core State Standards*, provides an overview of how the CCSS should influence leadership, teaching, and learning. The third handbook provides explicit suggestions aligned with the mathematics CCSS. The relationship of the Common Core to formative assessment processes and the practices of Professional Learning Communities and Data Teams for improvement and sustainability are the focus of the fourth handbook in the series.

The Common Core represents an unprecedented, united change effort throughout the United States, and nothing less than such an effort will prepare students for inhabiting the dynamic world of global connections, which is within their grasp today.

The Powerful Influence of the Learning Progressions in Planning for Instruction and Assessment

Maryann D. Wiggs

By its very nature, learning involves progression. To assist in its emergence, teachers need to understand the pathways along which students are expected to progress. These pathways or progressions ground both instruction and assessment.

—Heritage, 2008, p. 2

Among the most salient accomplishments in the design of the Common Core State Standards for English Language Arts and Literacy in History/Social Studies, Science, and Technical Subjects are the learning pathways that a student follows as he or she advances from one grade-specific standard to the next, leading to mastery of each college and career readiness (CCR) anchor standard. While the anchor standards taken together serve to provide focus on what matters most for college and career readiness in the area of English language arts, coherence is accomplished by the explicit articulation of knowledge and skills along the learning progressions. The specificity of the content within the learning progressions makes visible and clear the expectations for student learning (CCSSI, 2010a). In other words, the grade-specific standards clearly define competence at every level of schooling (Wiggs, 2011). This chapter focuses specifically on the utility of the learning progressions as a vehicle for educators to locate entry points for students in accessing valued learning targets, while supporting all students in advancing along the learning pathways toward preparedness for college, careers, and citizenship upon graduation from high school.

SYNTHESIS OF THE ENGLISH LANGUAGE ARTS COMMON CORE STATE STANDARDS

The college and career readiness anchor standards are the focal point for the learning trajectories embedded in the ELA Common Core State Standards document. The grade-specific standards, therefore, provide guidance to all K–12 teachers regarding the special role that each grade-level teacher holds in establishing the building blocks for the more complex learning to come. There is a one-to-one correspondence between each grade-specific standard and a college and career readiness anchor standard. Grade-specific standards define end-of-year expectations in each of the four literacy strands. The standards are based on a mastery model of learning whereby students are expected to demonstrate proficiency in each year's grade-specific standard and further advance knowledge and skills as they progress through the grades (CCSSI, 2010b, p. 8).

Having thorough knowledge of how each of the four literacy strands (reading, writing, speaking and listening, and language) work together in mutually reinforcing ways is critical for educators organizing the CCSS for instructional planning and assessment design. A more in-depth discussion on the topic of the design and organizational features of the Common Core State Standards for English Language Arts and Literacy in History/Social Studies, Science, and Technical Subjects is available in Chapter Two of *Navigating Implementation of the Common Core State Standards* (2011), the first book in the four-part *Getting Ready for the Common Core Handbook Series* from Lead + Learn Press.

Collectively there are just shy of 400 pages in the original ELA Common Core State Standards document and accompanying appendices, which can be accessed at www.corestandards.org. For a brief overview of the entire collection of ELA Common Core standards, Appendix A of this handbook provides readers with a short synthesis of the much larger document. The "Synthesis of the ELA CCSS" provides an overview of how the document is organized, includes a copy of each of the college and career anchor standards, highlights key features of each of the literacy strands, and provides readers with information about how to read the coding and numbering system unique to the ELA Common Core State Standards.

GRADE-SPECIFIC STANDARDS AND THE SPIRAL EFFECT

The "spiral effect" is a useful metaphor for further understanding how the learning progressions are structured to provide support for many more students to both access and accelerate through the learning pathways.

Consider the following two definitions from the Merriam-Webster online dictionary (www.merriam-webster.com):

> **Spiral** when used as an *adjective:* Of or relating to the advancement to higher levels through a series of cyclical movements.

Spiral when used as a *noun:* The path of a point in a plane moving around a central point while continuously receding from or approaching it.

The spiral effect metaphor relates to the ascending level of difficulty embedded in the content of each grade-specific standard as it approaches the college and career readiness anchor standard. The college and career readiness standards serve as the central point or significant learning expectation toward which all grade-specific standards aspire. As students move along the plane of a particular learning trajectory, they study the same expectation each year at ever-increasing increments of complexity and sophistication. The gradual cycling through repeated exposure to iterations of the same concepts and processes each year breaks complex learning expectations into manageable teaching and learning targets (Wiggs, 2011).

HOW TO USE LEARNING PROGRESSIONS AS A ROAD MAP FOR INSTRUCTION

"Spiral effect" tables provide models for how to read the grade-to-grade learning progressions that can be applied more broadly across all the ELA Common Core State Standards. To create the tables, the grade-specific standards related to each individual college and career readiness anchor standard are aligned next to one another to visually represent how learning is sequenced over time. At a glance, the tables provide a road map for the learning terrain to be navigated on the way to mastery.

The illustration in Exhibit 1.1: The Spiral Effect for CCR Reading Anchor Standard 3 demonstrates how students repeatedly practice mastered competencies from the year prior in the context of new competencies being "added" each year as the standard increases in complexity and sophistication. Notice how the new skills and concepts that are "added" to each grade level from the year prior are noted in **bold**.

HOW TO DESIGN SMALLER LEARNING PROGRESSIONS BY "UNWRAPPING" THE STANDARDS

The learning progressions in the ELA Common Core State Standards, depicted as vertically aligned grade-to-grade instructional sequences, have been engineered for student attainment. It is possible, at a glance, to view how learning is expected to be attained over time. Notice in Exhibit 1.2 how students in early elementary school begin the process of conducting short research projects that form the basis of the much more complex and sophisticated short and sustained research projects expected in high school. Notice also the density and complexity of the wording of Writing Standard 7 in grades 9–12. When each of the individual grade-specific standards is examined more closely, it is clear that within each standard a number of concepts and skills are represented, with varying degrees of hierarchy of cognitive demand embedded within.

By using the process of "unwrapping" the standards, as defined by Larry Ainsworth in his book *"Unwrapping" the Standards: A Simple Process to Make Standards Manageable* (2003), it is possible to zoom in to each grade-specific standard to reveal yet another layer of options for creating instructional learning sequences for students to both access and accelerate through grade-specific standards.

The Spiral Effect for CCR Reading Anchor Standard 3

Example of Grade-Specific Standards for Reading Standard 3

The example below illustrates how skills and concepts for end-of-year, grade-specific expectations for a given standard are both reinforced and expanded as students advance through the grades. The result is a ***"spiral effect"*** where students repeatedly practice mastered competencies from the year prior in the context of new competencies being "added" each year as the standard increases in complexity and sophistication. New skills and concepts "added" to each grade level from the year prior are noted in **bold.**

R.CCR.3	**CCR Reading Anchor Standard 3:** **Analyze how and why individuals, events, and ideas develop and interact over the course of a text.**	=
RL.11-12.3 Grade 11–12 students:	Analyze the **impact of the author's choices regarding how to develop and relate elements** of a story or drama **(e.g., where a story is set, how the action is ordered, how the characters are introduced and developed)**.	+
RL.9–10.3 Grade 9–10 students:	Analyze how **complex characters (e.g., those with multiple or conflicting motivations) develop over the course of a text,** interact with other characters, **and advance the plot or develop the theme.**	+
RL.8.3 Grade 8 students:	Analyze how particular **lines of dialogue or incidents** in a story or drama **propel the action, reveal aspects of a character, or provide a decision**.	+
RL.7.3 Grade 7 students:	**Analyze** how particular **elements** of a story or drama **interact (e.g., how setting shapes the characters or plot).**	+
RL.6.3 Grade 6 students:	Describe **how** a particular story's or drama's plot **unfolds in a series of episodes as well as how** the characters **respond or change as the plot moves toward resolution.**	+
RL.5.3 Grade 5 students:	**Compare and contrast two or more** characters, settings, or events in a story or drama, drawing on specific details in the text **(e.g., how characters interact)**.	+
RL.4.3 Grade 4 students:	Describe **in depth** a character, setting, **or event** in a story **or drama, drawing on specific details in the text (e.g., a character's thoughts, words, or actions).**	+
RL.3.3 Grade 3 students:	Describe characters in a story **(e.g., their traits, motivations, or feelings) and explain how their actions contribute to the sequence of events.**	+
RL.2.3 Grade 2 students:	Describe **how** characters in a story **respond to major events and challenges.**	+
RL.1.3 Grade 1 students:	**Describe** characters, settings, and major events in a story, **using key details.**	+
RL.K.3 Kindergarten students:	**With prompting and support, identify characters, settings, and major events in a story.**	+

Source: Adapted from CCSSI, 2010b, pp. 11, 12, 36, 38.

The Spiral Effect for CCR Writing Anchor Standard 7

Example of Grade-Specific Standards for Writing Standard 7

The example below illustrates how skills and concepts for end-of-year, grade-specific expectations for a given standard are both reinforced and expanded as students advance through the grades. The result is a ***"spiral effect"*** where students repeatedly practice mastered competencies from the year prior in the context of new competencies being "added" each year as the standard increases in complexity and sophistication. New skills and concepts "added" to each grade level from the year prior are noted in **bold.**

W.CCR.7	**CCR Writing Anchor Standard 7:** **Conduct short as well as more sustained research projects based on focused questions, demonstrating understanding of the subject under investigation.**	=
W.11–12.7 Grade 11–12 students:	Conduct short as well as more sustained research projects to answer a question (including a self-generated question) or solve a problem; narrow or broaden the inquiry when appropriate; synthesize multiple sources on the subject, demonstrating understanding of the subject under investigation.	+
W.9–10.7 Grade 9–10 students:	Conduct short **as well as more sustained** research projects to answer a question (including a self-generated question) **or solve a problem; narrow or broaden the inquiry when appropriate; synthesize multiple sources on the subject, demonstrating understanding of the subject under investigation.**	+
W.8.7 Grade 8 students:	Conduct short research projects to answer a question **(including a self-generated question),** drawing on several sources and generating additional related, focused questions **that allow for multiple avenues of exploration.**	+
W.7.7 Grade 7 students:	Conduct short research projects to answer a question**,** drawing on several sources and **generating additional related, focused questions for further research and investigations.**	+
W.6.7 Grade 6 students:	Conduct short research projects **to answer a question, drawing on several sources and refocusing the inquiry when appropriate.**	+
W.5.7 Grade 5 students:	Conduct short research projects that **use several sources** to build knowledge through investigation of different aspects of a topic.	+
W.4.7 Grade 4 students:	Conduct short research projects that build knowledge **through investigation of different aspects of a topic.**	+
W.3.7 Grade 3 students:	**Conduct short research projects that build knowledge about a topic.**	+
W.2.7 Grade 2 students:	Participate in shared research and writing projects (e.g., **read a number of books on a single topic to produce a report; record science observations**).	+
W.1.7 Grade 1 students:	Participate in shared research and writing projects (e.g., explore a number of **"how-to" books on a given topic and use them to write a sequence of instructions**).	+
W.K.7 Kindergarten students:	**Participate in shared research and writing projects (e.g., explore a number of books by a favorite author and express opinions about them).**	+

Source: CCSSI, 2010b, pp. 19, 21, 44, 46.

"Unwrapped" standards provide clarity as to what students must know (concepts) and be able to do (skills). When teachers take the time to analyze each standard and identify its essential concepts and skills, the result is more effective instructional planning, assessment, and student learning (Ainsworth, 2003, p. 1).

It is through the process of "unwrapping" that teachers are better able to manage and map out the sequence of instruction for students to meet grade-level expectations. Exhibit 1.3 illustrates the "unwrapped" Writing Standard 7 at the 11–12 grade span, which is identical to expectations in the 9–10 grade span. Notice the number of action verbs (skills) and the number of nouns and noun phrases (concepts) in the wording of this standard. It is only through the "unwrapping" process that the significant learning expectations that are embedded within the standards are revealed.

As a reminder, the grade-specific standards are written as end-of-year grade-level mastery expectations. Exhibit 1.4 takes the "unwrapped" standard example even further and illustrates how the concepts and skills revealed in the "unwrapped" standard can be mapped in an instructional sequence from less complex to more complex learning throughout the school year. The example in Exhibit 1.4 is for illustrative purposes; another educator mapping out the same "unwrapped" standard might very well arrive at a different instructional sequence with regard to how to map out the teaching of the concepts and skills in standard W.11–12.7.

"Unwrapping" the Standards

"Unwrapped" Standard W.11–12.7

STEP 1: Select the standard for the "unwrapping" process—**W.11–12.7**
STEP 2: Concepts—underline the key concepts, the important nouns or noun phrases.
STEP 3: Skills—circle or use CAPITAL LETTERS to identify verbs.

CONDUCT short as well as more sustained research projects to **ANSWER** a question (including a self-generated question) or **SOLVE** a problem. **NARROW** or **BROADEN** the inquiry when appropriate; **SYNTHESIZE** multiple sources on the subject, **DEMONSTRATING** understanding of the subject under investigation.

STEP 4: Create a Graphic Organizer
Next to each verb, list the approximate level of Bloom's Taxonomy of thinking skills.

Concepts (*What students need to know*):
- **Short research projects**
- **Sustained research projects**
- **Questions**
- **Self-generated questions**
- **Problem**
- **Inquiry**
- **Multiple sources on the subject**
- **Subject under investigation**

Skills (*What students must be able to do*):
- **CONDUCT**
- **ANSWER**
- **SOLVE**
- **NARROW OR BROADEN**
- **SYNTHESIZE**
- **DEMONSTRATE**

Bloom's Level	Graphic Organizer of "Unwrapped" Concepts and Skills
3-6	**CONDUCT** short research projects sustained research projects
2-4	**To ANSWER** a question a self-generated question
4	**To SOLVE** a problem
4	**NARROW or BROADEN** inquiry (when appropriate)
5	**SYNTHESIZE** multiple sources on the subject
2-3	**DEMONSTRATE** understanding of subject investigation

STEP 5: Determine Big Ideas—*These are enduring understandings students will remember long after the unit of study.*

1. **Research can be used to demonstrate understanding of a subject.**
2. **Focused questions guide my research.**
3. **Specific investigation strategies are used to conduct research.**

STEP 6: Write Essential Questions—*These guide instruction and assessment for all tasks, and the big ideas are answers to the essential questions.*

1. **What is the purpose of conducting research?**
2. **How do I decide what to research?**
3. **How do I conduct research?**

Example of Building an Instructional Sequence from an "Unwrapped" Standard

Instructional Learning Sequence for W.11–12.7				
Conduct short research	Conduct short research	Conduct short research	Conduct sustained research	Conduct sustained research
		To answer a question	To answer a question	To answer a self-generated question
	To answer a self-generated question	To solve a problem	To solve a problem	To solve a problem
To answer a question	Broaden inquiry	Narrow inquiry	Broaden inquiry	Narrow inquiry
Broaden inquiry	Synthesize resources	Synthesize multiple sources	Synthesize multiple sources	Synthesize multiple sources
Demonstrate understanding of the subject under investigation	Demonstrate understanding of the subject under investigation	Demonstrate understanding of the subject under investigation	Demonstrate understanding of the subject under investigation	Demonstrate understanding of the subject under investigation
TIME →				

HOW TO USE LEARNING PROGRESSIONS TO MAKE ADJUSTMENTS TO INSTRUCTION

> *The concept of learning progression offers one promising approach to developing the knowledge needed to define the "track" that students may be on, or should be on. Learning progressions can inform teachers about what to expect from their students. They provide an empirical basis for choices about when to teach what to whom.*
>
> —Consortium for Policy Research in Education, 2011, p. 12

Clearly articulated learning progressions are as useful for helping to point the way to where learning is going as they are for locating where the learner is at any given time on the continuum. Using formative assessment practices, teachers can elicit evidence of student proficiency of significant literacy concepts and skills based on what they know about the building blocks in the earlier grades for any given learning pathway.

> *Formative assessment involves a teacher in seeking evidence during instruction (evidence from student work, from classroom questions and dialog or one-on-one interviews, sometimes from using assessment tools designed specifically for the purpose, and so on) of whether students are understanding and progressing toward the goals of instruction, or whether they are having difficulties or falling off track in some way, and using that information to shape pedagogical responses designed to provide students with the feedback and experiences they may need to keep or get on track.*
>
> —Consortium for Policy Research in Education, 2011, p. 17

Gathering formative assessment data about the current state of student learning and the desired state of student learning yields explicitly clear information about where students are entering into the learning progression. While having a well-marked pathway provides a clear map of the journey for reaching instructional summits, adjustments to instruction along the route are dictated by variations in diverse learner needs.

The learning progressions articulated in the ELA CCSS are useful verbal descriptions of how learning is expected to progress over time. Collectively they serve as a general map of the terrain leading to college and career readiness. The progressions, however, are not perfect. As W. James Popham (2008) notes, "A learning progression isn't unerringly accurate." Further, variations in individual student learning needs will require refinement of the learning progressions to locate more discrete elements of the building blocks along the pathways. Particular students are likely to arrive at the same level of mastery of the intended grade-specific standards by arriving from a different learning progression altogether. While teachers will find the learning progressions to be powerful influences for instructional planning and assessment design, the progressions are not intended to be used as an exclusive checklist for learning.

The explicit expectations in the K–12 learning progression for W.CCR.7 are clearly visible as represented in Exhibit 1.4. By "unwrapping" the W.11–12.7 standard, as depicted in Exhibit 1.3, a grade 11–12 teacher can know specifically the concepts and skills articulated in the grade-specific standards. Further, the teacher can use this "unwrapped" standard exercise to create an instructional sequence for teaching the concepts and skills throughout the year, as illustrated in Exhibit 1.4.

Using formative assessment practices, the teacher can deter-

BOOK TWO EXHIBIT 1.5

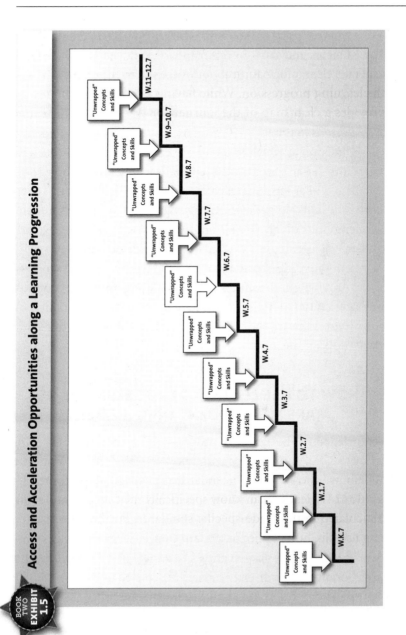

Access and Acceleration Opportunities along a Learning Progression

mine whether there are students who are not able to demonstrate key concepts and skills in this standard at the 11–12 grade level and may require building blocks leading up to the grade-level expectations. Using guidance from what is known about this learning progression, the teacher can look at prior learning expectations in grades 9–10, grade 8, grade 7, and so on, to determine the level at which students are demonstrating readiness to enter into (or access) the next level of learning (see Exhibit 1.5).

In a similar fashion, teachers can use the "unwrapped" concepts and skills along the learning progression to support student acceleration through the learning progression to enhance, extend, and enrich learning for students who already demonstrate proficiency in the grade-specific standards. Thus, the learning progressions provide opportunities for determining both access points and acceleration options for all students to engage in demonstrating progress toward the college and career readiness anchor standard expectations.

HOW TO USE LEARNING PROGRESSIONS AS MAPS FOR STUDENT INVOLVEMENT

Knowledge of the learning progressions used in concert with knowledge of formative assessment processes provides not only anchors for powerful classroom instructional practices for teachers, but also maps for students to become involved in monitoring their own progress toward college and career readiness.

Consider, for example, the communication challenges presented for students participating in a variety of conversations and collaborations with diverse partners as depicted in Exhibit 1.6: The Spiral Effect for Speaking and Listening Standard 1 (SL.CCR.1).

The Spiral Effect for Speaking and Listening Standard 1 (SL.CCR.1)

Example of Grade-Specific Standards for Speaking and Listening Standard 1		
The example below illustrates how skills and concepts for end-of-year grade-specific expectations for a given standard are both reinforced and expanded as students advance through the grades. The result is a **"spiral effect"** where students repeatedly practice mastered competencies from the year prior in the context of new competencies being "added" each year as the standard increases in complexity and sophistication. New skills and concepts "added" to each grade level from the year prior are noted in **bold.**		
SL.CCR.1	**CCR Speaking and Listening Anchor Standard 1:** **Prepare for and participate effectively in a range of conversations and collaborations with diverse partners, building on others' ideas and expressing their own clearly and persuasively.**	=
SL.11–12.1 Grade 11–12 students:	Initiate and participate effectively in a range of collaborative discussions (one-on-one, in groups, and teacher-led) with diverse partners on ***grades 11–12*** *topics, texts, and issues,* building on others' ideas and expressing their own clearly **and persuasively.** a. Come to discussions prepared, having read and researched material under study; explicitly draw on that preparation by referring to evidence from texts and other research on the topic or issue to stimulate a thoughtful, well-reasoned exchange of ideas. b. Work with peers **to promote civil, democratic** discussions and decision making, set clear goals and deadlines, and establish individual roles as needed. c. Propel conversations by posing and responding to questions that **probe reasoning and evidence; ensure a hearing for a full range of positions on a topic or issue;** clarify, verify, or challenge ideas and conclusions; **and promote divergent and creative perspectives.** d. Respond thoughtfully to diverse perspectives; **synthesize comments, claims and evidence made on all sides of an issue; resolve contradictions when possible; and determine what additional information or research is required to deepen the investigation or complete the task.**	+
SL.9–10.1 Grade 9–10 students:	**Initiate and participate** effectively in a range of collaborative discussions (one-on-one, in groups, and teacher-led) with diverse partners on ***grades 9–10*** *topics, texts, and issues,* building on others' ideas and expressing their own clearly and persuasively. a. Come to discussions prepared, having read **and** researched material under study; explicitly draw on that preparation by referring to evidence **from texts and other research** on the topic or issue **to stimulate a thoughtful, well-reasoned exchange of ideas.** b. **Work with peers to set rules** for collegial discussions and decision making (e.g., **informal consensus, taking votes on key issues, presentation of alternative views**), set clear goals and deadlines, and establish individual roles as needed. c. **Propel conversations** by posing **and responding** to questions that **relate the current discussion to broader themes or larger ideas; actively incorporate others into the discussion; and clarify, verify, or challenge ideas and conclusions.** d. **Respond thoughtfully to diverse perspectives, summarize points of agreement and disagreement,** and, when warranted, qualify or justify their own views **and understanding and make new connections** in light of the evidence **and reasoning** presented.	+

The Spiral Effect for Speaking and Listening Standard 1 (SL.CCR.1) *(continued)*

SL.8.1 Grade 8 students:	Engage effectively in a range of collaborative discussions (one-on-one, in groups, and teacher-led) with diverse partners on ***grade 8*** *topics, texts, and issues,* building on others' ideas and expressing their own clearly. a. Come to discussions prepared, having read or researched material under study; explicitly draw on that preparation by referring to evidence on the topic, text, or issue to probe and reflect on ideas under discussion. b. Follow rules for collegial discussions and **decision making**, track progress toward specific goals and deadlines, and establish individual roles as needed. c. Pose questions that **connect the ideas of several speakers** and respond to others' questions and comments with relevant **evidence**, observations, and ideas. d. Acknowledge new information expressed by others, and, when warranted, **qualify or justify** their own views **in light of the evidence presented.**	+
SL.7.1 Grade 7 students:	Engage effectively in a range of collaborative discussions (one-on-one, in groups, and teacher-led) with diverse partners on ***grade 7*** *topics, texts, and issues,* building on others' ideas and expressing their own clearly. a. Come to discussions prepared, having read or **researched material under study**; explicitly draw on that preparation by referring to evidence on the topic, text, or issue to **probe** and reflect on ideas under discussion. b. Follow rules for collegial discussions, **track progress toward** specific goals and deadlines, and establish individual roles as needed. c. Pose **questions that elicit elaboration and respond to others' questions and comments with relevant observations and ideas that bring the discussion back on topic as needed.** d. **Acknowledge new information expressed by others, and, when warranted, modify their own views.**	+
SL.6.1 Grade 6 students:	Engage effectively in a range of collaborative discussions (one-on-one, in groups, and teacher-led) with diverse partners on ***grade 6*** *topics, texts, and* ***issues,*** building on others' ideas and expressing their own clearly. a. Come to discussions prepared, having read or studied required material; explicitly draw on that preparation **by referring to evidence on the topic, text, or issue to probe and reflect on ideas** under discussion. b. Follow rules for **collegial discussions, set specific goals and deadlines, and establish individual roles as needed.** c. Pose and respond to specific questions **with elaboration and detail** by making comments that contribute to the **topic, text, or issue** under discussion. d. Review the key ideas expressed and **demonstrate understanding of multiple perspectives through reflection and paraphrasing.**	+

The Spiral Effect for Speaking and Listening Standard 1 (SL.CCR.1) *(continued)*

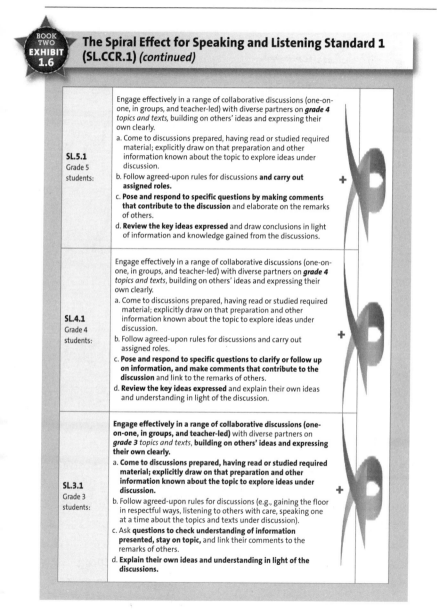

SL.5.1 Grade 5 students:	Engage effectively in a range of collaborative discussions (one-on-one, in groups, and teacher-led) with diverse partners on ***grade 4*** *topics and texts,* building on others' ideas and expressing their own clearly. a. Come to discussions prepared, having read or studied required material; explicitly draw on that preparation and other information known about the topic to explore ideas under discussion. b. Follow agreed-upon rules for discussions **and carry out assigned roles.** c. **Pose and respond to specific questions by making comments that contribute to the discussion** and elaborate on the remarks of others. d. **Review the key ideas expressed** and draw conclusions in light of information and knowledge gained from the discussions.	+
SL.4.1 Grade 4 students:	Engage effectively in a range of collaborative discussions (one-on-one, in groups, and teacher-led) with diverse partners on ***grade 4*** *topics and texts,* building on others' ideas and expressing their own clearly. a. Come to discussions prepared, having read or studied required material; explicitly draw on that preparation and other information known about the topic to explore ideas under discussion. b. Follow agreed-upon rules for discussions and carry out assigned roles. c. **Pose and respond to specific questions to clarify or follow up on information, and make comments that contribute to the discussion** and link to the remarks of others. d. **Review the key ideas expressed** and explain their own ideas and understanding in light of the discussion.	+
SL.3.1 Grade 3 students:	**Engage effectively in a range of collaborative discussions (one-on-one, in groups, and teacher-led)** with diverse partners on ***grade 3*** *topics and texts,* **building on others' ideas and expressing their own clearly.** a. **Come to discussions prepared, having read or studied required material; explicitly draw on that preparation and other information known about the topic to explore ideas under discussion.** b. Follow agreed-upon rules for discussions (e.g., gaining the floor in respectful ways, listening to others with care, speaking one at a time about the topics and texts under discussion). c. Ask **questions to check understanding of information presented, stay on topic,** and link their comments to the remarks of others. d. **Explain their own ideas and understanding in light of the discussions.**	+

The Spiral Effect for Speaking and Listening Standard 1 (SL.CCR.1) *(continued)*

SL.2.1 Grade 2 students:	Participate in collaborative conversations with diverse partners about ***grade 2*** *topics and texts* with peers and adults in small and large groups. a. Follow agreed upon rules for discussion (e.g., **gaining the floor in respectful ways**, listening to others with care, speaking one at a time about the topics and texts under discussion). b. Build on others' talk in conversations by **linking their comments to the remarks of others.** c. Ask **for clarification and further explanation as needed** about the topics and texts under discussion.	+
SL.1.1 Grade 1 students:	Participate in collaborative conversations with diverse partners about ***grade 1*** *topics and texts* with peers and adults in small and large groups. a. Follow agreed-upon rules for discussion (e.g., listening to others **with care, speaking one at a time** about the topics and texts under discussion). b. **Build on others' talk in conversations by responding to the comments of others through multiple exchanges.** c. **Ask questions to clear up any confusion about the topics and texts under discussion.**	+
SL.K.1 Kindergarten students:	**Participate in collaborative conversations with diverse partners about kindergarten topics and texts with peers and adults in small and large groups.** a. **Follow agreed-upon rules for discussions (e.g., listening to others and taking turns speaking about the topics and texts under discussion).** b. **Continue a conversation through multiple exchanges.**	+

Source: CCSSI, 2010b, pp. 23, 24, 49, 50.

Making learning clearly visible to students is a practical strategy for involving students in managing their own learning of the rigorous expectations outlined in the Common Core State Standards. Exhibit 1.7 provides one example of using a simple formative assessment tool that also engages students in becoming self-reflective about evaluating the degree to which they are making progress toward mastery of Speaking and Listening Standard 1 for grade 8.

Example of Involving Students in Self-Assessment

Speaking and Listening Standard 1 Grade 8 (SL.8.1) Formative Assessment Example			
Grade 8 Expectations*	**Implementation Effectiveness**		
Student Self-Reflection	**I make no attempt and/or do not implement this strategy effectively.**	**By practicing, I am continually demonstrating improvement on implementing this strategy.**	**I consistently and effectively implement this strategy.**
I come to discussions prepared, having read or researched material under study.			
I explicitly draw on my preparation by referring to evidence on the topic, text, or issue to probe and reflect on ideas under discussion.			
I follow rules for collegial discussions and decision making.			
I track progress toward specific goals and deadlines.			
I participate in defining individual roles, as needed.			
I pose questions that connect the ideas of several speakers and respond to others' questions and comments with relevant evidence, observations, and ideas.			
I acknowledge new information expressed by others, and, when warranted, qualify or justify my own views in light of the evidence presented.			
*An alternative self-assessment tool, using the learning progressions, might include aspects of the grade-specific standards above and below the student's current grade level, for example: **Grade 9**: I respond thoughtfully to diverse perspectives; summarizing points of agreement, and, when warranted, qualify or justify my own views and understanding and make new connections in light of the evidence and reasoning presented. **Grade 8:** I acknowledge new information expressed by others, and, when warranted, qualify or justify my own views in light of the evidence presented. **Grade 7:** I acknowledge new information expressed by others and, when warranted, modify their own views.			
My Improvement Goal			

SUMMARY

> *The fundamental reality is that an unused learning progression can't enhance anyone's instruction.*
>
> —Popham, 2008, p. 28

- The learning progressions within the ELA Common Core standards provide an architectural framework that enables teachers to keep learning moving as students demonstrate increasing expertise in the four strands of significant literacy concepts and skills.
- Knowing how the standards develop vertically from grade to grade and across strands enables teachers to know what to teach next or where to circle back to bring students forward.
- With expertise in using formative assessment processes, the skilled practitioner can determine what students are able to do independently, without teacher guidance, along the learning continuum.
- The skilled practitioner using formative assessment practices can determine where and when learning breaks down for individual students, and design instructional adjustments that support getting students back on track for learning within and across grade-level spans.
- The process of "unwrapping" the standards is a powerful practice to support instructional planning and assessment design. "Unwrapped" standards provide clarity regarding the concepts and skills embedded within the standards, and

provide guidance for teachers on mapping out smaller instructional learning progressions.

- Appendix B of this handbook provides a complete list of the learning progressions found in the Common Core State Standards for English Language Arts and Literacy in History/Social Studies, Science, and Technical Subjects.

References

Ainsworth, L. (2003). *Unwrapping the standards: A simple process to make standards manageable.* Englewood, CO: Lead + Learn Press.

Common Core State Standards Initiative (CCSSI). (2010a, June). Common Core State Standards (Webinar; PowerPoint presentation). Retrieved from www.corestandards.org

Common Core State Standards Initiative (CCSSI). (2010b, June). *Common Core State Standards for English language arts & literacy in history/social studies, science, and technical subjects* (PDF document). Retrieved from www.corestandards.org/assets/CCSSI_ELA%20Standards.pdf

Consortium for Policy Research in Education (CPRE). (2011, January). Paper: *Learning trajectories in mathematics: A foundation for standards, curriculum, assessment, and instruction.* Retrieved from www.cpre.org/ccii/images/stories/ccii_pdfs/learning%20trajectories%20in%20math_ccii%20report.pdf

Heritage, M. (2008). Paper: *Learning progressions: Supporting instruction and formative assessment.* Washington, DC: Council of Chief State School Officers.

Popham, W. J. (2008). *Transformative assessment.* Alexandria, VA: ASCD.

Wiggs, M. (2011). *Standards and assessment: The core of quality instruction.* Englewood, CO: Lead + Learn Press.

The "New" Reading—Rigor, Range, Reasoning, and Relationships

Angela Peery

Although the creators of the document insist that it does not prescribe any particular instructional methods, the Common Core State Standards for English language arts and literacy provide a mandate for how reading instruction must change so that students can meet the demands of the 21st-century "flat-world" workplace. Unlike most American standards documents of the past two decades, the Common Core standards are internationally benchmarked, deliberately spiraled, extremely specific, and richly embedded with the media and technology that now fill our daily lives. In other words, these standards are most likely far different from any that you have known, either as a student or as a teacher.

This chapter provides an overview of the entire ELA CCSS document and then discusses expectations in terms of four prominent features of the reading strand: rigor, range, reasoning, and relationships. These four embedded characteristics clearly differentiate Common Core reading, or the "new" reading, from reading expectations of the past.

OVERVIEW

The Common Core State Standards for English Language Arts and Literacy in History/Social Studies, Science, and Technical Subjects provide a "cumulative progression" (CCSSI, 2010a, p. 4) of grade-level learning expectations in four strands: reading, writing, speaking and listening, and language. Although these strands are separate, there is significant crossover in their substance, representing the integrated nature of literacy; for example, students write about their reading and orally present their research findings. Each of the strands contains college and career readiness anchor standards that unify the entire strand. These anchor standards also represent the culmination of all the grade-specific standards contained within each strand.

The standards are interdisciplinary. The K–5 document delineates learning goals in reading, writing, speaking and listening, and language without linking those goals to specific disciplines. The documents for grades 6–12 differ, however, with one document pertaining to English language arts specifically and another pertaining to literacy in history/social studies, science, and technical subjects. (Other subjects are not specifically mentioned.) In the 6–12 document for English language arts, the reading standards are applied separately to two types of text: literary and informational. The standards for writing, speaking and listening, and language are not subdivided. Also of note: the K–5 document, like its secondary counterpart, has separate standards for reading literary text versus informational text, but it also includes a section of standards on foundational skills (the basics of teaching reading).

There are ten anchor standards for reading and six for language. Although they appear outside of the reading strand, four of the six language anchor standards apply directly to reading. Three of these focus on vocabulary acquisition and use; the other is about how language functions in different contexts. (The remaining two of the six language anchor standards link directly to writing.)

RIGOR

Academic rigor is hard to define. It's similar to what Supreme Court Justice Potter Stewart famously said about pornography in 1964: "I know it when I see it." However, Richard Strong, Harvey Silver, and Matthew Perini (2001) provide a practical definition when they say, "Rigor is the goal of helping students develop the capacity to understand content that is complex, ambiguous, provocative, and personally or emotionally challenging" (p. 7).

Many scholars have decried the lack of rigor in English language arts instruction in the past few years, with Mike Schmoker being one of the loudest voices. Schmoker (2011) asserts that English language arts, more than any other discipline, has lost its way and is in desperate need of clarity (p. 93). And even though the Common Core standards stress cross-curricular literacy, there is a call to action for all those language arts teachers who, in recent years, have downplayed the use of complex texts and the requirement for students to read such texts independently. In fact, an entire anchor standard is dedicated to the *proficient, independent* reading of on-grade-level texts. There could be no clearer directive about increasing the rigor of reading instruction.

Unlike many recent state standards documents, the Common Core reading standards place *equal emphasis* on the difficulty of texts being read and the reading skills of the student. In the last decade, much attention has been paid (and rightly so) to ensuring that students are reading proficiently by the end of third grade. The federally funded program Reading First had this goal as its singular mission. However, initiatives like Reading First and Reading Recovery have placed far more emphasis on a student's fluency and comprehension than on the quality of the texts being read.

In even a quick review of the Common Core English language arts documents, one can easily tell that text complexity is important, because Appendix A allocates nine full pages to an explanation of this concept. Within those nine pages, a three-part model is presented. This model consists of three equally important components of text complexity: qualitative dimensions, quantitative dimensions, and reader/task considerations.

Briefly, qualitative dimensions are those aspects of complexity that can be assessed only by a careful human reader—factors such as hidden meanings, author's purpose, and specialized background knowledge that is needed to fully understand the text. Quantitative dimensions include those aspects of text that have often been used in determining reading levels—for example, the total number of words in the text and the lengths and structures of the sentences. Reader/task considerations include things personal and individual—factors such as a student's interest in the topic and motivation to read the text.

What does the three-part model mean to a classroom teacher? A teacher selecting texts for whole-class instruction must consider all three of the components equally. When guiding students in their self-selected reading, the teacher must also consider the three components and push students toward two interdependent goals: grade-level (or *above* grade-level) complexity, and independent reading. Schmoker and others (ACT, 2006; ACT, 2009; Bauerlein,

2011) argue that in recent years, teachers have paid more attention to the reader and/or the task than is warranted, and have thereby not engaged their students in reading quantitatively and qualitatively rigorous texts frequently enough.

Text complexity matters, because, as stated in Appendix A of the CCSS documents, "... A high school graduate who is a poor reader is a postsecondary student who must struggle mightily to succeed" (CCSSI, 2010b, p. 4).

RANGE

Secondary to the issue of text complexity, but still of urgent concern, is the issue of the range of texts with which students interact. Simply put, students must read both broadly and deeply in all subject areas.

In addition to dealing with complex texts as part of guided instruction and for independent practice, students need opportunities "to experience the satisfaction and pleasure of easy, fluent reading" (CCSSI, 2010b, p. 9). In other words, they should select and be matched with texts that they want to read and that are at a comfortable reading level for them. Matching readers to engaging texts should remain an important part of English language arts instruction so that students develop a lifelong love of reading.

The standards were written in alignment with the National Assessment of Educational Progress (NAEP) Reading Framework, which specifies that at grade 4, fully half of what students read should be informational text, with the other half being literary text. It logically follows that if students are reading the bulk of literary text during language arts instructional time, then in other subjects, *almost all the text studied should be informational in nature.* This is the only way that the recommended ratio can be achieved.

According to the NAEP framework, at grade 8, only 45 percent of what students read should be literary, and at grade 12, only 30 percent should be literary. Along with consideration of what students are reading in their non-English language arts classes, English teachers are cautioned to pay far greater attention to literary nonfiction than ever before (CCSSI, 2010a, p. 5). So English teachers must find the ideal combination of literary text (fiction, nonfiction, poetry, drama, etc.), and their non-English-teaching colleagues must do the "heavy lifting" with informational/explanatory text. The standards are clear that instruction and assessment must match the NAEP framework if students are to be successful in their postsecondary pursuits (CCSSI, 2010a, p. 5).

An entire appendix in the ELA CCSS is dedicated to providing examples of texts that meet the guidelines for rigor and range (Appendix B). Range is explicitly identified as one of the primary considerations in text selection (CCSSI, 2010c, p. 2). The lists of representative texts make it clear that students are expected to read literature across time periods, genres, styles, authors, and cultures. In history/social studies, science, and technical subjects, the sample texts focus on some of the most important and provocative topics related to those disciplines (slavery, the Civil War, gravity, mass, advances in technology).

A side note within the anchor standards for reading reinforces the message in Appendix B: ". . . Students must grapple with works of exceptional craft and thought whose range extends across genres, cultures, and centuries" (CCSSI, 2010c, p. 35). This same side note also mentions seminal United States documents (such as the Declaration of Independence), American classics, and Shakespearean dramas. In sum, broad and deep reading includes reading for one's own enjoyment, reading in order to understand complex texts of various genres, and reading works that are of historical and literary significance.

What should teachers do in response to the guidelines presented about range of reading? The standards present the ideas as "useful guideposts" for assisting teachers in selecting texts of "similar complexity, quality, and range for their own classrooms" (CCSSI, 2010a, p. 2). First, one should become familiar with the works and excerpts that are provided in Appendix B, considering the complexity, quality, and instructional value. Then, one might consider the units of instruction already planned and examine the reading that has traditionally been done (or that is recommended). Teachers can apply the NAEP Reading Framework percentages to see if there is a discrepancy. If there is a discrepancy, then several reflective questions could be asked: With what type of text do my students need more experience? How do I provide increased use of this type of text—which units, lessons, and topics can I supplement or revise? Only after these two questions are considered should a teacher seek specific resources.

REASONING

To reason is to think logically and to form conclusions or judgments. The emphasis on sound reasoning is a central component of nine of the 10 anchor standards for reading.

Anchor standard 1 is about the close reading of text and the ability to make logical inferences; it also specifies that students must cite evidence from the text in support of their inferences, conclusions, and judgments. This standard, then, goes far beyond simple comprehension. The ability to understand what any given text says explicitly is only a first step; inferences and conclusions make up the remainder of the standards statement. Valid inferences and logical conclusions require reasoning and should be a *constant focus* in reading instruction.

Anchor standard 2 is about the central ideas and themes of texts but also goes further than comprehension. There are two other parts to this anchor standard: a student must summarize the support for the central idea or theme and analyze the development of that central idea or theme. It is the analysis portion of this standard that forces students to apply the principles of logic and to dig deeper into each text.

Anchor standard 3 is about the development of ideas, people/characters, and events through the entirety of a text. This standard requires students not only to possess declarative knowledge (what the main idea or thesis is, who the characters or key people are, and what the sequence of events includes), but also to consider how these elements interact to create a total effect. Therefore, the standard goes beyond factual knowledge and includes conceptual knowledge. Students have to know the what, who, and when, but they also need to know the *how* and the *why*. They must know *how* the component parts work together plus *why* the author has crafted the *how* to achieve certain purposes and effects.

At grade level 2, the representation of anchor standard 3 for literary text is, "Describe how characters in a story respond to major events and challenges." This same standard at grade level 8 reads, "Analyze how particular lines of dialogue or incidents in a story or drama propel the action, reveal aspects of a character, or provoke a decision." One can clearly see from this progression across the years that students must know the *how* before determining the *why,* and the *why* becomes increasingly important as the student matures.

Anchor standard 4 focuses squarely on word choice, including the technical, connotative, and figurative meanings of the words and expressions used. This standard, like most of the anchor standards for reading, requires cognition at the analysis level. Students must interpret words and phrases used in a text and analyze how these choices impact the meaning and tone. Again, the *why* is important—*why* did the author choose the words that he did?

It is interesting to note that by the time one reaches anchor standard 4, the verb "analyze" has been used three times. The anchor standards are, by almost any educator's standards, cognitively very challenging.

The verb "analyze" appears again in anchor standard 5. This standard deals with text structure and how the overall structure is interdependent with its component parts (sentences, paragraphs, sections, chapters). Obviously this standard contains the element of logical reasoning. If students truly understand the overall structure of a text, then they should also be able to understand how that overall structure supports the central idea or theme and how that structure interacts with its component elements. Again we have more of the *how* and *why. How* is the text organized, and *why* is this the best organizational pattern for this particular text?

Anchor standard 6 is about author's purpose (for informational text) and point of view (for literary text). The standard actually uses the verb "assess," which makes it different from the other nine anchor standards. "Assess" implies one of the highest levels of cognition—evaluation. In this case, "assess" is used in the context of how purpose or point of view is inextricably linked with content and style. Students must use their reasoning skills to fully meet the intent of this standard. They must know the *what* (author's purpose or point of view), but the *how* is far more important. The *how* here, much like in anchor standard 3, is about the interaction of text elements with each other and in sum.

Anchor standard 7 is about not only reading basic, linguistic text but also understanding the use of visual, quantitative, and multimedia information when it appears with linguistic text. According to this standard, students must demonstrate basic comprehension and apply their higher-level thinking skills to text that has information in different formats. As a result of their thinking, they must then reach valid conclusions and judgments.

Anchor standard 8 is more directly focused on reasoning than most of the other reading standards. It states that students should dissect arguments based on the validity of the claims presented and on the quality of the evidence. This particular reading standard aligns nicely with the first anchor standard for writing, which is also about argumentation. Students must read and critique arguments for effectiveness and also write effective arguments themselves; these standards, even though they appear in two different strands, go hand in hand.

How does the reading skill of dissecting an argument play out across the grade levels? At grade 2, the standard demands that students describe how reasons used in an informational text support the specific points of the writer. At grade 8, the student must delineate the argument, evaluate the argument, evaluate the claims, assess the reasoning for soundness, determine whether or not the evidence is relevant and sufficient, and recognize irrelevant evidence.

The last standard with a focus on reasoning, anchor standard

9, is about comparing multiple texts written about similar themes or topics. Obviously students must complete careful readings of such texts and demonstrate basic comprehension before being able to compare and contrast the texts based on their arguments or literary merit.

What should an educator do in response to the push for increased critical thinking found in the reading standards? A good first step is to examine page 7 of the introduction to the Common Core State Standards (CCSSI, 2010a). This page is intended to provide a portrait of students who meet or exceed the requirements in the standards. Of special note are a couple of descriptors: these students display independence and "comprehend as well as critique" (CCSSI, 2010a, p. 7). The thrust for *independent, frequent application of reasoning skills* is evident in the full description. It's enough to make all teachers reflect on their teaching practices and question where they currently stand.

RELATIONSHIPS

This chapter will close with an exploration of several important relationships regarding the material within the CCSS document and the people who stand outside the document and are charged with making it come to life.

A striking feature of the standards is the section devoted to literacy in grades 6–12 in subjects other than English language arts. The literacy standards for history/social studies, science, and technical subjects "are not meant to replace content standards in those areas but rather to supplement them" (CCSSI, 2010a, p. 3). Teachers of these subjects must help students master reading, writing, speaking, listening, and language as they apply *in those fields.* And while some state standards documents in the past few years have addressed communication in disciplines other than English language arts, there has never been as much specific, comprehensive guidance offered to secondary teachers about how to integrate literacy instruction. Thus, the inclusion of this special section of standards is a monumental step toward helping secondary teachers see the critical relationship between literacy and all learning.

Another striking feature of the documents is the interconnectedness among the strands. Although there are separate strands for reading, writing, speaking and listening, and language, each set of standards supports the others. One can trace, for example, the close connections between anchor standard 8 in reading and anchor standard 1 in writing, which was shown earlier in this chapter.

The creators of the Common Core state that the division into strands (reading, writing, speaking and listening, and language) was only for "conceptual clarity" (CCSSI, 2010a, p. 4). Certainly the six anchor standards of the language strand could have been divided up and integrated within both the reading and writing strands, but this could have resulted in a far more unwieldy document.

Research and media do not occupy their own strands but are embedded throughout. In the reading strand, diverse media and formats are cited in anchor standard 7. In the writing strand, anchor standard 7 is about research projects, and anchor standard 8 is about using multiple sources of information. These two writing standards clearly connect to reading, for one must read in order to conduct research, and they also clearly include the use of technology and texts of diverse formats.

The connections between the reading standards and writing standards are the most plentiful and specific. The connections between the reading and writing of argumentation have already been examined in this chapter. It is also important to examine other genres across the two sets of standards. In the writing strand, informative/explanatory texts must be written; in the reading strand, they must be read, understood, analyzed, and evaluated.

If one simply lays the anchor standards for reading beside the anchor standards for writing and goes back and forth circling key words, general themes or "big ideas" become apparent. One is that understanding logical argument is highly important. Two: readers and writers must use evidence to support their conclusions and judgments. Three: a text is always composed of multiple components that have been thoughtfully manipulated by the writer in order to achieve desired effects.

Lastly, one of the most crucial relationships to understand is not within the words of the document but within the walls of each school. The authors claim, "The Standards insist that instruction in reading, writing, speaking, listening, and language be a shared responsibility. . ." (CCSSI, 2010a, p. 4). Students cannot reach the high levels of literacy required in our modern society without being strongly supported *across all grade levels and content areas.* In order to guide students to mastery of the Common Core, teachers, teacher-leaders, and administrators must remain steadfastly focused and committed—and they must provide the best instruction possible.

As Mike Schmoker has remarked, "The erosion of literacy is one of the most profound but insidious developments in modern schooling" (2011, p. 173). This erosion can be rectified—not quickly, not easily—but it *can* be rectified.

Thus we uncover the most important relationship of all—the relationship between a committed group of adults and the young people entrusted to their tutelage. American students must vastly improve their literacy skills in order to achieve academic and vocational success, and they can't do it alone—we have to lead the way.

SUMMARY

- The Common Core State Standards for English Language Arts and Literacy in History/Social Studies, Science, and Technical Subjects lay out a vision of what literate students must know and be able to do in the 21st century.
- The English language arts Common Core represents a rigorous, cumulative progression of expectations in the areas of reading, writing, speaking and listening, and language conventions. Each area (or "strand") contains from six to 10 college and career readiness anchor standards that unify it.
- The four separate strands have many connections to each other and support each other.
- Research and media are embedded throughout the strands.
- The English language arts CCSS are both subject-specific (to English language arts instruction) and interdisciplinary. For grades 6–12, specific expectations are outlined for the fields of history/social studies, science, and technical subjects.
- The reading standards place equal emphasis on *what is read* (the range of materials and the complexity of individual texts) and *how it is read* (students' reading skills). Students must read broadly and deeply in *all subject areas.*

- The reading standards place particular emphasis on informational text. Persuasive and argumentative texts take prominence.
- In order for students to meet the expectations represented in the reading standards, high levels of critical thinking are required.

References

ACT, Inc. (2006). *Reading between the lines: What the ACT reveals about college readiness in reading.* Iowa City, IA.

ACT, Inc. (2009). *The condition of college readiness 2009.* Iowa City, IA.

Bauerlein, M. (2011). Too dumb for complex texts? *Educational Leadership, 68*(5), 28–33.

Common Core State Standards Initiative (CCSSI). (2010a, June). *Common Core State Standards for English language arts & literacy in history/social studies, science, and technical subjects* (PDF document). Retrieved from www.corestandards.org/assets/CCSSI_ELA%20Standards.pdf

Common Core State Standards Initiative (CCSSI). (2010b, June). *Common Core State Standards for English language arts & literacy in history/social studies, science, and technical subjects: Appendix A* (PDF document). Retrieved from www.corestandards.org/assets/Appendix_A.pdf

Common Core State Standards Initiative (CCSSI). (2010c, June). *Common Core State Standards for English language arts & literacy in history/social studies, science, and technical subjects: Appendix B* (PDF document). Retrieved from www.corestandards.org/assets/Appendix_B.pdf

Schmoker, M. (2011). *Focus: Elevating the essentials to radically improve student learning.* Alexandria, VA: ASCD.

Strong, R., Silver, H., & Perini, M. (2001). *Teaching what matters most: Standards and strategies for raising student achievement.* Alexandria, VA: ASCD.

The "New" Writing—Sharing, Shifting, and Sustaining Student Writing

Lisa Cebelak

In the previous chapters, an overview of the Common Core State Standards for English Language Arts and Literacy in History/Social Studies, Science, and Technical Subjects was provided, with clarity given to the reading strand. This chapter provides a review of the writing strand in terms of four themes: sharing the responsibility, shifting the focus, sustaining student writing, and samples of proficient writing. These themes build on the characteristics of Common Core writing, or the core writing essentials defined as what is needed to be proficient in writing in the 21st century.

OVERVIEW

The writing strand for English language arts and literacy in history/social studies, science, and technical subjects contains both broad college and career readiness anchor standards and grade-specific or grade-band standards. The 10 college and career readiness anchor standards for writing are the same K–12. While the anchor standards are the same, a "note on range and content of student writing" is provided for further clarity for each of the following areas: K–5, 6–12 ELA, and 6–12 literacy in history/social studies, science, and technical subjects.

The grade-specific writing standards are grade-level specific for grades K–8 and in two-year grade bands (9–10 and 11–12) at the high school level. The writing standards are meant to complement the reading standards. For example, anchor standard 9 requires students to write about evidence from literary text (in the ELA classroom) and from informational text (in ELA, history/social studies, science, and technical subjects). The writing standards are also inseparable from the six language standards that specify language conventions for clear communication. The 10 anchor standards for writing are grouped by text types and purposes (anchor standards 1–3), production and distribution of writing (anchor standards 4–6), research to build and present knowledge (anchor standards 7–9), and range of writing (anchor standard 10). Here is a brief overview of each of the writing anchor standards.

Anchor standard 1 is about argumentative writing and the components needed in a logical argument. The Common Core places an emphasis on student ability to write sound arguments, as this is a critical skill for college and career readiness. Because this standard continues to state that an analysis of substantive topics or texts must occur in supporting claims by using valid reasoning and relevant and sufficient evidence, it directly supports the need for students to read critically. In grades K–5, "opinion" is the term used to reference argumentative writing in the grade-specific standards.

Anchor standard 2 is about informative/explanatory writing, that is, writing that conveys information accurately. This standard goes beyond writing when it calls for students to examine and convey complex topics or texts, and like anchor standard 1, directly supports reading critically with increasing text complexity. In order to write informative/explanatory text, students must use primary and secondary sources.

Anchor standard 3 is about narrative writing—narrative that is real or imagined. This standard states that a student must use effective techniques, such as dialogue, pacing, description, and well-chosen details, including using concrete words and sensory details; and well-structured event sequences, including using a variety of transitional words, phrases, and clauses. It is important to note here that the narrative standard does address many forms of creative writing. It is also important to note that this is the one writing standard that is not required of non-ELA teachers at the secondary level.

Anchor standard 4 is about producing a coherent piece of writing. This standard calls for grade-specific areas to be addressed in relation to anchor standards 1–3. In order to make sure that the development, organization, and style are appropriate to the task, purpose, and audience, one must address the grade-specific expectations for writing types.

Anchor standard 5 is about the writing process. This standard specifically calls for the need for planning, revising, editing, and rewriting in order to develop and strengthen student writing. It also encourages students to try a new approach to the writing process starting in fifth grade. This anchor standard also notes in the grade-specific standards that in the "editing" phase, students should show mastery of conventions as spelled out in the language standards 1–3 starting by third grade. Here, one cannot appropriately address anchor standard 5 without addressing the grade-specific expectations for "conventions of standard English" and "knowledge of language" as addressed in the language strand.

Anchor standard 6 is about students using technology to do two things. First, it calls for students to use technology for the purpose of producing and publishing writing. Second, it calls for students to interact and collaborate with others. Looking at the grade-specific standards, starting in kindergarten, students are to explore digital tools in order to publish writing. By fourth grade, students need to demonstrate a command of keyboarding skills in order to type at least one page in a single sitting. By grade 6, students should be able to type at least three pages in a single sitting. In ninth grade, students not only produce and publish their writing, but use technology to update individual or shared writing products.

Anchor standard 7 is about conducting research projects based on subjects that are under investigation. This calls for drawing on several sources and being a critical reader. It also reinforces the importance of analysis of text. The research projects should answer a question, and starting in grade 8, this includes a self-generated student question. In grades K–8, the grade-specific standards call for short research projects. Starting in ninth grade, the standard includes sustained research projects as well as short research projects. At the high school level, students need to be able to narrow or broaden the inquiry as needed and be able to synthesize multiple sources on a subject as part of demonstrating understanding of the subject being investigated.

Anchor standard 8 is about how to gather information for researching and touches on four key components. The first component calls for finding information in both print and digital sources. While in the early elementary years, sources should be provided for students; by sixth grade, students need to be able to gather information from many different print and digital sources *on their own.* The second component addresses the student's ability to assess the credibility and accuracy of each source (assessing the credibility starting in sixth grade and building on that skill by including accuracy by seventh grade). The third component addresses what students need to be able to do with the information. For instance, at the elementary level, students summarize their notes while at the secondary level, students quote or paraphrase the data and the conclusions of others. The fourth component of this standard addresses the avoidance of plagiarism. Another feature in the grade-specific standards is citing sources.

Anchor standard 9 is about the ability to draw evidence from both literary and informational texts in order to support analysis, reflection, and research. This standard begins in fourth grade and is directly connected to the reading standards. At each grade level, the grade-specific standard calls for applying the grade reading standards for literature or the grade reading standards for informational texts (elementary) or literacy nonfiction (secondary). The Common Core State Standards are internationally benchmarked, and a recurring pattern found in international assessment programs is that students are required to write in response to sources (CCSSI, 2010b, p. 41).

Anchor standard 10 is about the ability to write for shorter time frames, such as one or two class periods, and the ability to write over an extended amount of time. This standard will be discussed in more detail later on in this chapter.

SHARING THE RESPONSIBILITY

Writing standards are no longer the sole responsibility of the English language arts teacher. The Common Core State Standards *insist* that instruction of literacy be a shared responsibility (CCSSI, 2010a, p. 4). While this might be a common practice found at the elementary level because most instruction of all subjects comes from one teacher, it typically is not a shared practice among teachers at the secondary level.

To keep an integrated model of literacy at the secondary level, the standards are divided into two documents, one for ELA and one for history/social studies, science, and technical subjects. As stated in "Key Design Considerations," the Common Core introduction document, "this division reflects the unique, time-honored place of ELA teachers in developing students' literacy skills while at the same time recognizing that teachers *in other areas* must have a role in this development as well (CCSSI, 2010a, p. 4, emphasis added). Although literacy standards have been laid out for history/social studies, science, and technical subjects, the Common Core document strongly encourages that literacy standards in other subject areas, such as mathematics and health education, be modeled on these same literacy standards (both writing and reading) in order to have a strong school-wide literacy program (CCSSI, 2010a, p. 6).

In a report to the Carnegie Corporation of New York titled *Writing Next: Effective Strategies to Improve Writing of Adolescents in Middle and High Schools*, Graham and Perin declare that there is a writing proficiency crisis in our schools (2007, p. 3). There has been some progress toward proficiency made at the elementary level in recent years; however, the secondary levels have remained stagnant. It is important to note that the authors explain in this report that there has been recent focus on improving literacy of adolescent learners, but more attention has been given to reading than to writing (p. 7). The authors point out that "although reading and writing are complementary skills, whole development runs a roughly parallel course, they do not necessarily go hand in hand . . . therefore, although writing and reading are both vital aspects of literacy, they each require their own dedicated instruction" (p. 8).

In discussion of why writing is important, the authors share insight into two major roles writing plays within a school. The first role is that writing is a skill that uses many learned strategies to accomplish an end goal. The second role that writing plays is deepening a student's learning; in other words, using writing as a way to better understand content matter. Therefore, Graham and Perin's *Writing Next* refers to an earlier report titled *Reading Next*, in that the report continues to recommend that English language arts teachers teach reading and writing skills and that teachers of other content areas provide instruction in discipline-specific reading and writing (2007, p. 10). If 70 percent of students in grades 4–12 are low-achieving writers, then writing must be a shared responsibility of all teachers if we are to prepare our students for success in the 21st century.

Douglas Reeves recently wrote that every school district planning on implementing the Common Core State Standards should implement more nonfiction writing across the curriculum. Reeves argues that schools must make a substantial commitment to increase the amount of informational writing, in every grade level. He notes that the Common Core standards have blown the myth that non-ELA teachers are not teachers of writing. In fact, he states that "every teacher in every subject is responsible for helping students think critically, and writing is the best way to master that skill" (Reeves, 2011).

In order to implement the Common Core writing strand, every teacher in every grade, K–12, must play an integral part in increasing the amount of quality writing in their classrooms and must understand the types of writing that the Common Core is calling for.

SHIFTING THE FOCUS

The first three writing standards are each dedicated to different text types and purposes: argumentative, informative/explanatory, and narrative. These three text types are defined and described more in detail in Appendix A of the ELA standards document. The brief explanations of each below are summarized from Appendix A.

Argumentative

An argument is a reasoned, logical way of demonstrating that the writer's position, belief, or conclusion is valid (CCSSI, 2010b, p. 23). It is important to note that the Common Core places a strong emphasis on argumentative writing as a key factor for college and career readiness.

While many state standards have used "persuasive" writing versus argumentative, it is important to note the differences. A sound argument consists of reasonable claims rather than emotional appeals. Appendix A discusses this critical difference and notes that a shift in focus regarding argument writing must occur.

While all persuasion is not argumentation, all argumentation is intended to be persuasive. It is the element of logic that separates the two. Claims must be used in writing to support an argument with evidence given. In history/social studies, science, and technical subjects, argumentation is to focus on discipline-specific content. In the elementary levels, argumentative writing is called "opinion pieces." Because reasons are required, the opinion writing called out in grades K–5 directly builds support for the complexity needed by sixth grade, when writing arguments to support claims with clear reasons and relevant evidence is called for.

Informative/Explanatory

Informative/explanatory writing is different from argumentative in that it answers the questions "what," "why," or "how." Many state standards have called this type of writing "expository" writing in the past. The main thrust of this writing is to explain something in detail.

As with using the term "argumentative" instead of "persuasive," here "explanatory" now replaces "expository" for most teachers. Informative/explanatory writing is used when students are naming, describing, defining, or comparing or contrasting ideas, to list a few specifics. This form of writing can serve many purposes, including learning more about a topic and helping readers understand a process. As students progress through the grades, they will learn to use narrative within informative/explanatory writing as they learn to blend text types to achieve the more sophisticated style of writing expected starting in middle school.

Narrative

Narrative writing conveys experience, either real or imagined. Narrative writing can be used for many different reasons. Typically used as the main form of writing at the elementary level and mainly in ELA classrooms at the secondary level, it is important to note that the Common Core gives examples of how writing narratives can be used in other courses. For example, in science, students might write narratives to describe step-by-step procedures so other students can follow their procedures and see if they reach the same results. In history, students might write narrative accounts about individuals of historical significance.

While these broad types include many subgenres, it is these three main forms of writing that are reinforced K–12. At the elementary level, there is a major shift of moving away from mostly narrative writing to sharing the emphasis with argumentative and informative/explanatory writing. At the middle school level, more emphasis is placed on argumentative and informative/explanatory over narrative, and that emphasis continues to increase at the high school level. In fact, the distribution of communicative purposes by grade 12 in the 2011 National Assessment of Educational Progress (NAEP) Writing Framework shows that 40 percent of writing should be to persuade, 40 percent of writing should be to explain, and only 20 percent of writing should be to convey experience (CCSSI, 2010a, p. 5). This is the sum of writing that is to occur by the twelfth grade year for students across all courses, *not just in the ELA classroom.* In Appendix A, the Common Core document notes that "a 2009 ACT national curriculum survey of postsecondary instructors found that 'write to argue or persuade readers' was virtually tied with 'write to convey information' as the most important type of writing needed by incoming college students" (CCSSI, 2010b, p. 24). It is important to note that narrative skills are expected to continue to be developed after the elementary years; however, by sixth grade the Common Core requires that narrative elements be used effectively within arguments and informative/explanatory writing pieces. Derived from international models, the Common Core notes that writing arguments and writing informative/explanatory texts are the priorities in high school in order to be college and career ready.

While in the past, many state standards focused mainly on narrative writing at the elementary level, the Common Core places roughly equal emphasis on the three main forms. The distribution of communicative purposes by fourth grade requires 30 percent of writing to persuade, 35 percent of writing to explain, and 35 percent of writing to convey experience (CCSSI, 2010a, p. 5). By first grade, students should understand these three broad text types and be able to write for each purpose.

To be college and career ready, students need to be able to write as a way of demonstrating understanding of the subjects they are studying. Not only do students need to know and understand argument, informative/explanatory, and narrative forms, but they need to be able to combine different types of writing in order to write for proficiency in all subjects.

SUSTAINING STUDENT WRITING

By third grade, the ELA Common Core requires students to write *routinely* for short amounts of time, and over extended amounts of time for different tasks, purposes, and audiences. Anchor standard 10 in writing addresses the range of writing and calls for a range of discipline-specific tasks.

In shorter amounts of time (a class period or two) students might write on-demand essays. In the ELA Common Core, students are expected to be able to concentrate and write a quality first draft under time constraints. This is also a needed practice for state, district, or course summative assessments. It is important to note that the word *routinely* is used in the standard; this is a standard for grades K–5, and ELA 6–12, and it allows for a variety of writing assignments that are "writing to learn" in nature. In history/social studies, science, and technical subjects in grades 6–12, it is expected that writing must occur in classrooms frequently, if not daily!

When writing for extended periods of time (over days, weeks, or a semester), students are able to practice and gain growth in the writing process, including planning, revising, editing, rewriting, or trying a new approach as called for in anchor standard 8. Allowing for extended writing time also helps satisfy anchor standard 7, which requires not only short research pieces, but also more sustained research projects. When students are able to work on one piece of writing over a length of time, they are able to reflect, revise, and produce multiple copies of their work. This type of writing is needed for students to see themselves as growing and developing writers. Today, more than ever, students need to understand that product writing typically takes many drafts. It should be the rarity, not the norm, that a student turns in a first draft and calls it a "final" draft. Teachers of all content areas must allow time for students to review their writing and make improvements by writing multiple drafts as needed. Students must have time in every class devoted to writing as a way to learn content, and writing to produce products.

SAMPLES OF PROFICIENT STUDENT WRITING

Samples of student writing are given in Appendix C of the ELA CCSS. The writing samples are provided with annotations that explain the criteria met for the type of writing by grade level. The writing samples are considered proficient in that the requirements for the writing standard had been met. It is important to note that these samples represent a variety of classroom conditions, such as being written in class with teacher support, homework assignments, on-demand assessments, and so on.

These student samples are great examples for teachers to view in grade-level or department teams as a starting point to an exploration of what writing for each text type and grade level might look like according the ELA Common Core. Teachers could compare their students' writing to the student samples provided in Appendix C as a way to start discussions about what grade-level proficiency looks like. Teachers can use this model of annotation when viewing student work and collaborating with other teachers whether or not students are proficient according to certain writing standards. While the Common Core does not provide any rubrics or scoring guides for types of writing, it would be ideal for teachers to work collaboratively to create common rubrics by grade level (or grade bands). Having common writing rubrics not only provides teachers with a consistent form of assessment, but also provides students with clarity as to what is considered proficient writing for different text types at each grade level. A first step toward accurate writing assessment is for teachers of grade levels, grade bands, or departments to agree on what a proficient piece of writing looks like for each text type: argument, informational/explanatory, and narrative. To have actual samples with which to compare the writing of one's own students is an invaluable tool.

While the student samples are designed to provide artifacts for teachers with regard to what proficiency should look like for different types of writing, it would also be beneficial to share these examples and annotations with the students themselves. By viewing and discussing different writing samples, students grow as writers. Students need to see what good writing looks like. Teachers should share student work within the classroom as part of the writing process. Teachers could model the annotation process and students could practice annotating other students' work as a form of peer reviewing. Teachers might also save proficient student writing in different text types and under several conditions to create a "bank" of different types of writing that can be shared and discussed in the classroom.

SUMMARY

An increased amount of writing is being demanded by the Common Core State Standards. Writing is to be a shared responsibility instead of happening just in the English classroom. A shift in focus must occur, with students writing more argument and informational/explanatory texts, and less narrative text, especially at the high school level. With increased writing must come sustained focus that addresses short lengths of time (such as on-demand writing) and extended writing that allows for multiple drafts, in-depth research, and time for revision. And lastly, student samples of proficiency must be shared not only amongst teachers to collaboratively come to terms with what proficient writing looks like for different text types and grade levels, but also for students to view and discuss as valuable learning tools.

- The Common Core State Standards for English Language Arts and Literacy in History/Social Studies, Science, and Technical Subjects contain 10 broad college and career readiness anchor standards for grades K–12 with additional clarification notes and grade-specific content in three areas: K–5, 6–12 ELA, and 6–12 literacy in history/social studies, science, and technical subjects.
- The English language arts standards demand that instruction of literacy be a shared responsibility. Reading and writing standards are *in addition to* content taught outside of the English language arts classroom.
- The writing standards have many direct connections to the other English language arts standards.
- The writing standards place special emphasis on argumentative writing. Argument and informative/explanatory writing are now given equal status to narrative writing at the elementary level, with increasing prominence over narrative at the secondary level.
- Students must be able to write for short and extended amounts of time. The demand for nonfiction writing is called out and that writing is to occur *routinely* in all classrooms.
- Appendix C of the ELA CCSS standards provides student samples of different types of writing. Teachers should view and discuss and understand what proficient writing looks like at each grade level.

References

ACT. (2009). National curriculum survey. Retrieved Sept. 5. 2011, from www.act.org/research/policymakers/pdf/NationalCurriculum Survey2009.pdf

Biancarosa, G., & Snow, C. (2004). *Reading next: A vision for action and research in middle and high school literacy.* A report to the Carnegie Corporation of New York. Washington, DC: Alliance for Excellent Education.

Common Core State Standards Initiative (CCSSI). (2010a, June). *Common Core State Standards for English language arts & literacy in history/social studies, science, and technical subjects* (PDF document). Retrieved from www.corestandards.org/assets/CCSSI_ELA%20Standards.pdf

Common Core State Standards Initiative (CCSSI). (2010b, June). *Common Core State Standards for English language arts & literacy in history/social studies, science, and technical subjects: Appendix A* (PDF document). Retrieved from www.corestandards.org/assets/Appendix_A.pdf

Common Core State Standards Initiative (CCSSI). (2010c, June). *Common Core State Standards for English language arts & literacy in history/social studies, science, and technical subjects: Appendix C* (PDF document). Retrieved from www.corestandards.org/assets/Appendix_C.pdf

Graham, S., & Perin, D. (2007). *Writing next: Effective strategies to improve writing of adolescents in middle and high schools.* A report to the Carnegie Corporation of New York. Washington, DC: Alliance for Excellent Education.

Reeves, D. B. (2011, March). Getting ready for common standards. *American School Board Journal.*

The "New" Speaking and Listening—The Need for Rich Conversations and Showcasing Knowledge

Lisa Cebelak

In order to be able to readily adapt in the 21st century, students need many opportunities to participate in rich classroom discussions to develop their speaking and listening skills starting at a very early age. Students need multiple opportunities to collaborate with others in a variety of settings—in a large group, in small groups, or with a partner, for example—in order to acquire the skills called for in the speaking and listening strand of the Common Core. It is very apparent that students need to be able to contribute to discussions by sharing accurate and relevant information, to be able to listen to others' viewpoints, and to be able to address those viewpoints by developing and expanding ideas according to others' responses. Ultimately, students should be able to clearly articulate their viewpoints in a persuasive manner.

Students need to practice expanded forms of communication while learning speaking and listening skills, so it is difficult to separate technology from this strand. In fact, if our students are to be successful in the 21st century, we cannot separate technology from the Common Core ELA standards. Reading, writing, speaking, and listening are intertwined with technology, and our students need to be able to use all forms of communication. Students must have opportunities to learn and use technology (e.g., graphics, images, and combinations of text, embedded video, and audio) in order to enhance their presentations. Students today already use multimedia and see it as a means of expressing information to others, but they need guidance about how to use it in an academic setting. Teachers need to evolve with the fast-paced role of technology in the classroom and be ready to help students by giving them the experience of using technology in their discipline areas. With technology, there is the increasing need for students to adapt their speech and be able to demonstrate formal English on demand.

This chapter will provide an overview of the speaking and listening strand of the Common Core and discuss implications for each standard.

OVERVIEW

The Common Core State Standards for English Language Arts and Literacy in History/Social Studies, Science, and Technical Subjects contain four strands: reading, writing, speaking and listening, and language. The Common Core standards are divided into three grade-span sections: K–5, 6–12 for English language arts, and 6–12 for history/social studies, science, and technical subjects. Whereas the reading strand and writing strand are placed in all three sections, the speaking and listening strand and language strand are placed only in the first two sections: K–5 and 6–12 ELA. The reading and writing strands have 10 college and career readiness anchor standards each, but the speaking and listening and language strands only have six each. These six anchor standards are divided into two areas: comprehension and collaboration, and presentation of knowledge and ideas. Here is a brief overview of the six speaking and listening standards.

Anchor standard 1 is about being able to actively participate in classroom conversations because one is readily prepared. To have a rich discussion, one must be both an active listener and an active speaker. Students need many opportunities to work in diverse groups and be able to collaborate and build on each other's ideas.

Anchor standard 2 is about understanding multiple sources of information from different types of media and being able to evaluate and integrate that information.

Anchor standard 3 is about awareness of both the speaker's point of view and reasoning, and being able to evaluate a speaker's point of view by assessing the use of evidence and rhetoric.

Anchor standard 4 is about presenting information in a logical way so that an audience can understand the reasoning and evidence being presented.

Anchor standard 5 is about the ability to use digital media (e.g. graphics, audio, visual) to support presentations.

Anchor standard 6 is about being able to adapt one's speech to different contexts and tasks, and being able to demonstrate standard English when speaking when it's appropriate.

RICH CONVERSATIONS—COMPREHENSION AND COLLABORATION

The first three anchor standards of speaking and listening are under the subcategory of comprehension and collaboration. Anchor standard 1 calls for rich discussions to occur with diverse partners about grade-level topics, texts, and issues, both in small student groups and in teacher-led groups. When one takes a closer look at standard 1 at the grade-specific levels, it is important to understand the spiral effect of the Common Core standards to see the level of complexity built into this one standard based on collaborative conversations. At the K–2 grade band, students must be able to participate in discussions and be able to follow rules, such as taking turns to speak. In kindergarten, students should be able to continue a conversation on topic with many exchanges. In first and second grade, students should be able to build on others' input by responding and linking their comments to that input. They are also to ask questions for clarity or if additional information is needed.

At the 3–5 grade band, the collaborative discussions become more complex as students are to be actively engaged in many types of discussions by coming to discussions prepared. That means that students have to be able to read and/or study grade-level material in advance and refer to their studies in order to be ready for a rich discussion. Students must continue to follow the rules for discussion, but also start to have assigned roles in the process. At this level, students are expected to explain their ideas and eventually be able to review the key ideas and be able to form a conclusion based on their understanding of the discussion.

At the 6–8 grade band, engaging in a range of collaborative

discussions becomes more defined. For example, instead of just knowing the rules of discussion, students start to set specific goals and deadlines, track their progress, and define their own individual roles within groups if needed.

At the 9–12 grade band, the standard is the most complex, and demands that rich and structured conversations be led by students. For example, instead of just asking and answering questions within a discussion, the standard calls for high school students to be able to "propel conversations by posing and responding to questions that probe reasoning and evidence; ensure a hearing for a full range of positions on a topic or an issue; clarify, verify, or challenge ideas and conclusions; and promote divergent and creative perspectives" (SL.11–12.1c, CCSSI, 2010).

The second anchor standard under comprehension and collaboration focuses on comprehending what has been heard through a text read aloud or information given through other media. Looking at the grade-specific standards, we again notice the spiral effect.

At the K–2 grade band, students need to be prepared to ask questions if they do not understand and be able to answer questions about key details or describe the key details. It is important to note that the standards place emphasis in the early elementary years, and Appendix B contains many examples of read-aloud text exemplars to support teachers with this standard.

At the 3–5 grade band, students need to determine the main ideas and be able to paraphrase at times and summarize the information given.

At the 6–8 grade band, the phrase "a written text read aloud" is dropped and instead the focus is on "information presented in diverse media and formats (e.g., visually, quantitatively, orally)."

At this level, students work to interpret the information, analyze and explain how it relates to the topic of discussion, and, by eighth grade, analyze the purpose and evaluate the motives of the source.

At the 9–12 grade band, it is expected that students will go beyond analyzing by integrating multiple sources of information in their work. Not only should students be able to evaluate each source, but they should also be able to use this information to make informed decisions and solve problems. The standard also states that students should be able to acknowledge discrepancies as they come across them in their work.

Anchor standard 3, the last standard under the comprehension and collaboration category, focuses on evaluating a speaker's point of view and reasoning, and assessing the speaker's use of evidence and rhetoric. Here, the speaker is not identified, but could be the teacher, a student, a guest speaker, or even a media source such as a recorded lecture provided by a professor to supplement a topic studied in a course. Looking at the grade-specific standards, one can see the level of complexity increase throughout the years. At the K–2 grade band, this standard simply demands that students ask and answer questions if they need help, need additional information, or do not understand what is being said. At the 3–5 grade band, students are expected to not only ask and answer questions, but also elaborate and give details where appropriate, be able to identify the speaker's reasons and evidence given, and summarize the points the speaker makes. At the 6–8 grade band, students are listening to evaluate the speaker's claims, knowing which claims are supported with evidence and which claims are baseless. At the 9–12 grade band, students are evaluating the speaker's point of view by listening intently to his or her reasoning, use of evidence, and rhetoric. Students at this level are assessing the information being heard by noticing any false reasoning and distorted evidence along with paying attention to the speaker's word choice, tone, and specific points of emphasis being presented.

IDEAS FOR IMPLEMENTATION—COMPREHENSION AND COLLABORATION

Starting at the kindergarten level, it will be important for teachers to include students in making rules for classroom discussions. It should be clear that how we speak to each other and how we listen to each other are equally important. The rules for discussion could be posted in the classroom and (in later years) be part of a course syllabus. For teachers, modeling this type of conversation with guided practice will be needed until these rules become the norm in the classroom setting.

A research-based instructional strategy to use at the secondary level is the Socratic seminar. A Socratic seminar is a method of teaching that has a process for classroom discussion. When using this method, open-ended questions are used to get students engaged and to think critically, but this method goes a step further by requiring students to articulate clearly and express their opinions with confidence. This strategy covers all the basics of standard 1, and when implemented correctly, the student-led conversations can be very powerful discussions.

A starting point for some teachers might be to rethink the power of questioning. Questioning can be a strong instructional strategy that is simple to implement. According to John Hattie in *Visible Learning* (2009), questioning is the second most dominant teaching method. Teachers spend about 50 percent of their teaching asking questions; however, these questions are typically recall or procedural. Teachers can really improve instruction when they move away from lower-level questions and start asking higher-order questions. According to Marzano, Pickering, and Pollock in *Classroom Instruction That Works* (2001), higher-level questions produce more learning. At the elementary level, a teacher could read a text aloud and stop every now and then to ask a question to check for understanding. As a teacher, you can increase the rigor of your questioning by asking inferential and analytic questions. If a student asks a question, ask if another student can answer the question. This strategy will help to build collaboration and break the habit of students always looking to the teacher for the correct answer. By allowing other students to answer their peers' questions, it also provides different perspectives and reinforces the idea that more than one response may be correct.

At the secondary level, the questioning strategy is powerful in that students start to realize that they need to explain more, or defend their answers. Again, it is important for teachers to encourage other students to respond to their peers and model good questions so that students themselves become good questioners. There are many methods that enable teachers to call on a range of students. One easy method is to use index cards with a student name on each card (select a card, read the name, and call on the student, instead of simply calling on students who raise their hands). This method keeps all students on their toes because they know they could be called on at any time. I recommend placing the index card back into the stack so that each student might get called on multiple times, so that students don't think they are "finished discussing" for the day. The Common Core calls for students to be able to pose good questions as a part of having rich discussions. It is important to implement a method for calling on *all* students from day one.

Another strategy is note-taking. At the elementary level, one could start with a simple two-column note system. In the left-hand column, students could write key points (or list key words) being made by the speaker, and in the right-hand column, students could identify the reasons or evidence the speaker gives. By fifth grade, Cornell Notes could be introduced. Cornell Notes is a note-taking format that has a two-column design that is more sophisticated than a simple two-column note template because it includes a summary box at the bottom. It is important to review the proper way to use this method as teachers often tend to "fill in" the template for students. We want to make sure that students are "note-taking" with this process. Cornell Notes are typically used at the secondary level, but the method certainly applies to the Common Core's fifth-grade standard, as students are asked to summarize the points the speaker makes. Note-taking is a great way to keep students focused on what the speaker is presenting and to develop a system for listening for key points being made. It also allows students to start good study skill habits by learning to create their own notes, rather than using a worksheet. Student note-taking also allows for pair-shares and small-group collaboration when asked to share information. Teachers should look for structured ways to have students collaborate, and by implementing Socratic seminars, effective questioning, and note-taking, teachers are setting their classrooms up for rich conversations to occur in a variety of ways.

SHOWCASING WHAT YOU KNOW—PRESENTATION OF KNOWLEDGE AND IDEAS

The last three anchor standards for the speaking and listening strand are under the subcategory presentation of knowledge and ideas. Anchor standard 4 is about presenting information in a logical way so that an audience can understand the reasoning and evidence being presented. Looking closer at the grade-specific standards, we notice that kindergarteners are being asked to present by describing familiar things. In the K–2 grade band, it is expected that all students are able to tell a story, with many facts and details. They are also expected to speak audibly and in coherent sentences.

In grades 3–5, students leave the comfort of narrative and move to informative speech by having to report on a topic or text or even present an opinion. Again, it is expected that ideas are sequenced logically with facts and supporting details; however, this time it is to support main ideas or a theme, rather than tell a story. Students continue to be expected to speak clearly, and at the 3–5 grade band, the grade-specific language requires that they speak "at an understandable pace."

At the 6–8 grade band, the stakes are raised as students are required to present claims and findings and expand the sequencing of ideas to include emphasizing points, relevant evidence, valid reasoning, and well-chosen details. At this level, it is also expected that students will use eye contact, adequate volume, and clear pronunciation when presenting in class. At the 9–12 grade band, students continue to build on the skills learned in middle school, but complexity is added in that when they present, they must convey a clear perspective and address other perspectives, and know what is appropriate for their purpose and audience.

Anchor standard 5 is about the ability to use digital media (e.g., graphics, audio, visual) to support presentations. At the K–2 grade band, this means that students will add their own drawings or other visuals to descriptions. In second grade, the grade-specific standard requires that students also create audio recordings of stories or poems.

At the 3–5 grade band, students continue to create audio recordings that demonstrate fluid reading and add them to presentations along with other types of visual displays. By fifth grade, students are expected to include multimedia components to enhance their presentations.

At the 6–8 grade band, students continue to include multimedia (e.g., graphics, images, music) and visual displays, but must also integrate this technology to clarify claims, emphasize points, and to make the presentation overall more appealing.

At the 9–12 grade band, students are expected to make strategic use of digital media. By the end of high school, students should be able to readily use many forms of multimedia, and be able to use them purposefully for the sake of enhancing their highly engaging presentations.

The last anchor standard for speaking and listening under the subcategory presentation of knowledge and ideas is anchor standard 6. This standard is about adapting one's speech to different contexts and tasks, and demonstrating formal English in speaking when appropriate. Looking at the grade-specific standards, it is important to note that starting in first grade, the standard is in tandem with the language grade-level standards 1 and 3. At the K–2 grade band, students are practicing speaking clearly and audibly in the beginning years, and by the end of second grade, students are expected to talk in complete sentences in response to requested detail or clarification. (So, for example, when looking at the grade-specific standard for grade 2, SL.2.6, one would have to refer also to language standards 1 and 3 for second grade, noted as L.2.1 and L.2.3, for further clarity.)

At the 3–5 grade band, students continue to speak in complete sentences and start to learn and understand when formal English is needed (presenting in class), and when informal discourse is allowed (small groups or working in pairs). By the end of fifth grade, students must be able to adapt their speech in the classroom depending on the situation. At the secondary level, the focus becomes more about demonstrating command of formal English when appropriate. It is important to review the language grade-specific standards that will help to give clarity as to what is expected regarding expectations of formal English.

IDEAS FOR IMPLEMENTATION—PRESENTATION OF KNOWLEDGE AND IDEAS

It is important that students have a solid understanding of what is expected when giving presentations in class. A detailed rubric can easily address the three presentation of knowledge and ideas standards. While a rubric for content is something most teachers are experienced with, it important to include areas like presentation style, multimedia use, and speech in order to gauge if students are proficient when presenting in the classroom.

At all grade levels, it is important to address areas such as volume, pacing, and eye contact. Ideally, a teacher should model a proficient presentation in front of the class and have students mark on the rubric what the teacher did and have conversations about the presentation. A teacher could also videotape presentations to serve as future exemplars. When students have a rubric to study from before their presentations, it can help to ease anxiety, let them know exactly what proficiency looks like, and give them a chance to practice at home or with a peer beforehand. If they are not proficient in one of these areas, they can use the rubric to identify what they need to work on before their next presentation. Rubrics are also great ways for students to create self-selected goals.

One can also use rubrics for addressing multimedia. There are many categories here that can really help to strengthen a student's presentation, such as sequencing of media information, text types and fonts, audio, and visual, to name a few. Students need to know and understand what proficiency for multimedia looks like, and teachers need to be very specific about what it means to include multimedia in presentations. I have seen too many teachers simply state in directions to *be creative* when addressing this issue. Asking students to be creative does not teach them how to use media responsibly, and leaves students wondering "what exactly is the teacher looking for?" Another note: "Be creative" is not specific enough to be on a rubric, and is not part of the "unwrapped" standard.

Teachers can also use rubrics to address the formal English required when giving presentations. I would suggest including key words and details from the appropriate language standards as a guide for creating proficiency for this topic. A rubric here serves as a review for students and allows them to practice using formal English and adapting their speech for presentations.

Rubrics can be created for presentations in grades K–12. Teachers could work to set them up in a spiral-effect chart to model the Common Core standards. Rubrics are beneficial for both students and teachers. In addition to being used to "grade" presentations, rubrics can also help grade-level teachers share data about their students with teachers of other grade levels.

SUMMARY

Students need multiple opportunities to collaborate with their peers in the classroom setting. Teachers need to ensure that students work in diverse groups, with a partner, in small groups, and in larger group settings. In order to have rich conversations, rules need to be in place, and students must come to the classroom prepared. Students need to be able to ask and answer their own questions and initiate and participate in discussions. Students also need to be able to present information in a logical way, use media to enhance their presentations, and adapt their speech as needed and show command of formal English. The emphasis on speaking and listening is intertwined with other English language arts standards, and the spiral effect shows how the complexity of what students need to be able to do in order to have rich classroom discussions and when showcasing information for their peers increases through the grade levels.

- The ELA CCSS include six speaking and listening anchor standards that are categorized into two subgroups: comprehension and collaboration, and presentation of knowledge and ideas.
- The speaking and listening standards have many direct connections to other English language arts standards.
- The comprehension and collaboration standards call for student-led conversations with diverse partners in both small groups and larger group settings.

- The comprehension and collaboration standards call for students to integrate multiple sources of information and to evaluate a speaker's argument.
- The presentation of knowledge and ideas standards call for students to become proficient speakers and to be able to adapt their speech based on circumstances.
- The presentation of knowledge and ideas standards call for students to use multimedia to enhance their presentations.

References

Common Core State Standards Initiative (CCSSI). (2010, June). *Common Core State Standards for English language arts & literacy in history/social studies, science, and technical subjects* (PDF document). Retrieved from www.corestandards.org/assets/CCSSI_ELA%20Standards.pdf

Hattie, J. (2009). *Visible learning: A synthesis of over 800 meta-analyses relating to achievement.* New York: Routledge.

Marzano, R., Pickering, D., & Pollock, J. (2001). *Classroom instruction that works: Research-based strategies for increasing student achievement.* Alexandria, VA: ASCD.

So Much More Than Grammar—How the Language Strand of the Common Core Supports and Strengthens the Other Strands

Angela Peery

The Common Core State Standards for English Language Arts and Literacy in History/Social Studies, Science, and Technical Subjects include four strands: reading, writing, speaking and listening, and language. In contrast with the 10 college and career readiness standards that anchor the reading and writing strands, both the speaking and listening and language strands contain only six anchor standards each. So, the language strand is unified by six statements, and these statements reflect only three key areas: standard English conventions (grammar, usage, capitalization, punctuation, and spelling); knowledge of language (syntax, formal and informal discourse, English varieties and dialects); and vocabulary acquisition and use.

This chapter provides an overview of the language strand and then discusses the expectations within the three key areas (standard English conventions, knowledge of language, and vocabulary acquisition and use). The specific expectations are parsed to clarify what they actually mean and then are discussed in terms of how they support the other strands.

OVERVIEW

The college and career readiness anchor standards for language demand that students be able to do the following:

- Use standard English grammar and usage when writing and speaking (L.CCR.1).
- Use standard English mechanics (spelling, capitalization, and punctuation) in written products (L.CCR.2).
- Apply their understanding of language varieties and language uses to be more effective in their own writing and speaking and to more fully comprehend when they are reading or listening (L.CCR.3).
- Use word attack strategies to determine the meanings of unknown or unfamiliar words in all situations (L.CCR.4).
- Apply their understanding of the various meanings of words (denotations, connotations, nuances) and figurative language (L.CCR.5).
- Acquire and use increasingly complex academic vocabulary in reading, writing, speaking, and listening (L.CCR.6).

STANDARD ENGLISH CONVENTIONS

Observing the rules of Standard American English (SAE) in speaking and writing is important to a student's academic success, and grammar, usage, and mechanics figure prominently in the language strand. Indeed, these rules comprise the first two anchor standards and are described with incredible precision throughout the grades.

Conventions in the Lower Grades

When scrutinizing the band for kindergarten through grade 2, the trained eye notices several remarkable things. Standard L.K.1a says that students will "print *many* upper- and lowercase letters" (CCSSI, 2010, emphasis added). This stands in stark contrast to many state standards documents that have, for the past decade, directed teachers to ensure their kindergartners can print *all* the letters of the alphabet (both upper- and lowercase). In the Common Core, printing all the letters of the alphabet in both forms is required in grade 1, *not in kindergarten* (L.1.1a). Then, in grade 2, the standard about printing the letters disappears altogether. Because of the spiral nature of the Common Core, when a standard is no longer mentioned, mastery was expected at the end of the year in which the standard last appeared. So, by the end of first grade, all students should be able to print all uppercase and lowercase letters. The standards make that very clear.

Across the years of kindergarten through grade 2, the use of nouns is discussed, with more specificity about application at each level.

In kindergarten, students are to "use frequently occurring nouns and verbs" (L.K.1b), while in first grade, they are to know how to use several specific types of nouns—common, proper, and possessive (L.1.1b). This would be predicated upon students having both the declarative and procedural knowledge required; in other words, students must know what common, proper, and possessive nouns are, and they must know how to use all three types in various situations and contexts.

In grade 2, the expectations about nouns are clarified further by two standards. First, "Use collective nouns" (L.2.1a), and then, "Form and use frequently occurring irregular plural nouns," such as the words *fish* and *mice* (L.2.1b). Again, students must possess and use both declarative and procedural knowledge to meet the standards. They must know what collective and irregular plural nouns are (declarative knowledge), plus apply their knowledge in speaking and writing (procedural).

Grade 3 builds on the earlier grades by adding more application of noun skills: explaining their functions in sentences, using both regular and irregular plural nouns, and using abstract nouns (L.3.1a, b, and c). After grade 3, there is no more mention of the particulars of working with nouns. That doesn't mean students stop using nouns! It means that they continue to apply their proficient understanding of nouns in all that they do.

Of course, the first standard for each of these grade levels also contains specifics about much more than just nouns. Verbs, prepositions, and the concept of the complete sentence also feature prominently. The concept of the complete sentence, which is conceptual knowledge needed in order to become an effective writer, is rightly emphasized at the kindergarten and first-grade levels.

In a nutshell, in kindergarten, students are simply to use the most frequently occurring verbs and prepositions in our language (L.K.1b and L.K.1e). (It is reminiscent of the initial lessons in a Spanish language learning software program that requires the learner to repeatedly look at photographs and then pick the correct word for the prepositions *in, on, under,* and *beside.*) Verbs are necessary in order for a sentence to be a sentence, and most basic English sentences could also not be produced without the use of prepositions.

As for sentences at the kindergarten level, students are to produce and expand them, but not independently—rather, "in shared language activities" (L.K.1f). This particular expectation will pleasantly surprise hundreds of kindergarten teachers across the country who have been striving to help their kindergartners master creating complete sentences independently. That particular outcome now appears at grade 1, and is fully described as: "Produce and expand complete simple and compound declarative, interrogative, imperative, and exclamatory sentences in response to prompts" (L.1.1j). This statement is worded so clearly that there can be no doubt that our nation's first graders should be experienced in producing and expanding all four types of sentences by the end of the school year. And, this understanding and experience then goes with them to grades 2 and above—deepened over time.

In grade 2, particular attention is given to simple and compound sentences, and students are to "produce, expand, and rearrange" them (L.2.1f). This expectation is then made more rigorous in grade 3, when students are to produce not only simple and compound sentences, but complex ones as well (L.3.1i). In the Common Core, this is the first mention of complex sentences, which, by definition, require dependent clauses. A reasonable interpretation then follows: In kindergarten, students learn to form sentences. In first grade, they learn the basics of forming all four types of sentences. And, at grades 2 and above, they expand their skills by forming various types of sentences, utilizing phrases and clauses with the requisite use of prepositions and conjunctions.

Continuing with standard 1 in kindergarten through grade 2, there are some other notable features:

- Verb tense is first mentioned in grade 1 (L.1.1e).
- Subject-verb agreement is first mentioned in grade 1, noted as "matching verbs" (L.1.1c).
- Adjectives are first mentioned in grade 1, while adverbs are not mentioned until grade 2 (L.1.1f and L.2.1e).

Standard 2 mirrors standard 1 in its specificity, but this time, the focus area is mechanics (capitalization, punctuation, and spelling). Interestingly enough, the first kindergarten expectation about capitalization is one that has often appeared in state standards documents in first grade: capitalize the first word of a sentence and the pronoun "I" (L.2.2a). So, while kindergarten students are not held independently responsible for producing complete sentences, they are supposed to know these two very important capitalization rules. It's an interesting juxtaposition—or a possible misalignment. Don't students need to know how to write a sentence before they know to capitalize the first letter?

Kindergartners are also to recognize and name end marks (L.K.2b), while first graders must apply this skill as they write their own sentences (L.1.2b). First graders also take their capitalization skills one step further, applying them to dates and names of people (L.2.2a). In grade 2, students add holidays, product names, and geographic names to their capitalization repertoire (L.2.2a). It is perplexing that the capitalization of the titles of books, poems, and stories doesn't also appear in grade 2 or grade 1.

Perhaps the trickiest punctuation mark of all—the comma—does not appear in kindergarten, but does, for dates and items in a series, in first grade (L.1.1c). In second grade, the pesky comma must also be used with the greetings and closings of letters (L.2.2b). If these most common uses of the comma were truly mastered by our country's second-grade youngsters, imagine how the business world 15 or 20 years from now would figuratively sigh in relief!

Spelling is discussed in standard 2, starting with the phonetic spelling of "simple words" in kindergarten (L.K.2d); however, the document never defines "simple." Appendix A does describe tier-one, tier-two, and tier-three words (CCSSI, 2010, p. 33). One could logically assume that all tier-one words are prime for instruction in kindergarten—and, depending upon the needs of the students, some tier-two words as well.

In first grade, spelling expectations are more specific than in kindergarten. Students are to use conventional spelling for words with common spelling patterns and phonetic approximations for "untaught" words (L.1.1d and 1e). It is unclear in kindergarten and grade 1 what the expectation for "taught" words is—that is, words that are studied and practiced, those that appear on word walls, and so on. "Taught" is never clearly defined, providing teachers with another area of the Common Core to interpret and apply.

In grade 2, the use of reference materials such as glossaries and dictionaries is first cited as an aid to accurate spelling (L.2.2e). The use of reference materials to help a student spell accurately also appears through grade 5 (L.3.2g; L.4.2d; L.5.2e). Because of the spiral nature of the Common Core, teachers should expect students after grade 5 to be able to utilize all available resources in order to spell accurately when accurate spelling counts.

The only other notable feature regarding standard English conventions in grades kindergarten through 2 worth discussing is that other much-maligned punctuation mark—the apostrophe.

It is mentioned at grade 2 for contractions and "frequently occurring" possessives (L.2.2e) and then is *never mentioned again in the language strand.* This leaves one to wonder about "infrequently occurring" possessives (e.g., plural words that already end in "s") and rarer uses of the apostrophe, as in the special plurals of some nouns and/or acronyms (e.g., "Watch your p's and q's," "Here are some do's and don'ts. . . ," "The 1990's were marked by financial prosperity"). Where are these uses taught? Perhaps we can infer from the document that from grades 3 and up, we need to base our instruction about apostrophes on what students are showing us in their writing. When they need to learn a more sophisticated application, then that's the best time to teach it.

Conventions in the Upper Grades

In grades 6–12, standards 1 and 2 lose much of their specificity, but certain topics and issues rise to prominence. Again, the lack of specificity does not mean that teachers stop teaching about the finer uses of the conventions that have already been delineated. It means that students should be applying their conventions skills to increasingly more difficult writing and speaking.

Spelling is dispensed with by the inclusion of the same exact statement in all six grade levels in the upper grades: "Spell correctly" (L.6.2b; L.7.2b; L.8.2c; L.9–10.2c; L.11–12.2b). Inherent in this statement are the earlier expectations of students approximating accurate spelling, then being held accountable for spelling "grade-appropriate words," and lastly, using all available reference materials in order to be correct.

Next, a mastery of the basics of punctuation is evident, with only very specialized instances of sophisticated punctuation use noted.

At grade 6, students are to demonstrate mastery in using several types of punctuation (commas, parentheses, and dashes) with nonrestrictive elements (L.6.2a). This particular expectation is one that is marked with an asterisk, so that means the creators of the document knew that it would have to be supported not only in grade 6 but also in higher grades. Even adult writers continue to struggle with this particular convention, as evidenced in the sentences below, all taken from recent business communications I have received:

> Please read the following letter thoroughly as we have included some very important information regarding logistics. (Comma should be inserted after "thoroughly.")
>
> If you are facilitating a discussion please e-mail me any discussion questions you would like to have disseminated. (Comma should be inserted after first "discussion.")
>
> That Tuesday, which happens to be a long travel day for me is the only day when I can be on the call. (Additional comma is needed after "me.")

Interestingly enough, another tricky use of the comma appears in grade 7, and that is the use of commas with "coordinate adjectives" (L.7.2a). The correct application of commas with adjectives that are equal in intensity and are used together to describe a noun can be particularly confusing for youngsters, but is perhaps cognitively easier than the applications with nonrestrictive elements highlighted in grade 6. For example, many students would know that this sentence does not require commas between the adjectives "red" and "brick": "He lives in a red brick house." However, students may not understand the difference between a sentence like that and a sentence like this one: "She was a stubborn, demanding child."

The only punctuation conventions that appear in grade 8 are for students to apply commas, ellipses, and dashes to indicate pauses and breaks (L.8.2a) and ellipses to indicate omissions (L.8.2b). These very specific conventions are the only mentions of ellipses in the entire language strand. Dashes are mentioned in grade 6, are absent in grade 7, and then appear again in grade 8.

Having been a middle school, high school, and college instructor of writing, I'll admit that I expected to see ellipses also mentioned when they are applied to quotations. "To indicate pauses and breaks" is perhaps too general a statement to remind teachers of how students struggle to use ellipses effectively in quotations. Also, from my perspective as a writing teacher, I know that writers of all ages struggle with the effective use of dashes. For the document to not more clearly spiral the uses of the dash within the grade span 6–8 could lead to some misunderstanding by teachers. Being able to use a dash effectively is a hallmark of sophisticated writing. In order for students to attain mastery of its uses in grade 8, there must be practice in both grades 6 and 7, so ideally, teachers would provide plenty of modeling and practice *within the context of authentic writing* throughout the middle grades.

At grade band 9–10, the correct use of semicolons to join independent clauses is noted, and the correct application of colons preceding lists or quotations is also specified (L.9–10.2a and 2b). Of interest here is the fact that the skill of using a colon to precede a list is often taught in the earlier grades. For example, in the Indiana academic standards, this particular convention has been taught at the fifth-grade level. In the Connecticut standards, this convention has been taught in sixth grade.

At grade band 11–12, the only punctuation convention noted is correct hyphenation (L.11–12.2a). The rules for hyphenation are not discussed at any other grade level or band. This is also a standard that has been traditionally taught in earlier grades, but at a lower level of application—that is, being able to hyphenate a word appropriately when having to divide it manually in handwriting. The more sophisticated use of hyphens in most writing is applying them to compound adjectives (two or more adjectives that convey a single thought), a convention that sends even professional writers to their grammar or style handbooks.

The grammar and usage conventions specified in grades 6–12 range from several very concrete, detailed expectations about pronouns in grade 6 to the vague and abstract topic of "complex or contested usage" (L.11–12.1b).

Also of note in this section of the standards is the expectation that by the end of grade 7, students must be able to fluidly use all four sentence structures—simple, compound, complex, and compound-complex (L.7.1b). I have personally engaged in an informal action research project over the last several months in which I have displayed a collection of four sentences (one of each structure) for groups of educators and have challenged them to correctly identify each. In the largest group to date—approximately 200 people—only two educators could correctly identify the compound-complex sentence and explain its features to others. The results of my little experiment lead me to believe that it will be very difficult to help America's middle schoolers master the specifics of the four sentence structures so that all four become a regular part of their writing. Additionally, L.7.1b is not marked with an asterisk, meaning it is one of the standards that the authors of the Common Core did not identify for continuing support in the grades that follow. My personal suspicion is that teachers will have to continue to support their students, particularly with complex and compound-complex sentences, through the high school years.

Using verbs in both the active and passive voices is mentioned in grade 8 (L.8.1b) and nowhere else. Up until this point, only subject-verb agreement and verb tense have been mentioned, not voice. (Active and passive voice also appear in the grade-level expectations for standard 3, as discussed in the next section.)

The Common Core actually gets into a great level of detail about verbs, which may be unnecessary for most of the speaking and writing that students will do, even in their postsecondary education. The main thing students should remember about active and passive voice is that writing in active voice is always more forceful. Therefore, passive voice should be used sparingly, if at all. This lesson will serve them well in the middle grades, in high school, in college, and in graduate school and the workplace.

Knowledge of Language

As students mature, understanding the shades of meanings of various words is important. It is also important for students to understand when it is best to use Standard American English (for example, in most academic situations), which may or may not be the language of the home, family, and community. The use of informal discourse styles and nonstandard forms of English (such as African-American Vernacular English, or AAVE) often results in penalties for students when they are writing or speaking. Additionally, students whose first language is not English often struggle with idioms, colloquialisms, and other specialized components of SAE. Anchor standard 3 in the language strand deals with all such situations—and more. This standard is not only about using standard English, but also about using informal discourse styles, nonstandard forms of English, dialects, and many types of figurative language when they are appropriate.

The grade-level specifics of standard 3 begin at grade 2 with one clear expectation: "Compare formal and informal uses of English" (L.2.3a). Generally, "formal and informal uses" are interpreted as academic or businesslike speaking and writing versus casual, friendly speaking and writing. The Online Writing Lab of Purdue University gives this apt description:

> The level of formality you write with should be determined by the expectations of your audience and your purpose. For example, if you are writing a cover letter for a job application or a[n] ... academic essay, you would write in a formal style. If you are writing a letter to a friend, writing something personal..., you would use a more informal style. (owl.english.purdue.edu)

At grades 3, 4, and 5, this standard includes using words, phrases, and punctuation for both effect and precision. At these grade levels, variations of the English language are also mentioned—specifically, dialects and registers (L.5.3b). In grades 6–8, this standard again focuses on precision but adds concision (L.7.3a) in addition to style and tone (L.6.3b). Active and passive voices are referenced again, and the only reference to subjunctive mood is also made (L.8.3a). The inclusion of subjunctive mood is notable because many adults would be hard pressed to define and describe the indicative, subjunctive, and imperative moods of verbs. Ask yourself if you can differentiate among and give examples of each of these. If you weren't an English major, or if you're not a grammar aficionado, you might struggle. So, it's important to note the wording of the expectation at grade 8: "Use verbs in the ... subjunctive mood to achieve particular effects." As in many of the explicit grade-level expectations, this one is fairly obscure but is nonetheless essential for effective speaking and writing.

At grades 9–12, the standard changes slightly and becomes more global, basically demanding that students edit to conform to certain accepted style guides (L.9–10.3a) and that they consider the craft of writing effective sentences not only when writing, but also when reading (L.11–12.3a).

VOCABULARY ACQUISITION AND USE

The last three anchor standards in the language strand focus upon vocabulary. Specifically, they focus on context clues, word analysis, reference materials, figurative language, connotation, and discipline-specific vocabulary.

At the earliest grade levels (K–2), students must learn about multiple-meaning words, using both word parts and context as clues. Root words feature prominently in grades 1–5, with Greek and Latin roots being specified at grades 4 and 5. It is unclear which roots might be part of curriculum and instruction in grades 1–3, although certainly by grade 3, students should have some familiarity with common roots, like *graph* (autograph, biography) and *tele* (telephone, television).

Sentence-level context is identified as a clue to meaning in grades 1–3; context is broadened at grades 4 and 5 to include definitions, examples, restatements, cause-effect relationships, and comparisons, which may go beyond just the sentence in which any given unfamiliar word or phrase appears.

The correct pronunciation of any given word is first mentioned in grade 4 (L.4.4c), in the context of students using reference sources in order to determine both pronunciation and meaning. Prior to that grade level, this same standard focuses only on meaning, not on pronunciation.

Obviously, students should know how to pronounce the words they are using in their speaking and writing for maximum effect. Because academic content often gets considerably more difficult at grade 4, this particular standard calls the appropriate attention to more difficult words in all content areas. Students need to know how to move many words from their receptive vocabularies (words that are understood when read or heard) to their productive vocabularies (words they can use in speaking and writing).

At the high school grade bands, anchor standard 4 adds increased precision in word use by referencing etymology, which is not mentioned before that point.

Anchor standard 5 plays out in kindergarten and grade 1 by specifically citing "guidance and support from adults." At grade 2, students become independent in their understandings of word relationships and shades of meaning. The shades of meaning requirements, in particular, evolve from focusing only on verbs (in kindergarten) to verbs and adjectives (first grade) to closely related verbs and adjectives (second grade). There is also an interesting juxtaposition between kindergarten and first grade, in that at the kindergarten level, the standard says that students act out the meanings of various verbs, whereas in first grade, students define, choose, or act out the meanings. If students are "choosing" certain words, that implies that the choice takes place when creating a spoken or written product. This is different from distinguishing meanings (which implies reading and is much more passive) and from acting out meanings (which is an even less direct application).

At grades 4 and 5, anchor standard 5 becomes specific about idioms, adages, proverbs, synonyms, antonyms, and homographs (L.4.5b and 5c; L.5.5b and 5c). In grades 6–8, the denotation and connotation of words are specifically mentioned for the first time.

Anchor standard 6 differs significantly at the lower grade levels, but is the same at grades 9–12. The middle school version of this standard is also the same across all three grade levels and is just slightly less rigorous than the high school version; it lacks the idea of demonstrating independence when gathering vocabulary knowledge, and, of course, it also lacks the phraseology about "college and career readiness" that appears in the high school strands. The very slight differences across grade levels 6–12 make this particular standard perhaps the hardest of all in the language strand to pin down and relate directly to instruction.

At grades 3–5, standard 6 delineates quite a few different focal points. At grade 3, spatial and temporal relationships take precedence. At grade 4, "precise actions, emotions, or states of being" are highlighted, as are common words that are applied to specific topics, like the verb *endanger* when discussing animal preservation. Lastly, at grade 8, "contrast, addition, and other logical relationships" are specifically denoted. The words *however* and *nevertheless* are used as examples, which is interesting, because student writers even a few years beyond grade 5 often use such words incorrectly (such as using the adverb *however* when opposites don't appear on each side of it).

The three vocabulary acquisition and use standards in the language strand are indeed important, as they all have application across the disciplines. Additionally, there is abundant research about the amount of vocabulary that students need in order to be successful in school (Beck, et al., 2002; Graves, 2005; Marzano, 2004). Unfortunately for teachers, the vocabulary standards are not nearly as specific as the conventions standards in this strand, and therefore, teachers will need to study these standards closely and utilize other resources in order to best carry out the intent of the standards. The Common Core document "Appendix A: Research Supporting Key Elements of the Standards Glossary of Key Terms" contains several pages about the vocabulary standards in this strand and should be consulted frequently and closely.

SUMMARY

The language strand of the Common Core State Standards for English language arts and literacy contains six standards that focus on standard English conventions, knowledge of language, and vocabulary acquisition and use. The six standards are fleshed out across the grade levels with varying levels of specificity, with the most specific expectations in the conventions standards and the most vague in vocabulary, most notably standard 6 as it appears in grades 6–12.

The language strand does make several things very clear, however. First, nouns and verbs are the building blocks of spoken and written communication. Second, the concept of the complete, correct sentence is a critical conceptual learning component in the early years of schooling and for our students who are learning English as a new language. Third, various types of sentence structures are necessary for effective communication, and these structures are dependent on the use of phrases, clauses, and sophisticated punctuation, including most notably the semicolon and the comma. Fourth, spelling should be accurate—period! Students should be urged to use *all available resources* when checking their spelling for written products that have an audience other than one's self. Fifth, Standard American English should be applied in speaking and writing situations where it is desirable. Sixth, unfamiliar vocabulary can be "unlocked" by various methods when one is reading or listening, and lastly, it is always important to expand one's own vocabulary—both generally and in relation to subject matter.

References

Beck, I. L., McKeown, M. G., & Kucan, L. (2002). *Bringing words to life: Robust vocabulary instruction.* New York: Guilford Press.

Common Core State Standards Initiative (CCSSI). (2010, June). *Common Core State Standards for English language arts & literacy in history/social studies, science, and technical subjects: Appendix A* (PDF document). Retrieved from www.corestandards.org/assets/Appendix_A.pdf

Graves, M. F. (2005). *The vocabulary book: Learning & instruction.* New York: Teachers College Press.

Marzano, R. (2004). *Building background knowledge for academic achievement: Research on what works in schools.* Alexandria, VA: ASCD.

Purdue University. (2011). Online writing lab. Retrieved Sept. 4, 2011, from owl.english.purdue.edu/owl/resource/608/02/

Preparing for Common Core Implementation of Literacy Expectations

Thomasina D. Piercy

Today, literacy is standing on its hind legs and growing stronger daily. It is peering into education's door, which is now ajar—pried open by adolescents.

Educators have been talking about declining literacy data for decades. Once again, as depicted by the ACT 2010 College and Career Readiness report, data are indicating that just under one in four high school graduates met all four college readiness benchmarks for reading, English, science, and math (p. 8). Taking a moment to move this data from a chart into the reality of our adolescents' lives, three out of four of our *graduates* were *not* prepared for English composition, algebra, social science, and biology *first-year* college courses (ACT, 2010, p. 19). This comes four years after ACT's disturbing release of *Reading Between the Lines*, which stated that student readiness for college-level reading, in relation to being ready for college-level expectations, was at its lowest point in more than a decade (ACT, 2006, p. 2).

Data points continue to be as alarming as they are extensive. Research-based national reports calling for action have been relentless. Whether analyzing the Carnegie Corporation's *Time to Act* report, a call to action for revised, explicit literacy standards (2010, p. 52), or Achieve's *Aligned Expectations?* summary, which states, "To be ready for college, students need to be able to read and interpret a variety of complex texts, both fiction and nonfiction" (2007, p. 13), the insight gleaned provides clear direction.

At long last, decades of data are being acknowledged and addressed. Urgency reached a boiling point, not simply from years of aligned data, but due to fresh details, including Williamson's study (2008, p. 618) depicting a 265L (Lexile) gap between texts read near the end of high school and university texts. This is more than the Lexile difference between the end of fourth and seventh grades (MetaMetrics, 2011, p. 2). The specific reading capacities that differentiated students' ability to achieve ACT's benchmarks were students' ability to read, understand, and respond to questions about complex texts (CCSSI, 2010b, p. 2; ACT, 2006, p. 16).

American adolescents' dismal performance has contributed to our nation's focused efforts to put the stake in the ground, here and now, and set forth with a plan for high-level, common standards that are honest and hopeful. Honest in that there are no minced words about the fact that the standards are imperfect; hopeful in that the standards seriously raise expectations for text complexity as the artery of cognitive demand.

How prepared are we to look literacy in the face? Fortunately, national and state resources are collaborating on this effort. The Common Core State Standards Initiative has established increased expectations to strengthen education's literacy core in major disciplines for all students. Integrated throughout the kindergarten through grade 12 standards, including college and career anchor standards for reading, are key requirements that all students must be able to independently and proficiently comprehend texts of increasing complexity. Text complexity is defined as the inherent difficulty of reading and comprehending a text combined with consideration of reader and task variables (CCSSI, 2010b, p. 43). Providing this level of instruction prepares students for success, as opposed to needing remediation after graduation when they are embarking on their college and career journeys. Embedded throughout the standards are instructional expectations, including a focus on informational texts (such as historical and scientific texts). Expectations also include reading independence, including reducing the level of scaffolding, and increasing rigor by focusing on discipline-specific questions. With the standards released, there is much we can do to get ready for implementation of aligned literacy expectations.

Although the pace of change in some states has been increased by participation in the Race to the Top initiative, all states are facing significant literacy changes. Now is the time to prepare for the CCSS, even for the Race to the Top states that are already on a fast track for change. Avoiding the complexity of 21st-century literacy changes is no longer an option. With state leadership teams gearing up for the sea change stemming from the Common Core State Standards' expectations, it is time to widely open education's door and welcome literacy—with all its complexity. Since fear can accompany change when it is not understood, this chapter will take a closer look at how recent changes have impacted current literacy decisions. Then, recommendations for enthusiastically getting ready for the literacy initiatives embedded in the Common Core standards will be provided.

Groundwork for building a strong foundation capable of embracing the complexity surrounding literacy is enhanced by briefly revisiting what we have learned from "chaos theory." Although the word *chaos* implies disorder and confusion, chaos theory is about finding the underlying order in randomness. Just as it shapes understanding by establishing order out of confusion in other fields, chaos theory can articulate an understanding of the *relationships* between current educational practices and the increased Common Core expectations.

One aspect of chaos theory, phase space, describes a state where two unique variables of a system can coexist. A walk through our woods provides opportunities to notice the coexistence of two seasons—summer and winter. Green leaves peek out from beneath a blanket of white snow. Characteristics unique to each season are represented; the existence of one does not prevent the existence of the other. Getting ready for the Common Core standards requires a similar state of mind. We need to recognize and continue successful practices, while making a place at the table for new concepts. To begin, we must identify the current antecedents of student success that have contributed to increased achievement and need to be continued. Then, as in the phase space example, recommendations supporting increased Common Core State Standards expectations for what districts and schools can do now to prepare for the Common Core standards will be added to the existing best practices.

CURRENT SUCCESSFUL LITERACY ANTECEDENTS

While the CCSS are providing opportunities for changes in education, sustaining a variety of positive current practices will provide the foundation for students' success.

Literacy Leadership

As the Carnegie Corporation's report for advancing adolescent literacy explains, "critical thinking and effective communication has to be the center of everyone's efforts" (2010, p. viii). The need for communication about literacy has never been more vital, because "administrators can walk through the hallways and classrooms of a school and accomplish nothing if they do not begin with a clear and consistent idea of what effective instruction looks like and have the ability to communicate the elements of effective instruction in clear and unmistakable terms" (Reeves, 2009, p. 119). When literacy leadership includes disciplined practice, it becomes a sustainable process (Piercy and Piercy, 2011, p. 129). It is through disciplined practice that Gardner's premise, that "respectful and ethical minds cannot be outsourced" (2009), can be modeled, because when literacy leadership is disciplined, the work of leaders, actions of teachers, and achievement of students is connected. The literacy changes are challenging for all educators at every level, yet they are filled with enormous potential.

Invisible Excellence during Compelling Conversations

One student achievement process that closes the gap for students not yet meeting grade-level standards is "invisible excellence." Invisible excellence also closes the gap for students who are not yet demonstrating their full potential for comprehending at above-proficient levels by comprehending the "stretch" texts as recommended by the CCSS. When students achieve invisible excellence, it is a tribute to the students and to every teacher who believes in them.

The invisible excellence process arose from a question I asked in September as a new principal: "Why are you providing instruction two years below your students' enrolled grade level?" Teachers' responses included, "I don't know"; "I don't know anything about the decisions that were made prior to this year." One teacher after another explained that when previous teachers made decisions to not advance a student in reading or math, the rationale for those decisions was typically not clearly communicated between grades.

The leadership model of *Compelling Conversations* (Piercy, 2006) evolved naturally to confront the historically difficult norm of individual teachers making isolated decisions about student growth. By expanding decision making during regularly scheduled, individual conversations between each teacher and the principal about every student, these conversations increase support for teachers in establishing student goals. Those goals are considered "invisible excellence" goals when they are made for students who may not yet be achieving grade-level standards, but with high goals could achieve *more* than one year's growth during a school year. These are students who may not be on grade level this year, but who are not "failures." The same holds true for proficient students who have the potential to excel. Establishing high goals is motivational for all students, and backward mapping goals together with individual students focuses their attention as much as it incites a deep personal belief in themselves.

As explained by Achieve, "Too often, accountability has been thought of as punitive" (2010, p. 13). Current processes, including sanctions that have layers of consequences for schools that do not achieve "cut" scores, have established fear of accountability. Data is not good or bad; it simply provides information to guide decisions. But data is currently perceived in some cases as a device for determining what is broken so it can be fixed. The Common Core is not focused on avoidance of data or sanctions, but on establishing opportunities for revisiting previous practices to embrace a broader understanding of accountability for guiding and communicating decisions for all students. Data-based results are communicated throughout the current grade and content team. When this growth is communicated *between* grade levels, and the baton of student progress is not dropped over summer vacation, or between elementary, middle, and high schools, but held tightly when handed off to the next year's teachers, invisible excellence progress continues. And often invisible excellence progress expands, igniting progress in adjoining content areas, so that over the course of two years, a student's achievement gap is closed. In ways not measurable with traditional test scores, students achieve growth toward meeting grade-level standards.

Increasing communication horizontally within teaching

teams, and vertically between the principal and teachers, leads to accountable conversations between assistant superintendents and principals. These conversations increase in effectiveness when they continue between superintendents and their school boards. The data from compelling conversations is provided to the school's Data Teams to increase the transparency of student growth.

Data Teams

Data-driven decisions, as recommended by ACT (2010, p. 21), establish longitudinal prekindergarten through college (P–16) data systems. Through frequent monitoring of student growth, states will be able to ensure more students are prepared for work and college. Data is fruitless without a systematic process in place to identify students in need of academic interventions at an early stage in order to achieve grade-level standards, and to identify students who can excel beyond those standards. Providing evidence of successful interventions over time will inform the decisions of all educators touching the lives of each student.

At the school level, Data Teams (Allison, et al., 2010) are small grade-level or department teams composed of teachers and a Data Team leader who meet regularly to establish student goals, determine interventions, and frequently monitor student progress. They examine individual student work generated by common formative and performance assessment processes (Ainsworth, 2010). These collaborative meetings focus on the effectiveness of teaching and student learning. This process supports schools and districts in identifying instructional and leadership strategies that can become measurable indicators to support student progress and accountability.

Together, invisible excellence and the Data Teams process provide schools and districts with valuable structures to not only frequently monitor student growth, but also identify the timely instructional changes needed. These structures increase participatory accountability for all stakeholders.

High school, middle school, and elementary school students have acquired understanding about growth-monitoring structures. Student achievement gaps identified through the Adequate Yearly Progress expectations of the No Child Left Behind Act have, in some cases, been reduced. The standards-based educational model, including high standards, measurable goals, and required annual assessments, prepared educators for this current literacy reform.

COMMON CORE STATE STANDARDS: ACHIEVING INCREASED LITERACY EXPECTATIONS

While the literacy component of the Common Core may appear to be fearlessly standing on its hind legs and getting stronger, aspects of its structure are not unfamiliar. How do the core literacy components of the CCSS initiative compare with those of No Child Left Behind? The Common Core State Standards incorporate a standards-based approach, built on the foundation of current state standards. Both sets of standards clearly communicate what is expected of students. The Common Core expands the previous state standards by incorporating vertically aligned standards from kindergarten through grade 12, accompanied by college and career readiness anchor standards for reading, which are backward mapped down to kindergarten. Like the current standards, the Common Core standards describe what students should *un-*

derstand (not what they should *know*), and what students should be able to do. The Common Core does not specify *how* to teach the required concepts and skills. As with No Child Left Behind, assessment will be required and linked to the standards. Accountability will continue to be a cornerstone of the standards-based process, having an increased presence in the Common Core State Standards.

Although foundational similarities exit between both standards-based initiatives—No Child Left Behind and the Common Core State Standards—there are also additional literacy recommendations regarding what districts and schools can do to support the increased expectations of the Common Core State Standards that can coexist in "phase space" with current best practices.

GETTING READY FOR COMMON CORE STANDARDS *NOW*

It is time to open the door wide and look literacy in the face. In fact, we must take time now to make a place at the table of current successful literacy practice to support the new literacy expectations within the Common Core, which are distinct from those established by No Child Left Behind. The depth of literacy change requires focused preparation, beginning with an aerial view of the Common Core landscape at the district level. What can districts and schools do *now* to build a strong foundation for the increased literacy expectations of the Common Core?

Increasing understanding about the Common Core requires opportunities to unfold new knowledge based upon educators' prior knowledge. The following steps explain how to build district-

and school-level understanding about the causes of current successes. Then educators can move through the quadrants of the Leadership and Learning Matrix (Exhibit 6.1) from a low understanding of the reasons for success (or lack of success) to a high understanding. In this way, cause data—the actions of adults—can be positively identified and impacted today to influence future results.

STEPS FOR DEVELOPING CORE LITERACY ALIGNMENT

Getting districts and schools ready for the Common Core includes emphasizing the importance of aligning literacy at its core. The following are specific steps for getting ready to implement the Common Core State Standards.

Step 1: Create Opportunities for Rich Literacy Discussions

Initiate dialogue by providing an overview from a current state debriefing, such as from the Partnership for Assessment of Readiness for College and Careers, or the SMARTER Balanced Assessment Consortium. With the Leadership and Learning Matrix (Exhibit 6.1) (Besser, et al., 2008, p. 20) projected on a screen, ask each participant to analyze which quadrant currently indicates the district's student achievement progress. Ask participants to place their responses in writing on self-adhesive notes, then place the notes on the screen, or on a large chart of the matrix, inside the appropriate quadrant. Proceed with a discussion of positive approaches that should be sustained. Repeat the process with a different color of notes, analyzing which quadrant indicates the

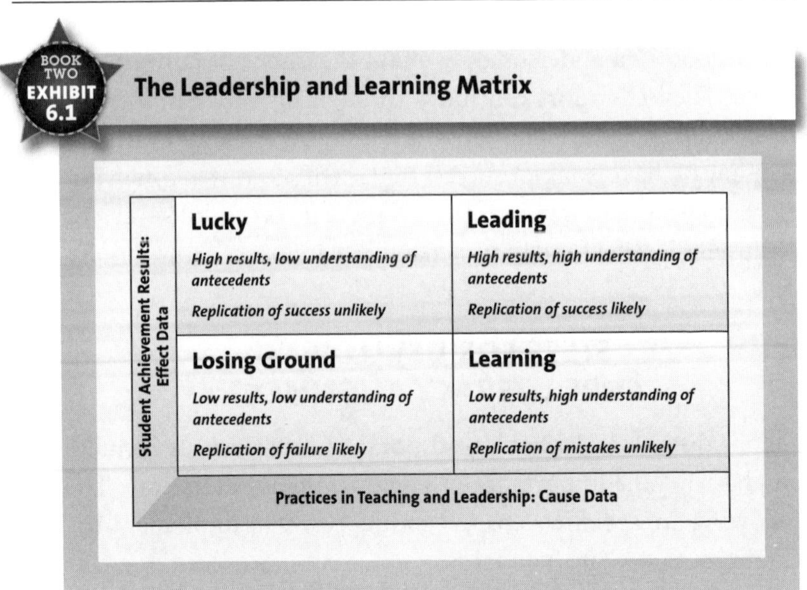

district's preparation for implementing the Common Core State Standards initiative. Display and discuss, while a recorder types the rich questions on a frame displayed on the screen. Point out the differences in responses to each question. These questions will provide a blueprint for next-step actions for the district and school leaders.

BOOK TWO
EXHIBIT 6.1
The Leadership and Learning Matrix
Student Achievement Results: Effect Data
Lucky
High results, low understanding of antecedents
Replication of success unlikely
Leading
High results, high understanding of antecedents
Replication of success likely
Losing Ground
Low results, low understanding of antecedents
Replication of failure likely
Learning
Low results, high understanding of antecedents
Replication of mistakes unlikely
Practices in Teaching and Leadership: Cause Data

Step 2: Align ELA CCSS with Assessment, Curriculum, and Instruction

Display a talking points PowerPoint frame that includes four bullets representing the components that must be in alignment for a guaranteed, viable curriculum:

- The Common Core State Standards

- Assessment
- Curriculum
- Instruction

Continue the dialogue, encouraging questions to surface by asking participants to generate questions they have about each of the components, including curricula learning progressions, in relation to the Common Core standards.

Record all questions in a PowerPoint frame on the screen to provide evidence of the current status of awareness and uncertainty on each of the four specific points. Examples of the kinds of participant questions that may result from steps 1 and 2 and that can guide district and school leadership direction include:

- How can we begin building a foundation of understanding to support the CCSS?
- How will our leadership roles need to change?
- With some state models providing professional development directly to *school-based* teams, how can communication at the *district* level be improved to support systemic change?
- How will the budget deficit impact leadership responsibilities?
- How can we sustain areas of successful student achievement while implementing CCSS-aligned curriculum and assessments?
- How can Data Teams support increased accountability expectations as they relate to teacher and principal responsibilities?

- How can the Common Core standards, state and district curricula, and instruction be clarified?
- What place will our current district formative assessments have in the new plan?
- How will expectations for student placement be impacted throughout the district?

As a team, prioritize the questions to determine next steps. Begin developing a transition plan, including strategies and a timeline.

Step 3: Complete a Rigor Inventory of Available Complex Texts for Each Grade Level

Determine the rigor and type of texts students are expected to read and comprehend proficiently and independently. Include more complex texts as "stretch" texts, including short texts of high complexity that extend beyond students' reading levels. Increase informational texts at all levels, beginning with elementary levels (K–5) having an equal split between informational text and literature, and proceeding through late high school having 70 percent informational text and 30 percent literature.

Step 4: Expand Academic Vocabulary Instruction

Initiate a focus on systematically building general academic vocabulary. Include all grade levels and the core disciplines. Although the language standards include the rules of standard written and spoken English, they focus on understanding words and phrases, their relationships, and acquiring new vocabulary, with specific emphasis on general academic and domain-specific words and phrases. Students will benefit from reading informational texts at the beginning of elementary school. Age-appropriate content knowledge and vocabulary in history/social studies, science, and the arts will increase students' capacity to comprehend increasing levels of complex text (CCSSI, 2010a, p. 33).

Although the Common Core State Standards require states and districts to prepare for numerous new curricular and assessment practices, the expectation for vocabulary instruction to provide continued practice via the three-tiers-of-words model (Beck, McKeown, and Kucan, 2002) is encouraging. Providing support for teachers to expand their focus on tier-two words will support students' comprehension of complex text, because tier-two vocabulary is not discipline specific. Then, content-area instructors can expand students' tier-three discipline-specific vocabulary.

Step 5: Compare Concepts and Skills in the ELA CCSS with Those Required in the Current District Curriculum

The purpose here is not to replicate new, state-developed, aligned curricula, but rather to develop a foundational awareness of the depth of concepts and skills in the Common Core. Beginning with an analysis process, select a few examples of priority standards in the CCSS to compare with current district curricula.

Using a rubric of 1 to 3, with 1 representing a minimal match between the concepts and skills in the new standards and the existing curriculum, and 3 representing a high level of correspondence, begin the analysis by asking, "Of the concepts and skills required by the Common Core, which are included in our district curriculum? How strong is the match between our current curricular standards and the CCSS? A matrix provides an excellent tool for this process. The intention is to develop district- and school-level awareness of the currently required concepts and skills that are strongly aligned (at level 3) with the new CCSS, and the specific concepts and skills with minimal or no alignment. (For example, when looking closely at the Common Core content, implications for increased availability of complex text will be apparent.) Concepts and skills having the least correlation (level 1) will indicate areas needing immediate focus for development of next steps. This process identifies implications for further focus, and facilitates the cross-discipline collaboration required for smooth Common Core implementation.

Step 6: Determine Curricular Voids by Analyzing the Curricular Crosswalk

Where are the greatest skills and concepts gaps in your district? Many schools find that there is less than a 50 percent match, or correspondence, between concepts and skills in the CCSS and the current state curriculum. Further analysis may indicate that the greatest gaps exist at the middle and high school levels. Drilling deeper, specific Common Core standards that might have little or no crossover with current state standards may include the literacy standards for history/social studies, science, and technical subjects. When expectations are high for explicit connections between the CCSS and current standards, the crosswalk typically becomes most narrow. Honest evaluations of the existing curricula will guide accurate alignment of the CCSS, curriculum development, and instruction—the foundation for excellence in future student achievement.

Step 7: Analyze Levels of Rigor Expected in the ELA CCSS

"Unwrapping" the concepts and skills within a standard establishes connections between the CCSS, current state standards, and curricular content. Providing an overview of the concepts using the "unwrapping" model, to guide participants in reflecting on the significant increase in rigor within the CCSS, will provide rationale for embracing changes while reducing possible frustration.

A set of 10 ELA CCSS standards for literacy in history/social studies in grades 6–12 aims to increase instructional attention to precise details, evaluation of arguments, synthesis of complex information, and reading of complex texts with independence and confidence. An example of "unwrapping" a literacy in history/social studies standard that addresses key ideas and details follows:

> Grades 9–10 Common Core State Standard for literacy in history/social studies (RH.9–10.1, CCSSI, 2010a): "Cite specific textual evidence to support analysis of primary and secondary sources, attending to such features as the date and origin of the information."
>
> "Unwrapping" this standard for rigor, students need to be able to CITE and ANALYZE. Explicit instruction will include concepts of <u>identifying specific textual evidence</u> as it relates to the <u>date</u> and <u>origin of information</u> (Ainsworth, 2010, p. 121).

Determining the level of rigor in each standard through the "unwrapping" process provides clarity about the level of cognitive demand needed in the assessment. The level of explicit instruction required for students to achieve the expectations within the standard, as indicated by aligned assessment tasks, must also be aligned with the cognitive demand of the standard. Focusing on the "unwrapped" concepts and skills to guide assessment and instruction will directly increase achievement of a guaranteed curriculum (Marzano, 2003, pp. 22–24), and as a result, students will be able to increase their capacity to read and comprehend increasingly complex text. A guaranteed curriculum is one that gives teachers clear guidance about the content to be addressed in particular courses for specific grades. Also, a guaranteed curriculum cannot be disregarded or replaced with different content.

Step 8: Analyze Current Expectations for Digital Reading and Writing

Determine areas where students can increase their use of technology to enhance their reading and writing. To support opportunities for additional use of technology, increase integration of online and offline learning. Analyze current barriers preventing students in your district from making optimum use of technology. For example, consider piloting the use of electronic readers with a small targeted population of students. Specific features such as increased font size, audible options (device reads to students to improve their fluency), discrete turning of pages that prevents others from noticing a student's slower pace, and a built-in dictionary that resembles the texting process are motivational for at-risk readers. Initiating an instructional pilot study, such as the use of electronic readers with English language learners or special education students, can bring to light the technology restrictions that need to be addressed. Addressing barriers with a manageable pilot program paves the path to expanding relevant opportunities for all students.

SUMMARY

When teachers and leaders are provided with a strong rationale for implementing the Common Core, an urgency that drives decisions develops naturally. Communicating the urgent need to close the achievement gap of our graduates leads to shared responsibility among all educators, including those responsible for our youngest learners.

Preparing to implement the Common Core begins with identifying the practices that currently produce positive results. Examples of successful current practices in districts and schools include strong literacy leadership, invisible excellence goals developed during compelling conversations, and the Data Teams process.

Achieving increased expectations as defined by the Common Core State Standards begins with developing core literacy alignment through the following steps:

Step 1: Create opportunities for rich literacy discussions

Step 2: Align ELA CCSS with assessment, curriculum, and instruction

Step 3: Complete a rigor inventory of available complex texts for each grade level

Step 4: Expand academic vocabulary instruction

Step 5: Compare concepts and skills in the ELA CCSS with those required in the current district curriculum

Step 6: Determine curricular voids by analyzing the curricular crosswalk

Step 7: Analyze levels of rigor expected in the ELA CCSS

Step 8: Analyze current expectations for students' digital reading and writing

Making time for assessing perspectives on the current reality of student performance and comparing these perspectives with the CCSS expectations will generate vital questions. These questions will guide decisions to generate opportunities, overcome potential barriers, and support individual districts and schools in preparing for their students' future success.

References

Note: This chapter includes excerpts from Disciplinary Literacy: Redefining Deep Understanding and Leadership for 21st-Century Demands *(Piercy and Piercy, 2011).*

Achieve. (2007). *Aligned expectations? A closer look at college admissions and placement tests.* Retrieved Sept. 9, 2011, from www.achieve.org/files/Admissions_and_Placement_FINAL2.pdf

Achieve. (2010). *On the road to implementation: Achieving the promise of the Common Core State Standards.* Retrieved Sept. 9, 2011, from www.achieve.org/files/FINAL-CCSSImplementationGuide.pdf

ACT. (2006). *Reading between the lines: What the ACT reveals about college readiness in reading.* Retrieved Sept. 9, 2011, from www.act.org/research/policymakers/pdf/reading_report.pdf

ACT. (2010). *The condition of college & career readiness.* Retrieved Sept. 9, 2011, from www.act.org/research/policymakers/cccr10/pdf/ConditionofCollegeandCareerReadiness2010.pdf

Ainsworth, L. (2010). *Rigorous curriculum design: How to create curricular units of study that align standards, instruction, and assessment.* Englewood, CO: Lead + Learn Press.

Allison, E., Besser, L., Campsen, L., Cordova, J., Doubek, B., Gregg, L., Kamm, C., Nielson, K., Peery, A., Pitchford, B., Rose, A., Ventura, S., & White, M. (2010). *Data teams: The big picture—Looking at data teams through a collaborative lens.* Englewood, CO: Lead + Learn Press.

Beck, I., McKeown, M. G., & Kucan, L. (2002). *Bringing words to life: Robust vocabulary instruction.* New York: Guilford.

Besser, L., Almeida, L., Anderson-Davis, D. M., Flach, T., Kamm, C., & White, S. (2008). *Decision making for results: Data-driven decision making.* Englewood, CO: Lead + Learn Press.

Carnegie Corporation. (2010). *Time to act: An agenda for advancing adolescent literacy for college and career success.* New York.

Common Core State Standards Initiative (CCSSI). (2010a, June). *Common Core State Standards for English language arts & literacy in history/social studies, science, and technical subjects* (PDF document). Retrieved from www.corestandards.org/assets/CCSSI_ELA%20Standards.pdf

Common Core State Standards Initiative (CCSSI). (2010b, June). *Common Core State Standards for English language arts & literacy in history/social studies, science, and technical subjects: Appendix A* (PDF document). Retrieved from www.corestandards.org/assets/Appendix_A.pdf

Marzano, R. J. (2003). *What works in schools: Translating research into action.* Alexandria, VA: ASCD.

MetaMetrics. (2011). *The Lexile framework for reading: Matching readers with texts.* Retrieved Sept. 9, 2011: *Lexile-to-grade correspondence,* www.lexile.com/about-lexile/grade-equivalent/grade-equivalent-chart/; *Text complexity grade bands and Lexile bands,* www.lexile.com/using-lexile/lexile-measures-and-the-ccssi/text-complexity-grade-bands-and-lexile-ranges/; *Lexile codes,* www.lexile.com/about-lexile/lexile-codes/; *Common Core standards and text complexity,* lexile.com/using-lexile/lexile-measures-and-the-ccssi/

Piercy, T. (2006). *Compelling conversations: Connecting leadership to student achievement.* Englewood, CO: Lead + Learn Press.

Piercy, T., & Piercy, W. (2011). *Disciplinary literacy: Redefining deep understanding and leadership for 21st-century demands.* Englewood, CO: Lead + Learn Press.

Reeves, D. B. (2009). *Leading change in your school: How to conquer myths, build commitment, and get results.* Alexandria, VA: ASCD.

Williamson, G. L. (2008). A text readability continuum for postsecondary readiness. *Journal of Advanced Academics, 19*(4), 602–632.

Text Complexity Structures: Comprehending Increased Levels of Complex Text

Thomasina D. Piercy

The text complexity focus throughout the Common Core State Standards is like the "hemi under the hood." As an integral component, the text complexity aspect is the hallmark of the ELA CCSS. It reveals the depth of educators' commitment to providing American students with every opportunity to be prepared to meet all future global challenges. The Common Core does not hesitate to acknowledge the magnitude and ramifications of the current void of complex texts in education. The ELA CCSS document offers no pretext of an easy fix or an ideal solution. In fact, had the seriousness of the 20-year decline of National Assessment of Educational Progress (NAEP) scores been addressed with equal determination prior to 2001, the U.S. Congress might not have had to intervene by passing the No Child Left Behind Act. With insight and humility, the Common Core addresses the national text complexity instructional void.

This chapter describes structures that can support districts and schools in preparing for the increased expectations within the ELA CCSS. These structures will illuminate a path for expanding the capacity of district leaders and teachers to increase text complexity levels for students. The text complexity implementation recommendations for districts and schools provide a route toward confident selection of complex texts aligned with both the cognitive demand of the CCSS and the needs of the readers. The concepts embedded in this path will expand teacher understanding during each step of preparing for ELA CCSS implementation.

DEFINING AND UNDERSTANDING TEXT COMPLEXITY

The CCSS defines text complexity as "the inherent difficulty of reading and comprehending a text combined with consideration of reader and task variables; in the Standards, a three-part assessment of text difficulty that pairs qualitative and quantitative measures with reader-task considerations" (CCSSI, 2010b, p. 57). Students must demonstrate an increasing ability to "discern more from and make fuller use of text, including making an increasing number of connections among ideas and between texts..." (CCSSI, 2010a, p. 8).

Text complexity is typically represented as a continuum of simple texts compared to complex texts. The three degrees of complexity provided by ACT are: uncomplicated, more challenging, and complex (ACT, 2006, p. 14). Achieve recommends that "educators can evaluate the complexity and importance of texts by considering ways in which students' assigned reading meets expectation for complexity, rigor and exposure to important fundamental works in American and world literature" (Achieve, 2011).

EMBRACING THE NEED FOR INCREASED TEXT COMPLEXITY

Questions frequently asked about text complexity include: "Why does text complexity matter?" "Why is it a significant focus throughout the ELA CCSS document?" "Why hasn't text complexity been a priority previously?" As described earlier, a significant Lexile gap exists between texts read near the end of high school and university texts. One skill that differentiated students who achieved above-the-benchmark scores in the reading section of the ACT college admissions test from those who did not was their ability to read, understand, and respond to questions about complex texts.

The ACT research contributed to increasing the focus on text complexity in the Common Core. Although educators have long been aware of the importance of increasing students' capacity to comprehend text of increasing difficulty, the key connection text complexity plays in students' success in school and their future college and career success provides much insight. It informs educators that it is not students' ability to infer or answer questions about main ideas that leads to success as much as their ability to read, understand, and respond to questions about complex texts. This research clarified the need to expand pedagogy that focuses not only on critical thinking and literacy actions but also on applying those concepts with complex texts. Put simply, if students are unprepared for comprehending at the level of cognitive function demanded by complex texts, they will not possess the capacity to be successful with the texts that are certain to be in their future work or college pathways (CCSSI, 2010b, p. 2; ACT, 2006, p. 16).

INCREASING TEXT COMPLEXITY ACROSS GRADE LEVELS

Throughout school, students are expected to increase their capacity to read and comprehend increasing levels of complex texts. The combination of the increase of text complexity aligned with the depth of cognitive demand within the task, such as discipline-specific questions, generates higher levels of rigor. Although text complexity is not a new concept, it has been an expectation that has been absorbed by the "haystack" of educational assumptions. As a vague required outcome without the benefit of specific, measurable standards, the expectation for text complexity became the lost needle in the haystack.

The Common Core's impact on the alignment of the intended, delivered, and achieved curricula is providing explicit structure for increasing students' comprehension of complex text. Significantly increasing each grade level's expectations for complex text, beginning at grade 2 and continuing through grade 12, articulates what students must be able to understand. Additionally, including standard 10 in every grade level, beginning at kindergarten, establishes a standard presence for text complexity within the Common Core, as an integral artery of rigor. In Exhibit 7.1, standard 10 is presented in a backward-mapped format as a scaffold to guide instructional expectations through grade 12 and college and career readiness. In the exhibit, changes in expectations between grade levels are noted in bold to prevent the baton of progress from being dropped between grades.

STRUCTURES FOR GUIDING SELECTION OF APPROPRIATE LEVELS OF COMPLEX TEXTS

Currently, there are published lists of texts identified for specific grade levels. These levels, such as the those provided in Lexile Framework for Reading (MetaMetrics, 2011), *The Continuum of Literacy Learning* (Pinnell and Fountas, 2007), and from publishers of leveled basal readers, have guided student progression. Included among teacher resources are trade books that have exact grade levels stamped right on the back. How easy is that? The problem has been that such measures have provided teachers with different recommendations for the same texts. Although these lists provide quick solutions to help make complicated decisions, teachers have long recognized the discrepancy problem.

The ELA CCSS documents have looked this literacy problem directly in the face. The text leveling issue is *directly* addressed by the Common Core. This does not mean that an *easy* solution is provided; there is no easy solution to leveling complex texts, because the only path to confronting the problem is understanding. The Common Core's Three-Part Model for Measuring Text Complexity (CCSSI, 2010b) contributes a depth of knowledge about each dimension. Informed teachers armed with deep understanding will not need to rely solely on published recommendations, which may have discrepant levels. National leaders recognize the need to improve the process and increase accuracy.

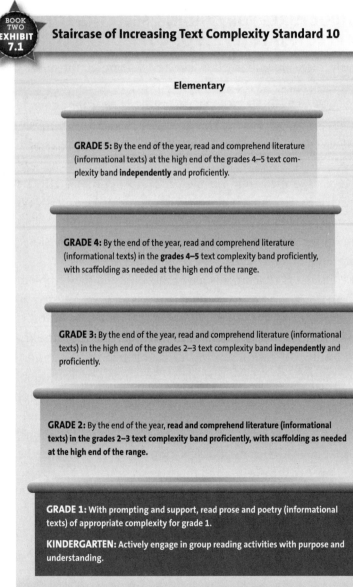

Staircase of Increasing Text Complexity Standard 10

Elementary

GRADE 5: By the end of the year, read and comprehend literature (informational texts) at the high end of the grades 4–5 text complexity band **independently** and proficiently.

GRADE 4: By the end of the year, read and comprehend literature (informational texts) in the **grades 4–5** text complexity band proficiently, with scaffolding as needed at the high end of the range.

GRADE 3: By the end of the year, read and comprehend literature (informational texts) in the high end of the grades 2–3 text complexity band **independently** and proficiently.

GRADE 2: By the end of the year, **read and comprehend literature (informational texts) in the grades 2–3 text complexity band proficiently, with scaffolding as needed at the high end of the range.**

GRADE 1: With prompting and support, read prose and poetry (informational texts) of appropriate complexity for grade 1.

KINDERGARTEN: Actively engage in group reading activities with purpose and understanding.

Grade-level text complexity demands begin at grade 2.

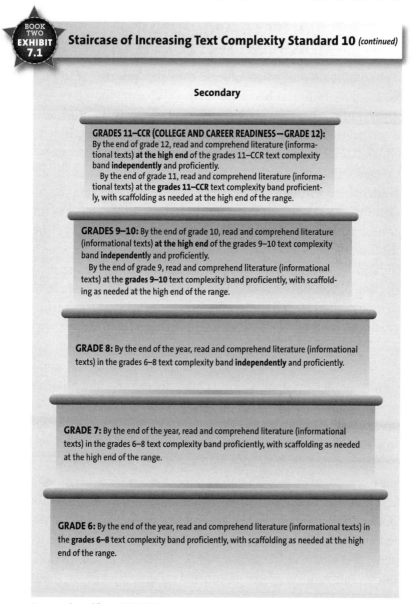

Staircase of Increasing Text Complexity Standard 10 *(continued)*

Secondary

GRADES 11–CCR (COLLEGE AND CAREER READINESS—GRADE 12): By the end of grade 12, read and comprehend literature (informational texts) **at the high end** of the grades 11–CCR text complexity band **independently** and proficiently.

By the end of grade 11, read and comprehend literature (informational texts) at the **grades 11–CCR** text complexity band proficiently, with scaffolding as needed at the high end of the range.

GRADES 9–10: By the end of grade 10, read and comprehend literature (informational texts) **at the high end** of the grades 9–10 text complexity band **independently** and proficiently.

By the end of grade 9, read and comprehend literature (informational texts) at the **grades 9–10** text complexity band proficiently, with scaffolding as needed at the high end of the range.

GRADE 8: By the end of the year, read and comprehend literature (informational texts) in the grades 6–8 text complexity band **independently** and proficiently.

GRADE 7: By the end of the year, read and comprehend literature (informational texts) in the grades 6–8 text complexity band proficiently, with scaffolding as needed at the high end of the range.

GRADE 6: By the end of the year, read and comprehend literature (informational texts) in the **grades 6–8** text complexity band proficiently, with scaffolding as needed at the high end of the range.

Source: Adapted from CCSSI, 2010a.

THREE COMPONENTS FOR MEASURING TEXT COMPLEXITY

The combination of what students read and how they read provides a clear future path to improvement. The emphasis is on two aspects of reading: the sophistication of the texts the student is expected to be able to read and comprehend, and the skill with which students are able to read. A text complexity "staircase" is defined within standard 10. This standard is integrated into the kindergarten through grade 12 CCSS. The staircase begins its ascent in grade 2 and continues its grade-by-grade increase to the college and career readiness level. The intention is to set clear, measurable expectations for students to acquire deep understanding and demonstrate their comprehension, including making connections between texts and using explicit textual evidence to demonstrate their full understanding. Included in the text complexity concept of the CCSS is the expectation for students to expand their capacity to evaluate the accuracy of information.

The three factors included in the Common Core text complexity model are qualitative evaluations of texts, quantitative evaluations of texts, and matching text to reader and task (CCSSI, 2010b, p. 4). The qualitative evaluation identifies levels of meaning, structure, language conventionality and clarity, and knowledge demands. Quantitative evaluation of text includes readability measures based on word length or frequency, sentence length, and text cohesion. The element of matching text to reader and task honors reader variables such as motivation, knowledge, and experiences; and task variables such as purpose and the complexity generated by the task assigned and the questions posed. Quantitative evaluations are often conducted using computer programs designed for the purpose, but decisions about the qualitative aspects of texts and those about matching text to reader and task are made by teachers. The next section delves into fundamental concepts that can help guide teachers through the process of evaluating texts on these levels.

GUIDING TEXT SELECTION WITH QUALITATIVE TEXT COMPLEXITY FACTORS

Text complexity descriptions are based on a progression of complexity to guide the selection of appropriately complex texts for each grade level (CCSSI, 2010b, pp. 4–6). Text elements, in addition to instructional concepts and skills that align with the specific standard, must be considered when selecting texts. Due to the range of these considerations, they may not be attached to specific grade levels. Even when they are connected to grade levels, it is beneficial for teachers to be informed of, and refer to, the text elements or factors to confirm that a selection is best aligned with their students' needs and instructional objectives. The ELA CCSS are organized under two types of texts: informational texts and literary texts.

Exhibit 7.2, Four Qualitative Text Complexity Factors, provides the CCSS elements in a chart format. The chart has an interactive design to allow it to be used by teachers and teams for analyzing the qualitative complexity of a text by checking the appropriate column. The column with the most factors checked indicates whether the text is simple or complex.

The chart in Exhibit 7.2 indicates that a complex text is usually considered to be complex because it includes a purpose that is implicit, having multiples levels of meaning or a subtext requir-

Four Qualitative Text Complexity Factors

TEXT FACTORS	*Easy Factors: Simple Text*	*Simple Text Factors* ✓	*Difficult Factors: Complex Text*	*Complex Text Factors* ✓
1a. PURPOSE (Informational texts) **1b. LEVELS OF MEANING** (literary texts)	Explicitly stated purpose Single level of meaning; easier to read		Implicit purpose, may be hidden or obscure Multiple levels of meaning; author's literal message is intentionally different from his/her subtext or underlying message, as in satires	
2. STRUCTURE	Simple, well-marked, clear, explicit, and conventional structures Informational text does not deviate from common genres; has simple graphics, if needed at all, or graphics are supplementary to the meaning Literary text is in chronological order, has traits of a common genre		Implicit, complex structures Informational text conforms to norms and conventions of a specific discipline; has sophisticated graphics whose interpretation is essential to understanding; graphics provide an independent source of information within the text Literary text has unconventional structures, flashbacks, flash-forwards, manipulations of time and sequence, out of chronological order	
3. LANGUAGE CONVENTION-ALITY AND CLARITY	Literal, clear, contemporary, familiar, and conversational		Figurative, ironic, ambiguous, purposefully misleading, unfamiliar language, discipline-specific vocabulary	
4. KNOWLEDGE DEMANDS: **a. Discipline/ Content Knowledge** **b. Life Experiences** **c. Cultural/ Literary Knowledge**	a. Few assumptions are made about extent of reader's life experiences and knowledge; incorporates everyday knowledge; few if any references to other texts b. Simple themes; everyday experiences; familiarity with genre conventions; single perspective or similar to one's own perspective c. Everyday knowledge; familiarity with genre conventions; few references, allusions to other texts		a. Numerous assumptions are made about extent of reader's life experiences; extensive, specialized, depth of cultural, literary, and discipline-specific knowledge; high intertextuality (references to other texts) b. Sophisticated, multiple themes; different experiences from one's own; multiple perspectives different from one's own c. Cultural and literary knowledge contributes to understanding; high intertextuality	

Source: Adapted from CCSSI, 2010a.

ing literacy actions such as inferring; a structure that is discipline-specific, requiring synthesis with understanding of graphics and unconventional structures; language conventionality and clarity that is figurative, ambiguous, or having discipline-specific vocabulary; and knowledge demands that include assumptions about the extent of the reader's life experiences. Additional resources on the topic include Achieve's elements of text complexity (2007) and ACT's six aspects of text complexity (2006).

In addition to analyzing qualitative measures of text complexity, quantitative measures and reader-task considerations must be included when considering text complexity due to the interplay of all three aspects. Exhibit 7.3 provides teachers with an interactive chart to use after completing the chart in Exhibit 7.2 to ana-

Assessing Text Complexity with Multiple Measures

Qualitative Measures	Quantitative Measures	Reader-Task Considerations	Recommended Placement
Text Factors: Levels of meaning; Structure; Language; Knowledge demands	**Text Dimensions:** Word length or frequency; Sentence length; Text cohesion as measured by: Coh-Metrix, Lexile Framework, Flesch-Kincaid Grade Level, Dale-Chall, ATOS	**Considerations:** Motivation, knowledge, and experiences; Task's purpose and complexity; Cognitive demand of questions	**Informed Judgment:** ✔ Using your qualitative indicators and the quantitative results, along with reader and task considerations, what conclusions can you reasonably draw about the use of this text with the identified students? ✔ Explain why or why not it is an appropriate challenge. ✔ Describe the discrepancies you needed to resolve.

lyze the Common Core's three components for measuring text complexity to determine a recommendation for specific texts. Teachers will apply their informed judgment using the qualitative indicators from Exhibit 7.2 combined with quantitative measures and reader-task considerations to explain why or why not the text provides an appropriate challenge. An opportunity to discuss and resolve discrepancies is included.

In addition to the qualitative text complexity factors depicted in the CCSS, a six-point scale for analyzing the difficulty level of reading passages was developed by Achieve (2007, p. 48). The characteristics used by Achieve to define the six levels include vocabulary, predictability of text organization, complexity of syntax, level of abstractness, familiarity of the topic, and number of concepts introduced in the passage. Being aware of the difficulty level of the text, and the level of cognitive complexity and reasoning required of the students by the text, supports teachers in text selection. Intentionally increasing students' interaction with complex text will increase their capacity to comprehend with deep understanding.

MATCHING TEXT TO READER AND TASK ELEMENTS

Qualitative and quantitative elements focus specifically on the inherent complexity of the text itself. But there are unique variables specific to the readers, including motivation, knowledge, and experiences. While matching text to reader and task requires focusing on the reader's unique variables, there are also important variables related to particular tasks, such as the purpose for the lesson and the vital complexity generated by the specific task assigned and the questions posed by the teacher or students. Both the task assigned and the questions posed are based upon the selection of appropriately complex text. Together, the student's qualities and the objective of the assignment need to be carefully considered in conjunction with the selected text. It is the interplay of all aspects, when aligned with a specific standard, that increases students' capacity to deeply understand increasingly complex texts (Exhibit 7.4).

Readers must have three dispositions to comprehend complex text: they must be willing to concentrate, pause, and probe; think uninterruptedly; and think deeply (Bauerlein, 2011, pp. 28–32). With text complexity being recognized as a main contributor to students' future success, much focus has been placed on its potential.

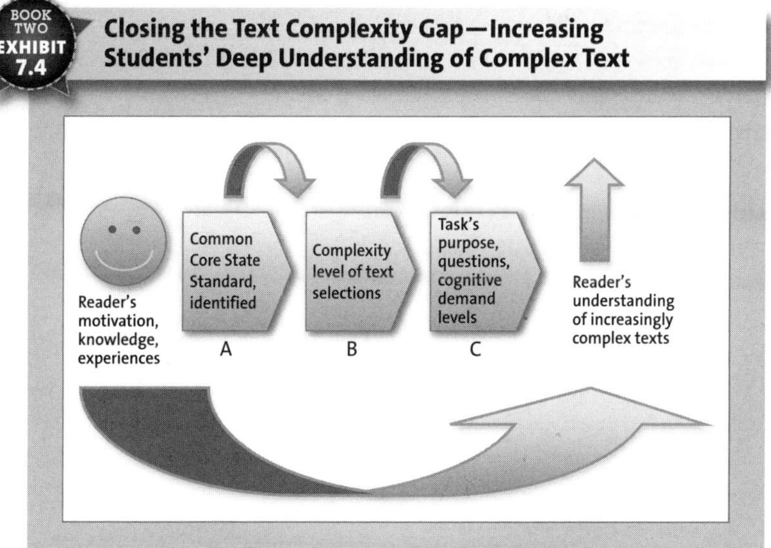

SUMMARY

This chapter has focused on supporting increased levels of complex text for grades 2–12, but the topic of text complexity cannot be considered in isolation from analyzing the level of rigor in each standard because it is through "unwrapping," or unpacking, the Common Core standards that the level of cognitive demand, which informs the selection of specific complex texts, is determined. Likewise, formative performance assessments must be designed in alignment with the level of cognitive demand within selected complex texts and the specific standards being focused on in the lesson. The disciplinary literacy instruction model provides a naturally integrated model for planning and delivering thoroughly aligned, integrated instruction and assessment at high levels of complexity. Selecting appropriate levels of complex text, using multiple measures, can help increase student achievement. Together, these key points provide a path that leads to increased understanding about complex text selection. Structures to support teachers during implementation of the high expectations in the CCSS included the text complexity staircase, qualitative text complexity factors, and the elements of matching text to reader and task. The following concepts can help educators implement the ELA CCSS text complexity expectations:

- Defining and understanding text complexity
- Embracing the need for increased text complexity
- Increasing text complexity across grade levels
- Using structures to guide selection of complex texts
- Three components for measuring text complexity

- Guiding text selection with qualitative text complexity factors
- Matching text to reader and task elements

It is important to note that literacy is a rapidly evolving field receiving significant attention at the moment. Efforts are being made at this time, as indicated in the Common Core document, to improve complex text identification methods. Teachers are being charged with higher expectations and they need much more support, including simplified and accurate models for determining text complexity levels. Getting ready for the Common Core requires an awareness of and general understanding about the important role of text complexity in literacy education.

References

Note: This chapter includes excerpts from Disciplinary Literacy: Redefining Deep Understanding and Leadership for 21st-Century Demands *(Piercy and Piercy, 2011).*

Achieve. (2007). *Aligned expectations? A closer look at college admissions and placement tests.* Retrieved Sept. 9, 2011, from www.achieve.org/files/Admissions_and_Placement_FINAL2.pdf

Achieve. (2011). *English and communication benchmarks, grades 4–12: Acquiring information*, retrieved Sept. 9, 2011, from www.achieve.org/node/948; *English and communication benchmarks, grades 4–12: Understanding text complexity*, retrieved Sept. 9, 2011, from www.achieve.org/node/946; and *English and communication benchmarks, grades 4–12: Procedure for ranking reading passages by level of demand*, retrieved Sept. 9, 2011, from www.achieve.org/node/946

ACT. (2006). *Reading between the lines: What the ACT reveals about college readiness in reading.* Retrieved Sept. 9, 2011, from www.act.org/research/policymakers/pdf/reading_report.pdf

Bauerlein, M. (2011). Too dumb for complex texts. *Educational Leadership, 55*(5), 28–32.

Common Core State Standards Initiative (CCSSI). (2010a, June). *Common Core State Standards for English language arts & literacy in history/social studies, science, and technical subjects* (PDF document). Retrieved from www.corestandards.org/assets/CCSSI_ELA%20Standards.pdf

Common Core State Standards Initiative (CCSSI). (2010b, June). *Common Core State Standards for English language arts & literacy in history/social studies, science, and technical subjects: Appendix A* (PDF document). Retrieved from www.corestandards.org/assets/Appendix_A.pdf

MetaMetrics. (2011). *The Lexile framework for reading: Matching readers with texts.* Retrieved Sept. 9, 2011: *Lexile-to-grade correspondence,* www.lexile.com/about-lexile/grade-equivalent/grade-equivalent-chart/; *Text complexity grade bands and Lexile bands,* www.lexile.com/using-lexile/lexile-measures-and-the-ccssi/text-complexity-grade-bands-and-lexile-ranges/; *Lexile codes,* www.lexile.com/about-lexile/lexile-codes/; *Common Core standards and text complexity,* lexile.com/using-lexile/lexile-measures-and-the-ccssi/

Pinnell, G. S., & Fountas, I. C. (2007). *The continuum of literacy learning grades K–8: Behaviors and understandings to notice, teach, and support.* Portsmouth, NH: Heinemann.

Increasing Students' Deeper Understanding of Complex Texts with Disciplinary Literacy Instruction

Thomasina D. Piercy

The disciplinary literacy model demonstrates how to increase focus on literacy in different disciplines. Such integrated instruction supports the Common Core curricular crosswalk in areas where it is most narrow for districts. Integrated into the disciplinary literacy instructional model is the use of complex text. The components of this model address the Common Core's intention to close the achievement gap of graduates entering into careers and college by incorporating complex text aligned with questions requiring an equal level of cognitive demand.

Considering the significant impact of increasing levels of complex text that students are expected to read and comprehend, instruction must be the focus. Recently, disciplinary literacy studies have contributed to the urgency for instructional changes to support students' deep understanding of complex text. For, as Gardner reminds us, "Knowledge of facts is a useful ornament but a fundamentally different undertaking than thinking in a discipline" (2008, p. 32). Disciplinary literacy studies and literature, including Shanahan and Shanahan (2008), Carnegie Corporation (2010), Snow and Moje (2010), McConachie and Petrosky (2010), McKeown, Beck, and Blake (2009), and Wineburg (2001), are disclosing significant findings that dispute long-accepted "reading in the content area" and "reading across the curriculum" strategies as students proceed to more challenging texts at the secondary level. These findings provide a starting point for instructional change. This chapter provides a path composed of four steps for implementing disciplinary instruction with complex texts.

Literacy skills and strategies are not as generalizable as was once thought. The "inoculation model" described by Shanahan and Shanahan (2008) depicts the overreliance on instruction of basic reading skills at the basic literacy level for guiding adolescent readers' comprehension needs in specific content areas. The disciplinary literacy model of instruction instead supports students in comprehending discipline-specific complex text.

STEP 1: CONSIDER THE THREE LEVELS OF LITERACY INSTRUCTION

3. Disciplinary Literacy—"Literacy skills specialized to history, science, mathematics, literature, or some other subject."

2. Intermediate Literacy—"Literacy skills common to many tasks, including generic comprehension strategies, common word meanings, and basic fluency."

1. Basic Literacy—"Literacy skills such as decoding and knowledge of high frequency words that underlie all reading tasks." (Shanahan and Shanahan, 2008)

Different disciplines require specific aligned actions for unique learning that each discipline demands, as practiced by historians, mathematicians, literary critics, and scientists. According to Shanahan and Shanahan, "We have spent a century of education beholden to the generalist notion of literacy learning—the idea that if we just provide adequate basic skills, from that point forward kids with adequate background knowledge will be able to read anything successfully" (2008, p. 41).

The limited success of the "reading in the content area" approach is due in part to not recognizing the cognitive demands of each discipline.

After a snowfall, what do you notice about the landscape in the northern United States? In winter, everything is one color. Literacy instruction needs to be aligned *differently* for each discipline.

Literacy is not a generalizable one-color season. Gardner agrees, "It is essential for individuals in the future to be able to think in the ways that characterize the major disciplines" (2008, p. 31). Disciplinary literacy identifies literacy skills and actions that teach students how to meet the unique cognitive demands within the different content areas to achieve deep understanding.

Exhibit 8.1 depicts the distinct qualities of each discipline. It represents the need to recognize that in addition to having different discipline-specific information, each discipline has unique literacy demands. These literacy demands are not generalizable. Yet, when all disciplines work together, students benefit. Working in tandem, literacy and content knowledge create deep understanding.

STEP 2: PAVE THE PATH FOR DISCIPLINARY LITERACY INSTRUCTION ALIGNED WITH THE CCSS

Some frequently asked questions about disciplinary literacy include:

- How well do current disciplinary literacy expectations and practices align with CCSS expectations? When the cross-walk of commonality between new standards and current curricula is narrow, much attention is needed to increase cross-fertilization across the disciplines.
- How can I begin planning disciplinary literacy instruction aligned with the high expectations for increased text complexity (such as in primary source documents and science lab reports) depicted in the ELA CCSS?

Disciplinary Literacy

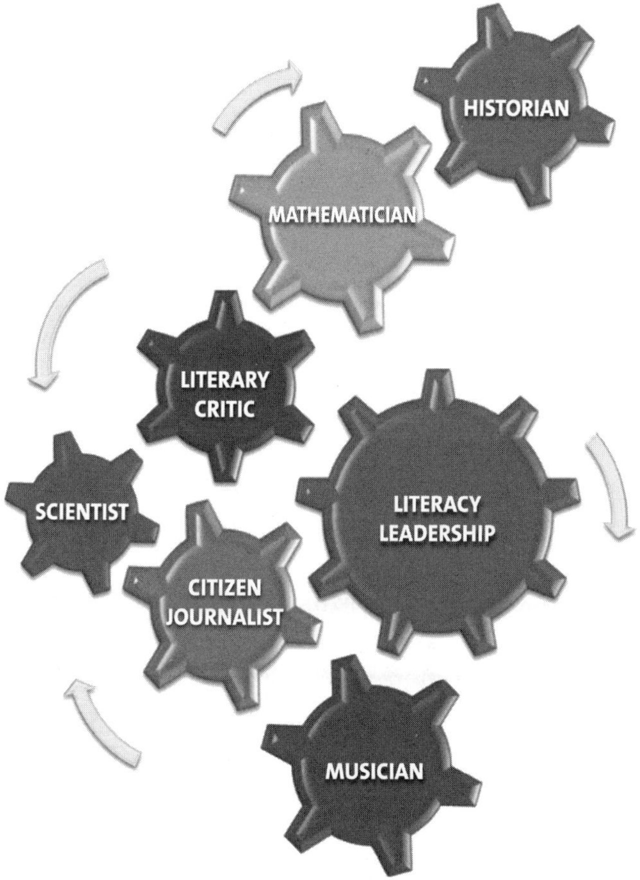

HISTORIAN

MATHEMATICIAN

LITERARY CRITIC

SCIENTIST

LITERACY LEADERSHIP

CITIZEN JOURNALIST

MUSICIAN

- How effectively do current English language arts formative performance assessments measure students' capacity to demonstrate the skills and concepts required in the Common Core literacy standards for history/social studies and science/technical subjects?
- How can I provide literacy instruction in my content area that connects the cognitive demand of discipline-specific complex texts to students' deep understanding?
- What would a student need to understand and be able to do to read like an expert in a specific discipline?
- How can professional development in the disciplinary literacy model contribute to increased capacity for teachers in different disciplines to provide instruction aligned with the high expectations of the Common Core?
- How can dialogue and collaboration with content-area teachers support adolescents' disciplinary literacy skills?

Achieving a guaranteed, viable curriculum begins with standards. A guaranteed curriculum provides teachers with clear guidance about the content to be taught, while a viable curriculum ensures there is sufficient time in the school year for the curriculum to be delivered to students (Marzano, 2003, p. 24). Focusing on specific standards provides time for explicit instruction. Examples in this chapter focus on the Common Core State Standards for literacy in history/social studies. The Common Core standards are organized by grade level, and the rigor of each standard increases through the grade levels. Exhibit 8.2 provides an example of scaffolded CCSS literacy standards in history/social studies. (Standards for K–5 reading in history/social studies, sci

Scaffolded Dynamic Connections Between Standards and Text Complexity

Grades	Common Core State Reading Standards for Literacy in History/Social Studies: Key Ideas and Details	Intertwining of text complexity elements and aligned instruction with high cognitive demand	Common Core State Reading Standards for Literacy in History/Social Studies: Range of Reading and Level of Text Complexity
Grades 11–12 students	**STANDARD 1 (RH.11–12.1):** Cite specific textual evidence to support analysis of primary and secondary sources, **connecting insights gained from specific details to an understanding of the text as a whole.**		**STANDARD 10 (RH.11–12.10):** By the end of **Grade 12**, read and comprehend history/social studies texts in the grades **11–CCR** text complexity band independently and proficiently.
	Instructional Tip: *When juniors and seniors do not connect insights about details to their understanding of the entire text, checking the previous standards can provide suggestions for differentiation. For this standard, students may require instruction that focuses on details such as the date or origin of information.*		***Increasing Text Complexity:*** *Progressing through grade levels, students should read and comprehend text of increasing complexity. Selection of complex texts aligned with the CCSS is informed by the text complexity factors in Exhibit 7.2 in Chapter 7. Alignment of the standard, text, and task requires the task to be of equally high cognitive demand.*
Grades 9–10 students	**STANDARD 1 (RH.9–10.1):** Cite specific textual evidence to support analysis of primary and secondary sources, **attending to such features as the date and origin of the information.**		**STANDARD 10 (RH.9–10.10):** By the end of **Grade 10,** read and comprehend history/social studies texts in the grades **9–10** text complexity band independently and proficiently.
	Instructional Tip: *When freshmen and sophomores do not demonstrate understanding of the important information the date and origin of the text can provide, checking the previous standard provides differentiation support. For this standard, students may benefit from additional opportunities to analyze primary and secondary sources and cite specific textual evidence. Advanced students would benefit from the concepts/skills in bold at the next level (attending to the date or origin of the information).*		***Increasing Text Complexity:*** *As students progress through grade levels, they should comprehend discipline-specific texts of increased complexity. For the literacy standards, this will include factors such as expectations for high intertextuality and discipline-specific vocabulary.*
Grades 6–8 students	**STANDARD 1 (RH.6–8.1):** Cite specific textual evidence to support analysis of primary and secondary sources.		**STANDARD 10 (RH.6–8.10):** By the end of Grade 8, read and comprehend history/social studies texts in the grades 6–8 text complexity band independently and proficiently.

ence, and technical subjects are integrated into the K–5 standards. College and career readiness standards work together with the literacy standard.)

The information in Exhibit 8.2 provides a visual representation of the dynamic intertwining of expectations in the Common Core. The CCSS provide the entrance to a bridge that can close the achievement gap for American students. Once educators get past the entrance, progress across the bridge is made by increasing parallel expectations for comprehending texts of greater complexity. Instruction must then be aligned with rigor that is equal to the standard.

To provide instruction with rigor equal to the demand of the standard, the standard should be "unwrapped" to determine the concepts and skills it includes (Ainsworth, 2010, p. 121). The full "unwrapping" process, which is explicitly described in Ainsworth's *Rigorous Curriculum Design*, involves highlighting the concepts and skills included in the standard: "The concepts are the important nouns or noun phrases and the skills are the verbs" (2010). During the "unwrapping" process, the teachable concepts (indicated by the nouns) are underlined. The words that describe what students are to do (indicated by the verbs) are circled or written in capital letters. Providing educators with professional development in this "unwrapping" process for aligning instructional rigor with the expectations in the standards would provide an excellent opportunity to prepare districts for the CCSS.

For example, the CCSS literacy in history/social studies standard RH.6–8.6 states: "Identify aspects of text that reveal an author's point of view or purpose (e.g., loaded language, inclusion or avoidance of particular facts)" (CCSSI, 2010a).

"Unwrapping" this standard for rigor, students need to be

able to IDENTIFY. This standard requires teaching the concepts of identifying the author's point of view and purpose. These are indicated by specific and perhaps loaded language used in the text, particular explicit facts in the text, and possibly obvious omission of facts.

Expecting students to "identify" evidence may appear to be a skill requiring a lower level of rigor, since it is in level 2 (understanding) out of the six levels in Bloom's Taxonomy (Bloom, 1956; Anderson and Krathwohl, 2000). However, for students to be able to identify as demanded in this standard requires students to "understand," or construct meaning, which demands a higher level of cognitive skill, for they must apply critical thinking to infer and analyze language that can be loaded with subtle bias to achieve an author's purpose—stated or unstated. Included in this standard's expectation is the assumption that students will be able to independently read complex texts in the discipline, and students must be able to differentiate between primary and secondary sources. Therefore, this standard may initially appear to be of a lower level of demand, but when the integrity of the purpose is considered, the level of rigor is moderate, rather than low. The "unwrapping" process guides the development of a standards-based curriculum. "Unwrapping" standard RH.6–8.6 revealed that the texts that are to be selected must have a level of complexity equal to that of the cognitive demand of the "unwrapped" standard, and that the task must require students to apply a high level of cognitive skill.

Connecting "unwrapped" priority standards with a complex text requires considering qualitative factors. Exhibit 8.3 depicts connections between complex texts and disciplinary literacy instruction. Moving through Exhibit 8.3: A. The standard would be "unwrapped" for rigor; B. A complex text would then be selected

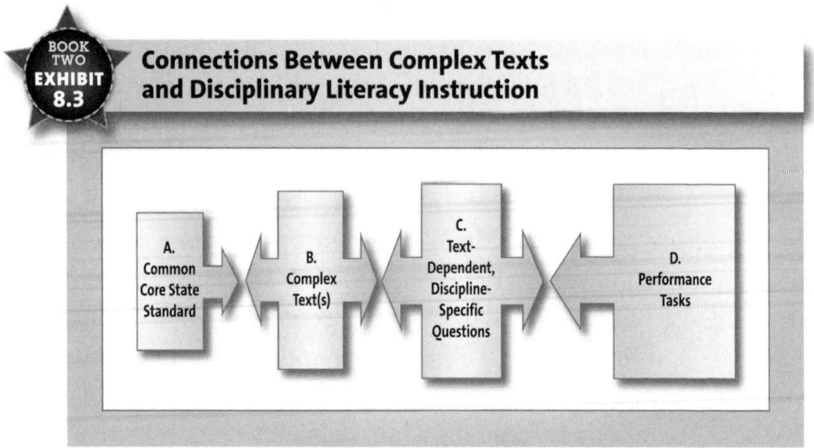

for the lesson; and C. Questions of high cognitive demand requiring text evidence would be generated. These questions must direct students to the text while stimulating thinking at higher cognitive levels. Instruction would include two to four performance tasks.

STEP 3: ALIGN PERFORMANCE TASKS

Performance tasks incorporate research-based learning progressions to evaluate the concepts and skills of the CCSS. These learning progressions define how students acquire the knowledge and skills called for in the standards. Results of performance tasks designed to align with the cognitive demand of specific standards provide teachers with formative information about students' progress during the year. As a result, decisions about instruction can be modified to support student growth. The necessity of aligning the rigor of performance tasks to the standards increases the need to provide discipline-specific instruction.

STEP 4: READ LIKE AN EXPERT—THE DISCIPLINARY LITERACY INSTRUCTIONAL MODEL

Reading like an expert is different for each discipline. Reading like a historian does not mean memorizing one isolated fact after another; comprehending history requires high-level critical thinking. Historians look for and consider information from the past. Their questioning establishes insightful connections with the present and enhances their understanding about the changing future. When reading history, the key is to view written text as a "speech act" (Wineburg, 2001, p. 66). A speech act is a communication produced by a specific person at a point in history to fulfill a purpose arising from personal motives and intentions, which may have an impact on individuals or society. Historians comprehend far beyond the words to understand the actions of people.

The following questions are examples that contain cognitive demand sufficiently robust to promote comprehension of *Narrative of the Life of Frederick Douglass, An American Slave*, by Frederick Douglass (1845), from CCSS Appendix A (2010b, p.11) and Common Core literacy standards RH.6–8.1: "Cite specific textual evidence to support analysis of primary and secondary sources," and RH.6–8.6: "Identify aspects of a text that reveal an author's point of view or purpose (e.g., loaded language, inclusion or avoidance of particular facts)."

- What three points of conflict, relevant to the time period, represent Frederick Douglass' frustrations? Provide textual evidence.
- Extend your understanding by describing two points of conflict a professional and successful person representing a minority race would include in a memoir today.

- Determine an emotional conflict Frederick Douglass' message created within you, or may create within others. Provide textual evidence for the source of this conflict.

These questions illustrate alignment between literacy standards from the CCSS and the determination of the level of rigor within the standard. They are based on a complex text of equal cognitive demand. The dynamics of the CCSS insist on applying teacher judgment when matching reader to text and task. These questions reflect one stage (stage B of "reading like a historian") of the disciplinary literacy instructional model, which guides students to read like experts in multiple disciplines.

The four stages in the investigation model for disciplinary literacy instruction are context, text, impersonal subtext, and personal subtext. Each stage is supported with questions that an expert might use to investigate the information in order to acquire deep understanding.

Stage A: **Context**—Piecing together clues to construct the "frame" used to surround the author's thoughts.

Stage B: **Text**—Weaving the author's thoughts and intentions with words, phrases, and sentences to produce a "fabric within the frame" to communicate with the reader.

Stage C: **Impersonal Subtext**—Investigating deeply to uncover the author's purpose, plan, and motives, and intentions that are either explicitly stated or implicitly buried by the author under layers of text.

Stage D: **Personal Subtext**—Upon deeper investigation, uncovering patterns and constructing meanings the author did not intend to reveal but which inadvertently are a part of the composition of the text.

Implementation of fully integrated disciplinary literacy instruction is grounded in alignment with the CCSS from planning through assessment.

Current state literacy standards rarely include content areas outside of the English language arts arena. The Common Core's decision to include literacy standards in history/social studies, science, and technical subjects recognizes that literacy standards for specific content areas are vital for an education that is no longer fragmented, but representative of the global environment that students are being educated to thrive within. It is important to highlight that teachers with skills in specific disciplines are critical for ensuring students acquire the content knowledge and skills required in each field of study. The literacy standards for history/social studies, science, and technical subjects offer guidance on the reading and writing requirement within those content areas, and it is through reading and writing that students increase their content knowledge. This focus is a significant change for both teachers of English and teachers of other content areas. To support these unparallel literacy standards, "and move from implicit or informal expectations to establishing a connection between standards in history/social studies, science and technical subjects and the CCSS, states will need a strong implementation strategy to ensure their impact in grades 6–12" (ACT, 2010, p. 24).

It is important for students to be provided with every opportunity to steadily increase progress in specific content areas. Monitoring progress with regularly scheduled Data Team meetings and with compelling conversations scheduled at least once per marking period with principals and school leaders can provide continuous support for students, teachers, and schools. School cultures depend on increased face-to-face communication during times of change to maintain trust, a significant criteria for achievement. To increase reading level expectations, as required in CCSS ELA standard 10, literacy instruction will need to expand into the main disciplines. Closing the college and career achievement gap requires that students increase their content knowledge. Educators must keep in mind the integrity of the CCSS while developing discipline-specific questions. Questions that are aligned with the rigor of the standards require discipline-specific information. Students must provide text-based evidence with attention to precise details in their responses, and their responses must demonstrate their ability to evaluate arguments, including the author's subtext.

SUMMARY

Literacy is receiving increased attention today as a result of the demand for students and adults to focus upon deeper understanding, dynamic connections with information, and the realization that the Internet is not simply a source of entertainment but an extension of adolescent lives. One role of education is to teach the literacy actions and skills that will support adolescents in becoming enthusiastic learners in different content areas, and responsible communicators of knowledge. The four steps in the disciplinary literacy process described in this chapter provide support for students to help them read complex texts with deep understanding.

Step 1: Consider the Three Levels of Literacy Instruction. Shanahan and Shanahan (2008) identified the levels as basic literacy, intermediate literacy, and disciplinary literacy. It is at the disciplinary literacy level that skills are specialized to comprehend complex texts specialized to history, science, mathematics, literature, or some other subject.

Step 2: Pave the Path for Disciplinary Literacy Instruction Aligned with the CCSS. Connections between the cognitive demand in the ELA CCSS and levels of text complexity are dynamic. It is through the "unwrapping the standards" process that connections are strengthened between rigor in the CCSS and students' assessed achievement.

Step 3: Align Performance Assessment. Aligning performance assessments having rigor equal to the demand of specific standards and complex texts increases student achievement. Over time, instruction aligned with the Common Core's rigor will close the achievement gaps of graduates.

Step 4: Read Like an Expert—The Disciplinary Literacy Instructional Model. The components of disciplinary literacy instruction (context, text, impersonal subtext, and personal subtext) guide students in comprehending complex text. A fully integrated and aligned instructional process begins with "unwrapping" the skills and concepts in the CCSS standards, developing performance assessments, and planning aligned discipline-specific instruction.

As Gardner explained, "More knowledge now lies in the spaces between, or the connections across, the several disciplines" (2008, p. 44). In the future, adolescents must learn how to synthesize knowledge and how to extend it in new and unfamiliar ways. The world is within their grasp, and we have the opportunity and responsibility for better preparing each and every student *now* to enthusiastically embrace literacy and its complexity.

References

Note: This chapter includes excerpts from Disciplinary Literacy: Redefining Deep Understanding and Leadership for 21st-Century Demands *(Piercy and Piercy, 2011).*

ACT. (2010). *The condition of college & career readiness.* Retrieved Sept. 9, 2011, from www.act.org/research/policymakers/cccr10/pdf/ConditionofCollegeandCareerReadiness2010.pdf

Ainsworth, L. (2010). *Rigorous curriculum design: How to create curricular units of study that align standards, instruction, and assessment.* Englewood, CO: Lead + Learn Press.

Anderson, L. W., & Krathwohl, D. R. (2000). *A taxonomy for learning, teaching, and assessing: A revision of Bloom's taxonomy of educational objectives.* Needham Heights, MA: Allyn & Bacon.

Carnegie Corporation. (2010). *Time to act: An agenda for advancing adolescent literacy for college and career success.* New York.

Common Core State Standards Initiative (CCSSI). (2010a, June). *Common Core State Standards for English language arts & literacy in history/social studies, science, and technical subjects* (PDF document). Retrieved from www.corestandards.org/assets/CCSSI_ELA%20Standards.pdf

Common Core State Standards Initiative (CCSSI). (2010b, June). *Common Core State Standards for English language arts & literacy in history/social studies, science, and technical subjects: Appendix A* (PDF document). Retrieved from www.corestandards.org/assets/Appendix_A.pdf

Gardner, H. (2008). *Five minds for the future.* Boston, MA: Harvard Business School Press.

Marzano, R. J. (2003). *What works in schools: Translating research into action.* Alexandria, VA: ASCD.

McConachie, S. M., & Petrosky, A. R. (2010). *Content matters: A disciplinary literacy approach to improving student learning.* Pittsburgh, PA: University of Pittsburgh of the Commonwealth System of Higher Education.

McKeown, M. G., Beck, I. L., & Blake, R. G. (2009). Rethinking reading comprehension instruction: A comparison of instruction for strategies and content approaches. *Reading Research Quarterly, 44*(3), 218–253.

Shanahan, T., & Shanahan, C. (2008). Teaching disciplinary literacy to adolescents: Rethinking content. *Harvard Educational Review, 78*(1), 40–59.

Snow, C., & Moje, E. (2010). Why is everyone talking adolescent literacy? *Phi Delta Kappan, 91*(6), 66–69.

Wineburg, S. (2001). *Historical thinking and other unnatural acts: Charting the future of teaching and the past.* Philadelphia, PA: Temple University Press.

Teaching Strategies for Reading for Information in the English Language Arts Common Core

Cathy J. Lassiter

The Common Core insists that literacy be a shared responsibility among all educators, and the inclusion of standards for not only reading, writing, and mathematics, but also speaking and listening and language usage, demonstrates a commitment to improving the literacy of all students. In this chapter, teaching strategies aligned with the English language arts CCSS standards specifically targeted at reading for information will be discussed. The strategies can and should be used in all subject areas, as all teachers are teachers of reading. According to research by Billmeyer and Barton of McREL (Mid-continent Research for Education and Learning), in *Teaching Reading in the Content Areas: If Not Me, Then Who?*, "Improvements in higher-level reading skills cannot come about simply by an emphasis on reading instruction in isolation from the other work students do in school. Students must learn to read in all content areas. Every teacher must be a reading teacher" (1998, p. 57).

The ELA CCSS places a significant emphasis on students managing and understanding informational texts at increasing levels of complexity as they progress through the system. Therefore, the teaching strategies that follow for reading for information are intended for teachers in all content areas. They are based on the six assumptions about learning proposed by McREL: 1. Learning is goal-oriented; 2. Learning is the linking of new information to prior knowledge; 3. Learning involves organizing information; 4. Learning is the acquisition of cognitive and metacognitive structures; 5. Learning occurs in phases, yet is nonlinear; and 6. Learning is influenced by cognitive development (Billmeyer and Barton, 1998). These research-based strategies are aligned to the Common Core standards for reading, writing, and speaking and listening.

TEACHING STRATEGY 1

Model and teach the steps to becoming a strategic and reflective reader, also known as metacomprehension: 1. planning for reading; 2. monitoring reading; and 3. evaluating reading comprehension.

Planning for Reading

Teachers who take the time to explicitly share metacomprehension techniques with their students will find that students attain higher levels of comprehension in both narrative and informational reading. In planning for reading, strategic readers preview the reading for content, scope, and organization.

It is important for teachers do this aloud with the class to provide students with the context for this action and the benefits of it. During the preview, students activate prior knowledge about the topic and begin to make predictions about the content of the reading (Billmeyer and Barton, 1998). They may ask each other questions in a think-pair-share format to accomplish this, or engage in a whole-group discussion asking questions and making predictions. The teacher should set a purpose for the reading following the predictions. Why are students reading? What should they seek to learn?

Finally, the teacher should discuss what specific reading skills will be helpful to the students as they read. Walking students explicitly through a preview of a reading selection each time reading is required will help them develop the habit of previewing. Eventually, the teacher can instruct the students to "conduct their preview," and step back from the explicit step-by-step instruction.

Monitoring Reading

As students read, they enter the monitoring phase of their metacomprehension work. Students who are successful at monitoring have two simultaneous thinking functions underway. First, they are engaged with the reading based on their preview, as they seek to confirm their predictions and answer questions. They strive to meet the purpose set for the reading by the teacher. And second, they are also assessing their progress on these tasks. They adjust their reading as needed to achieve the purpose (Billmeyer and Barton, 1998). For example, they slow down, reread certain sentences, and use context clues to determine meaning.

Teachers can assist students in developing these thinking functions by reading short passages aloud and pointing out the thinking strategies as they go along. This can be accomplished by reading the first paragraph aloud and then having students read a paragraph independently. The students then share their monitoring techniques with the class when they are finished. Building on their comments, the teacher reads the next passage aloud, pointing out the thinking again, and then having students read and share their thinking with a partner. Again, once students develop the habit of performing these simultaneous functions while they read, their comprehension will improve and become deeper.

Evaluating Reading

The third step in the metacomprehension strategy is teaching students to evaluate their understanding of the reading selection. Students accomplish this by summarizing the main ideas once reading is completed. They return to the purpose stated by the teacher and assess their achievement related to it. Students also return to their original predictions and questions and determine if their predictions were accurate, and if their questions were answered in the reading selection.

The teacher can complete the activity by asking students to share with their partner, share with the class as a whole, write a summary of what they learned and what more they want to learn, or use graphic organizers to record their success. Teachers need to pose questions that require students interpret and personalize the reading—in other words, make the reading their own (Billmeyer and Barton, 1998).

Also, teachers may ask students to come up with a way to demonstrate their understanding of the reading and the strategies they used to comprehend the information. It is important for students to be able to explain how they previewed the reading, monitored their reading as they went along, and evaluated their success by determining how well they used their strategies and how well they understood the information. Asking process questions can assist students with their comprehension. Questions that promote metacomprehension can help students plan for and monitor their comprehension and evaluate the effectiveness of the reading skills they use. Examples of these types of questions appear in Exhibit 9.1.

The teaching strategies described on previous pages for reading are directly aligned to the ELA CCSS reading for information standards. Exhibit 9.2 is an example of a CCSS learning progression in reading that the strategies address.

TEACHING STRATEGY 2

Teach both metacomprehension and metacognition.

The elements of metacomprehension—planning for reading, monitoring reading, and evaluating reading—are a form of general metacognitive skills that help students become more aware of and in control of their own thinking. Students learn these strategies with explicit instruction from highly competent teachers.

The most effective way to teach metacognition is to begin with direct instruction of the levels of thinking. Teachers should explain the levels of thinking and engage students in lessons that require them to compare and contrast, analyze, synthesize, evaluate, judge, and defend ideas they encounter in their informational reading. The teacher models what thinking sounds like when an analysis is underway; this is commonly called a "think-aloud." The teacher talks through the stages the brain is going through when a thinking skill is used. Students hear what happens in the brain of a person

Sample Reading Metacomprehension Questions

Before **Reading Questions**	***During*** **Reading Questions**	***After*** **Reading Questions**
Preview the passage and discuss what you think it will be about.	What do you think the main idea of the reading is so far?	What were the main ideas of the reading passage?
What are some things you already know about the topic?	What mental images came to your mind as you read?	Did you change your view on the main idea as you finished the reading?
What reading skills do you plan to use while you read?	Is the information in this reading similar to anything else you have read? In what ways?	Did you accomplish your reading goals?
What is your purpose for reading?	What were you wondering about as you were reading?	What strategies worked best for you while reading?
What will you be required to do with the information you learn from the reading?	How are your reading strategies working for you so far?	What parts of the passage did you find most interesting? Most difficult?
How will you know you understood the information?	Should you start to use different strategies to enhance your comprehension of the reading?	Were you able to make connections from this passage to passages you read previously? What were the connections?
What organizational tools will you have handy while you read? (Cornell notes, graphic organizer, vocabulary organizer, etc.)	What kind of tool will fit best for taking notes on this reading passage?	Has your thinking changed as a result of reading this passage? How?

Source: Billmeyer and Barton, 1998.

who is using a skill such as analyzing, evaluating, or synthesizing. They then practice, following the teacher's lead, by sharing how their thinking progresses as they complete the given task.

Reading Learning Progression

Reading Learning Progression for Informational Text	
Grade Level	**Standard**
Grade 1 **RI.1.2**	Identify the main idea and retell key details of a text.
Grade 3 **RI.3.2**	Determine the main idea of a text and explain how it is supported by key details; summarize the text.
Grade 5 **RI.5.2**	Determine two or more main ideas of a text and explain how they are supported by key details; summarize the text.
Grade 7 **RI.7.2**	Determine two or more central ideas in a text and analyze their development over the course of the text; provide an objective summary of the text.
Grades 9–10 **RI.9–10.2**	Determine a central idea of a text and analyze its development over the course of the text, including how it emerges and is shaped and refined by specific details; provide an objective summary of the text.
Grades 11–12 **RI.11–12.2**	Determine a central idea of a text and analyze its development over the course of the text, including how they interact and build on one another to provide a complex analysis; provide an objective summary of the text.

Source: CCSSI, 2010.

Practice doing these kinds of think-alouds, modeled by the teacher, will help make metacognitive skills automatic as students tackle various learning tasks, as described above with the meta-comprehension strategies. Ineffective readers are often not aware that their thinking and their comprehension of the information is not strong. When teachers verbalize their thoughts while reading aloud to students, the students learn how to create mental pictures, deal with unfamiliar vocabulary, revise predictions, and make connections. Students will also learn what thinking strategies work best for them, and they will realize that not everyone will use the same strategy at the same time. Metacognition is highly individual. Teachers can foster metacognition in their students when they ask and/or encourage students to do the following as part of their daily routine (Foster, et al., 2002):

- Explain the learning task in their own words.
- Express what they plan to do before, during, and after the work.
- Consider which of their personal strengths and interests are relevant to completing the task.
- Set goals for future learning based on assessing which strategies worked best this time and which ones they think they should keep or change.
- Explain what was working through the task and what it taught them about themselves as learners.

TEACHING STRATEGY 3

Emphasize and use the technical language of the content area and explicitly teach the content-area vocabulary.

John Hattie, researcher and author of *Visible Learning: A Synthesis of over 800 Meta-Analyses Relating to Achievement* (2009), involving millions of students and 15 years of research, found that explicit instruction in vocabulary had an effect size of .67 and is considered a highly effective practice on his scale for improving student comprehension. Hattie writes, "the most effective vocabulary teaching methods included providing both definitional and contextual information, involved students in deeper processing, and gave students more than one or two exposures to the words they were to learn" (2009, pp. 131–132).

The researchers at McREL agree with Hattie. They write that, "research over the past ten years reveals that vocabulary knowledge is the single most important factor contributing to reading comprehension" (Billmeyer and Barton, 1998, p. 19). Additionally, Marzano, Pickering, and Pollock, authors of *Classroom Instruction That Works*, had similar findings. They conclude that, ". . . an analysis of the research provides a strong case for systematic instruction in vocabulary at virtually every grade level" (2001, pp. 124–127). They offer guidance to teachers instructing students on vocabulary terms and phrases. They suggest that: 1. Students must encounter words in context more than once to learn them; 2. Instruction in new words enhances learning those words in context; 3. One of the best ways to learn a new word is to associate an image with it; 4. Direct vocabulary instruction works; and 5. Direct instruction on words that are critical to new content produces the most powerful learning (2001). As teachers begin to plan units of study, it is critical that the technical terms or new vocabulary students will encounter in their reading be identified in advance and plans made to explicitly teach the words.

One method supported as effective is Marzano's five-step process, or instructional sequence, for vocabulary instruction (Marzano, Pickering, and Pollock, 2001). This technique allows for multiple opportunities to learn new terms in discipline-specific content. When students encounter a new word in their reading or in class, the teacher presents students with a brief explanation or description of the term. The teacher also presents a visual or nonlinguistic representation of the new term. Students then generate their own description of the term and create their own visual to represent the term. Students check their explanations and representations for accuracy. Teachers can incorporate these five steps creatively into their lessons and students will enjoy learning new words and deepen their understanding of the content.

Another method for teaching vocabulary is the Frayer Model. The Frayer Model (Frayer, Frederick, and Klausmeier, 1969) is a word categorization activity. Although created several decades ago, teachers and content experts alike support the method as very effective in modern classrooms, due to the relational method of the strategy. Students analyze terms for their essential and nonessential attributes, and they determine examples and nonexamples of the concept, much like the concept attainment strategy used in many classrooms today. A four-square graphic organizer may be used to help students organize their thinking. Teachers explain the graphic organizer and either have students draw one or give them one on a handout. Using an easy word first, the teacher demonstrates how the model works and conducts a think-aloud with the class for each of the boxes in the model. Students then work in pairs or small groups to complete a model for the new term(s) they encounter in their reading or in class. Teachers can post the visuals in the room and use them as an integral part of instruction for the duration of the unit of study. Exhibit 9.3 is an example of a blank Frayer Model graphic organizer.

There are many other strategies for teaching vocabulary to improve reading comprehension of informational texts. These in-

BOOK TWO EXHIBIT 9.3

Frayer Model

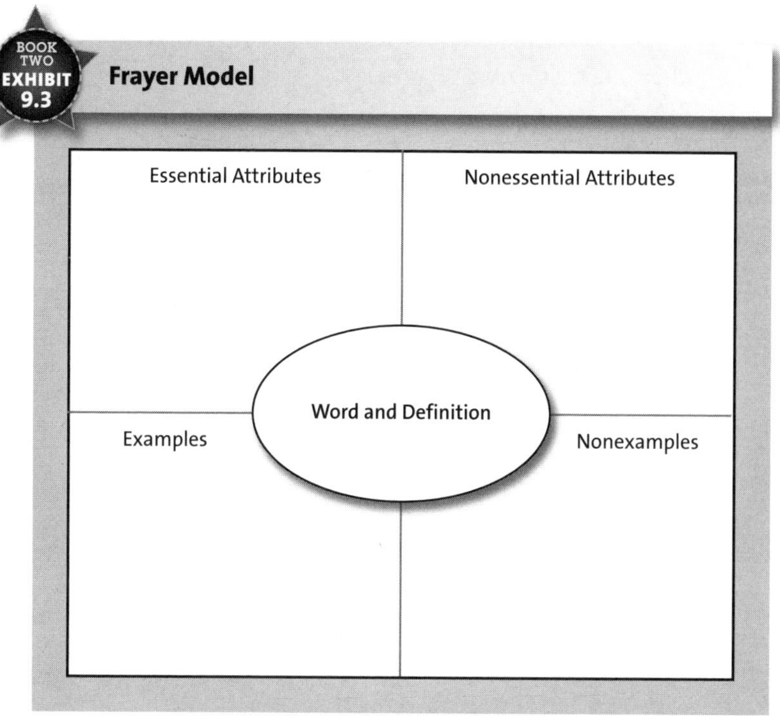

clude semantic mapping, word splash, concept attainment, and others. Content-area vocabulary differs greatly from the vocabulary that students learn in English class. The technical language of the content area distinguishes it from other content areas with the unique labels that the discipline uses to identify important subject-specific concepts. It is important to note that vocabulary strategies are essential to student mastery of content information and are supported by the literacy standards in the Common Core. Exhibit 9.4 provides a learning progression from the CCSS which relates to vocabulary strategies for all content areas.

Vocabulary Learning Progression

Vocabulary Learning Progression for Informational Text	
Grade Level	**Standard**
Kindergarten RI.K.4	With prompting and support, ask and answer questions about unknown words in a text.
Grade 2 RI.2.4	Ask and answer questions to help determine or clarify the meaning of words and phrases in a text.
Grade 4 RI.4.4	Determine the meaning of general academic or domain-specific words or phrases in a text relevant to a grade 4 topic or subject area.
Grade 6 RI.6.4	Determine the meaning of words and phrases as they are used in a text, including figurative, connotative, and technical meanings.
Grade 8 RI.8.4	Determine the meaning of words and phrases as they are used in a text, including figurative, connotative, and technical meanings; analyze the impact of specific word choices on meaning and tone, including analogies or allusions to other texts.
Grades 9–10 RI.9–10.4	Determine the meaning of words and phrases as they are used in a text, including figurative, connotative, and technical meanings; analyze the cumulative impact of the specific word choice on meaning and tone (e.g., how the language of a court opinion differs from that of a newspaper).
Grades 11–12 RI.11–12.4	Determine the meaning of words and phrases as they are used in a text, including figurative, connotative, and technical meanings; analyze how an author uses and refines the meaning of a key term or terms over the course of a text (e.g., how James Madison defines "faction" in *Federalist No. 10*).

Source: CCSSI, 2010.

SUMMARY

The CCSS ELA standards require that our students think critically, read and write proficiently, and develop and defend their ideas effectively.

As teachers, we must ensure that students are explicitly taught metacomprehension and metacognitive skills at the earliest grades and we must reinforce those skills through graduation. Students who monitor their own learning and regulate their thinking based on the given task develop high-level thinking skills that are transferrable between content areas. These skills, along with quality content instruction, will propel students to mastery learning in all content areas. Teachers of all content areas at all grades should take the time to teach students the steps to becoming strategic and reflective readers.

All teachers must take note of the research regarding explicit vocabulary instruction, and take steps to incorporate those strategies into their daily teaching routines. No matter which strategies a teacher uses to teach vocabulary, the key is the mindset with which the teacher approaches the work. Enthusiasm and passion about learning new words and concepts displayed by the teacher will transfer to the students. Students need to feel that learning new concepts and words helps them make meaning and improves their reading. They will also learn that vocabulary development is not only important to learning the subject matter, but is also a lifelong skill.

- In order to meet the requirements of the ELA CCSS, all teachers must be teachers of reading.
- Six assumptions about learning proposed by McREL in

Teaching Reading in the Content Areas: If Not Me, then Who? (Billmeyer and Barton, 1998) are:

1. Learning is goal-oriented.
2. Learning is the linking of new information to prior knowledge.
3. Learning involves organizing information.
4. Learning is the acquisition of cognitive and metacognitive structures.
5. Learning occurs in phases, yet is nonlinear.
6. Learning is influenced by cognitive development.

- Teaching strategies for reading for information include:
    1. Teach the steps to becoming a strategic and reflective reader, also known as metacomprehension: planning for reading, monitoring reading, and evaluating reading comprehension.
    2. Teach metacognitive skills in addition to metacomprehension skills. These can be taught by making students do the following as part of the daily classroom routine (Foster, et al., 2002):
        - Explain the learning task in their own words.
        - Express what they plan to do before, during, and after the work.
        - Consider which of their personal strengths and interests are relevant to completing the task.
        - Set goals for future learning based on assessing which strategies worked best this time and which strategies they think they should keep or change.
        - Explain what was working through the task and what it taught them about themselves as learners.

3. Emphasize and use the technical language of the content area and explicitly teach the content-area vocabulary.

References

Billmeyer, R., & Barton, M. (1998). *Teaching reading in the content areas: If not me, then who?* Aurora, CO: McREL.

Carmichael, S., Martino, G., Porter-Magee, K., & Wilson, W. (2010). *The state of the State Standards—and the Common Core—in 2010.* Washington, DC: Thomas B. Fordham Institute.

Common Core State Standards Initiative (CCSSI). (2010, June). *Common Core State Standards for English language arts & literacy in history/social studies, science, and technical subjects* (PDF document). Retrieved from www.corestandards.org/assets/CCSSI_ELA%20Standards.pdf

Foster, G., Sawick, E., Schaffer, H., & Zalinski, V. (2002). *I think, therefore I learn.* Ontario: Pembroke.

Frayer, D. A., Frederick, W. C., & Klausmeier, H. J. (1969). *A schema for testing the level of concept mastery.* Technical Report no. 16. Madison, WI: University of Wisconsin Research and Development Center for Cognitive Learning.

Hattie, J. (2009). *Visible learning: A synthesis of over 800 meta-analyses relating to achievement.* New York: Routledge.

Marzano, R., Pickering, D., & Pollock, J. (2001). *Classroom instruction that works: Research-based strategies for increasing student achievement.* Alexandria, VA: ASCD.

Synthesis of the ELA CCSS

Synthesis of the Common Core State Standards for English Language Arts and Literacy in History/Social Studies, Science, and Technical Subjects

PREPARED BY

Maryann D. Wiggs,

Professional Development Associate,

The Leadership and Learning Center

Source: ***Common Core State Standards for English Language Arts & Literacy in History/Social Studies, Science, and Technical Subjects***, June 2010.
Retrieved from: Common Core State Standards Initiative Web site: www.corestandards.org.

Common Core State Standards: Design & Organization for English Language Arts & Literacy in History/Social Studies, Science, and Technical Subjects

The K–12 Standards	Grade-Specific Standards				Strand-Specific College & Career Readiness (CCR) Anchor Standards
• The ELA standards document is comprised of three main sections: a K–5 content section, a 6–12 content section, and a section for 6–12 literacy in history/social studies, science, and technical subjects. • Three appendices accompany the main document. • The K–5 and 6–12 content sections are divided into four strands: Reading, Writing, Speaking and Listening, and Language. • The 6–12 literacy in history/social studies, science, and technical subjects section is divided into two strands: Reading and Writing. • The K–5 literacy standards for history/social studies, science, and technical subjects are embedded within the K–5 content strands.	• Grade-specific standards define end-of-year expectations. • Each grade-specific standard corresponds to the same-numbered CCR anchor strand and standard. • Standards use individual grade levels in K–8 to provide useful specificity; the Standards use two-year bands in grades 9–12 to allow flexibility in high school course design.				• The CCR anchor standards define literacy expectations for college and workforce readiness. • CCR anchor standards are divided into four strands: Reading, Writing, Speaking and Listening, and Language. • Each strand is headed by a strand-specific set of CCR anchor standards that is identical across all grades and content areas.
Section I: Standards for ELA & Literacy in History/Social Studies, Science, and Technical Subjects K–5	**K–5**	**6–8**	**9–10**	**11–12**	**CCR Anchor Standards**
❖ **Reading Standards for Literature K–5 (RL)** ❖ **Reading Standards for Informational Text K–5 (RI)**					Aligned to 10 **Reading Strand** Standards
❖ **Reading Standards: Foundational Skills K–5 (RF)**					
❖ **Writing Standards K–5 (W)**					Aligned to 10 **Writing Strand** Standards
❖ **Speaking and Listening Standards K–5 (SL)**					Aligned to 6 **Speaking and Listening** Standards
❖ **Language Standards K–5 (L)**					Aligned to 6 **Language Strand** Standards
Section II: Standards for English Language Arts 6–12	**K–5**	**6–8**	**9–10**	**11–12**	**CCR Anchor Standards**
❖ **Reading Standards for Literature 6–12 (RL)** ❖ **Reading Standards for Informational Text 6–12 (RI)**					Aligned to 10 **Reading Strand** Standards
❖ **Writing Standards 6–12 (W)**					Aligned to 10 **Writing Strand** Standards
❖ **Speaking and Listening Standards 6–12(SL)**					Aligned to 6 **Speaking and Listening** Standards
❖ **Language Standards 6–12 (L)**					Aligned to 6 **Language Strand** Standards
Section III: Standards for Literacy in History/Social Studies, Science, and Technical Subjects 6–12	**K–5**	**6–8**	**9–10**	**11–12**	**CCR Anchor Standards**
❖ **Reading Standards for Literacy in History/Social Studies 6–12 (RH)**					Aligned to 10 **Reading Strand** Standards
❖ **Standards for Literacy in Science and Technical Subjects 6–12 (RST)**					Aligned to 10 **Reading Strand** Standards
❖ **Writing Standards for Literacy in History/Social Studies, Science, and Technical Subjects 6–12 (WHST)**					Aligned to 6 **Writing Strand** Standards

Appendix A provides supplementary material on reading exemplars and foundational skills, definitions of writing, the role of speaking and listening, an overview of progressive language skills, a glossary of terms, and a detailed discussion on text complexity. Contains 43 pages.
Appendix B provides numerous sample texts illustrating the complexity, quality, and range of reading appropriate for various grade levels with accompanying sample performance tasks. The standards intentionally do not offer a reading list, as school districts and states must decide on curriculum. Contains 183 pages.
Appendix C provides annotated samples demonstrating at least adequate performance in student writing at various grade levels. Contains 107 pages.

<table>
<tr><th colspan="4">CCSS: English Language Arts (ELA) "Reading Strand"</th></tr>
<tr><td colspan="3">Grade-Specific Reading Standards
(Grade-appropriate end-of-year expectations aligned to CCR Reading anchor standards)</td><td rowspan="2">Strand-Specific College & Career Readiness (CCR)
Anchor Standards for Reading
Note: The same 10 CCR anchor standards for Reading apply to both literary & informational text, including texts in history/social studies, science, and technical subjects.</td></tr>
<tr><td>K–8</td><td>9–10</td><td>11–12</td></tr>
<tr><td colspan="3" rowspan="14">❖ K–12 Reading Standards for Literature (RL)
❖ K–12 Reading Standards for Informational Text (RI)
Key Features of the Reading Standards:
• K–5 Reading standards represent a balance between the reading of literature and the reading of informational text. The K–5 literacy standards for history/social studies, science, and technical subjects are embedded within the K–5 content strands.
• 6–12 Reading standards require much greater attention to a specific category of informational text—literary nonfiction.
• The Reading standards mandate certain critical types of content for all students, including classic and contemporary literature, classic myths and stories from around the world, foundational U.S. documents, seminal works of American literature, and the writings of Shakespeare.
• The ELA standards insist that instruction in reading, writing, speaking and listening, and language be a shared responsibility within the school.
• The Standards require that students demonstrate: an increasing sophistication of what they read and the skill with which they read, a steadily growing ability to discern more from and make fuller use of text, make an increasing number of connections among ideas and between texts, consider a wider range of textual evidence, and become more sensitive to inconsistencies, ambiguities, and poor reasoning in texts.
• Standard 10 defines a grade-by-grade "staircase" of increasing text complexity that rises from beginning reading to the college and career readiness level. Refer to Appendix A for a complete explanation of text complexity and how it is measured.</td><td>Key Ideas and Details</td></tr>
<tr><td>1. Read closely to determine what the text says explicitly and to make logical inferences from it; cite specific textual evidence when writing or speaking to support conclusions drawn from the text.</td></tr>
<tr><td>2. Determine central ideas or themes of a text and analyze their development; summarize the key supporting details and ideas.</td></tr>
<tr><td>3. Analyze how and why individuals, events, and ideas develop and interact over the course of a text.</td></tr>
<tr><td>Craft and Structure</td></tr>
<tr><td>4. Interpret words and phrases as they are used in a text, including determining technical, connotative, and figurative meanings, and analyze how specific word choices shape meaning or tone.</td></tr>
<tr><td>5. Analyze the structure of texts, including how specific sentences, paragraphs, and larger portions of the text (e.g., a section, chapter, scene, or stanza) relate to each other and the whole.</td></tr>
<tr><td>6. Assess how point of view or purpose shapes the content and style of a text.</td></tr>
<tr><td>Integration of Knowledge and Ideas</td></tr>
<tr><td>7. Integrate and evaluate content presented in diverse media and formats, including visually and quantitatively, as well as in words.</td></tr>
<tr><td>8. Delineate and evaluate the argument and specific claims in a text, including the validity of the reasoning as well as the relevance and sufficiency of the evidence.</td></tr>
<tr><td>9. Analyze how two or more texts address similar themes or topics in order to build knowledge or to compare the approaches the authors take.</td></tr>
<tr><td>Range of Reading and Level of Text Complexity</td></tr>
<tr><td>10. Read and comprehend complex literature and informational texts independently and proficiently.</td></tr>
<tr><td colspan="3">❖ Reading Standards: K–5 Foundational Skills (RF)
• Print Concepts (K–1)
• Phonological Awareness (K–1)
• Phonics and Word Recognition (K–5)
• Fluency (K–5)</td><td>Decoding the Numbering System for the Reading Standards:
R.CCR.6 = Reading Strand, CCR Anchor, Standard 6
RI.4.3 = Reading, Informational Text, Grade 4, Standard 3
RL.8.5 = Reading, Literature, Grade 8, Standard 5</td></tr>
</table>

<table>
<tr><th colspan="4">CCSS: English Language Arts (ELA) "Reading Strand"
• Literacy Standards for History/Social Studies
• Literacy Standards for Science and Technical Subjects</th></tr>
<tr><th colspan="3">Grade-Specific Reading Standards
(Grade-appropriate end-of-year expectations aligned to CCR Reading anchor standards) →</th><th>Strand-Specific College & Career Readiness (CCR)
Anchor Standards for Reading</th></tr>
<tr><th>6–8</th><th>9–10</th><th>11–12</th><td>Note: The same 10 CCR anchor standards for Reading apply to both literary and informational text, including texts in history/social studies, science, and technical subjects.</td></tr>
<tr><td colspan="3" rowspan="14">❖ Reading Standards for Literacy in History/Social Studies 6–12 (RH)
❖ Reading Standards for Literacy in Science and Technical Subjects (RST)

Key Features of the Reading Standards for Literacy in History/Social Studies, Science, and Technical Subjects:
• The ELA standards insist that instruction in reading, writing, speaking and listening, and language be a shared responsibility within the school. This interdisciplinary approach to literacy is based on extensive research establishing the need for college- and career-ready students to be proficient in reading complex informational text independently in a variety of content areas.
• Students must have knowledge of domain-specific vocabulary.
• By senior year of high school, the ELA standards indicate that 70 percent of the sum of student reading across the grades should be informational text.
• In history and social studies, students need to be able to analyze, evaluate, and differentiate primary and secondary sources.
• When reading scientific and technical texts, students need to be able to gain knowledge from challenging texts that often make extensive use of elaborate diagrams and data to convey information and illustrate concepts.
• The reading standards for literacy in history/social studies, science, and technical subjects are meant to complement the specific content demands of the disciplines, not replace them.</td><th>Key Ideas and Details</th></tr>
<tr><td>1. Read closely to determine what the text says explicitly and to make logical inferences from it; cite specific textual evidence when writing or speaking to support conclusions drawn from the text.</td></tr>
<tr><td>2. Determine central ideas or themes of a text and analyze their development; summarize the key supporting details and ideas.</td></tr>
<tr><td>3. Analyze how and why individuals, events, and ideas develop and interact over the course of a text.</td></tr>
<tr><th>Craft and Structure</th></tr>
<tr><td>4. Interpret words and phrases as they are used in a text, including determining technical, connotative, and figurative meanings, and analyze how specific word choices shape meaning or tone.</td></tr>
<tr><td>5. Analyze the structure of texts, including how specific sentences, paragraphs, and larger portions of the text (e.g., a section, chapter, scene, or stanza) relate to each other and the whole.</td></tr>
<tr><td>6. Assess how point of view or purpose shapes the content and style of a text.</td></tr>
<tr><th>Integration of Knowledge and Ideas</th></tr>
<tr><td>7. Integrate and evaluate content presented in diverse media and formats, including visually and quantitatively, as well as in words.</td></tr>
<tr><td>8. Delineate and evaluate the argument and specific claims in a text, including the validity of the reasoning as well as the relevance and sufficiency of the evidence.</td></tr>
<tr><td>9. Analyze how two or more texts address similar themes or topics in order to build knowledge or to compare the approaches the authors take.</td></tr>
<tr><th>Range of Reading and Level of Text Complexity</th></tr>
<tr><td>10. Read and comprehend complex literature and informational texts independently and proficiently.</td></tr>
</table>

CCSS: English Language Arts (ELA) "Writing Strand"

Grade-Specific Writing Standards *(Grade-appropriate end-of-year expectations aligned to CCR Writing anchor standards)*			Strand-Specific College & Career Readiness (CCR) Anchor Standards for Writing *Note: The same 10 CCR anchor standards for Writing cover numerous text types and subject areas, and apply to writing in history/social studies, science, and technical subjects.*
K–8	**9–10**	**11–12**	

❖ **K–12 Writing Standards (W)**

Key Features of the Writing Standards:

- The ability to write logical arguments based on substantive claims, sound reasoning, and relevant evidence is a cornerstone of the Writing standards, with opinion writing—a basic form of argument—extending down into the earliest grades.
- Research—both short, focused projects and longer-term, in-depth, inquiry research—is emphasized throughout the standards.
- Annotated samples of student writing accompany the standards (Appendix C) and help establish adequate performance levels in writing arguments, information/explanatory texts, and narratives in the various grades.
- The ELA standards insist that instruction in reading, writing, speaking and listening, and language be a shared responsibility within the school.
- The Standards emphasize an integrated model of literacy; thus, each standard need not be a separate focus for instruction and assessment. For example, when editing writing, students address Writing standard 5 as well as Language standards 1–3. When drawing evidence from literary and informational text per Writing standard 9, students are also demonstrating their comprehension skill in relation to specific standards in Reading.

Decoding the Numbering System for the Writing Standards:

W.CCR.7 = Writing Strand, CCR Anchor, Standard 7
W.5.1a = Writing, Grade 5, Standard 1a.

Text Types and Purposes

1. Write arguments to support claims in an analysis of substantive topics or texts, using valid reasoning and relevant and sufficient evidence.
2. Write informative/explanatory texts to examine and convey complex ideas and information clearly and accurately through the effective selection, organization, and analysis of content.
3. Write narratives to develop real or imagined experiences of events using effective technique, well-chosen details, and well-structured event sequences.

Production and Distribution of Writing

4. Produce clear and coherent writing in which the development, organization, and style are appropriate to task, purpose, and audience.
5. Develop and strengthen writing as needed by planning, revisiting, editing, rewriting, or trying a new approach.
6. Use technology, including the Internet, to produce and publish writing and to interact and collaborate with others.

Research to Build and Present Knowledge

7. Conduct short as well as more sustained research projects based on focused questions, demonstrating understanding of the subject under investigation.
8. Gather relevant information from multiple print and digital sources, assess the credibility and accuracy of each source, and integrate the information while avoiding plagiarism.
9. Draw evidence from literary or informational texts to support analysis, reflection, and research.

Range of Writing

10. Write routinely over extended time frames (time for research, reflection, and revision) and shorter time frames (a single sitting or a day or two) for a range of tasks, purposes, and audiences.

<table>
<tr><th colspan="4">CCSS: English Language Arts (ELA) “Writing Strand”
• Writing Standards for Literacy in History/Social Studies, Science, and Technical Subjects</th></tr>
<tr><th colspan="3">Grade-Specific Writing Standards
(Grade-appropriate end-of-year expectations aligned to CCR Writing anchor standards) →</th><th>Strand-Specific College & Career Readiness (CCR)
Anchor Standards for Writing</th></tr>
<tr><th>6–8</th><th>9–10</th><th>11–12</th><td>Note: The CCR anchor standards for Writing in history/social studies, science, and technical subjects are the same 10 CCR anchor standards for Writing in the English language arts standards.</td></tr>
<tr><td colspan="3" rowspan="15">❖ 6–12 Writing Standards for Literacy in History/Social Studies, Science, and Technical Subjects (WHST)

Key Features of the Writing Standards for Literacy in History/Social Studies, Science, and Technical Subjects:
• The ELA standards insist that instruction in reading, writing, speaking and listening, and language be a shared responsibility within the school.
• The Writing standards require that students be able to incorporate narrative elements effectively into arguments and informative/explanatory texts.
• The Standards require that students use domain-specific vocabulary in their writing.
• In history and social studies, students must be able to incorporate narrative accounts into their analysis of individuals and events of historical significance.
• In science and technical subjects, students must be able to write precise enough descriptions of the step-by-step procedure they use in their investigations or technical work that others can replicate them and (possibly) reach the same results.
• Students need to be able to use technology strategically when creating, refining, and collaborating on writing. They have to become adept at gathering information, evaluating sources, and citing material accurately, reporting their findings from their research and analysis of sources in a clear and concise manner.
• These Writing standards for literacy in history/social studies, science, and technical subjects are meant to complement the specific content demands of the disciplines, not replace them.

Decoding the Numbering System for the Writing in History/Social Studies, Sciences and Technical Subjects Standards:

W.CCR.2 = Writing Strand, CCR Anchor, Standard 2
WHST.8.1a = Writing, Grade 8, Standard 1a.</td><th>Text Types and Purposes</th></tr>
<tr><td>1. Write arguments to support claims in an analysis of substantive topics or texts, using valid reasoning and relevant and sufficient evidence.</td></tr>
<tr><td>2. Write informative/explanatory texts to examine and convey complex ideas and information clearly and accurately through the effective selection, organization, and analysis of content.</td></tr>
<tr><td>3. Write narratives to develop real or imagined experiences of events using effective technique, well-chosen details, and well-structured event sequences.</td></tr>
<tr><th>Production and Distribution of Writing</th></tr>
<tr><td>4. Produce clear and coherent writing in which the development, organization, and style are appropriate to task, purpose, and audience.</td></tr>
<tr><td>5. Develop and strengthen writing as needed by planning, revisiting, editing, rewriting, or trying a new approach.</td></tr>
<tr><td>6. Use technology, including the Internet, to produce and publish writing and to interact and collaborate with others.</td></tr>
<tr><th>Research to Build and Present Knowledge</th></tr>
<tr><td>7. Conduct short as well as more sustained research projects based on focused questions, demonstrating understanding of the subject under investigation.</td></tr>
<tr><td>8. Gather relevant information from multiple print and digital sources, assess the credibility and accuracy of each source, and integrate the information while avoiding plagiarism.</td></tr>
<tr><td>9. Draw evidence from literary or informational texts to support analysis, reflection, and research.</td></tr>
<tr><th>Range of Writing</th></tr>
<tr><td>10. Write routinely over extended time frames (time for research, reflection, and revision) and shorter time frames (a single sitting or a day or two) for a range of tasks, purposes, and audiences.</td></tr>
</table>

<table>
<tr><th colspan="4">CCSS: English Language Arts (ELA) “Speaking and Listening Strand”</th></tr>
<tr><td colspan="3">Grade-Specific Speaking and Listening Standards
(Grade-appropriate end-of-year expectations aligned to CCR Speaking and Listening anchor standards) →</td><td rowspan="2">Strand-Specific College & Career Readiness (CCR) Anchor Standards for Speaking and Listening</td></tr>
<tr><td>K–8</td><td>9–10</td><td>11–12</td></tr>
<tr><td colspan="3" rowspan="8">❖ K–12 Speaking and Listening Standards (SL)

Key Features of the Speaking and Listening Standards:
• The ELA standards insist that instruction in reading, writing, speaking and listening, and language be a shared responsibility within the school.
• The Standards emphasize effective communication practices.
• The Standards require that students gain, evaluate, and present increasingly complex information, ideas, and evidence through listening and speaking as well as through media.
• An important focus of the Speaking and Listening standards is academic discussion in one-on-one, small-group, and whole-class settings. Formal presentations are one important way such talk occurs, but so is the more informal discussion that takes place as students collaborate to answer questions, build understanding, and solve problems.
• Media and technology are integrated throughout the standards.

Decoding the Numbering System for the Speaking and Listening Standards:

SL.CCR.4 = Speaking and Listening Strand, CCR Anchor, Standard 4
SL.9–10.1d = Speaking and Listening, Grade 9–10, Standard 1d.</td><td>Comprehension and Collaboration</td></tr>
<tr><td>1. Prepare for and participate effectively in a range of conversations and collaborations with diverse partners, building on others’ ideas and expressing their own clearly and persuasively.</td></tr>
<tr><td>2. Integrate and evaluate information presented in diverse media and formats, including visually, quantitatively, and orally.</td></tr>
<tr><td>3. Evaluate a speaker’s point of view, reasoning, and use of evidence and rhetoric.</td></tr>
<tr><td>Presentation of Knowledge and Ideas</td></tr>
<tr><td>4. Present information, findings, and supporting evidence such that listeners can follow the line of reasoning and the organization, development, and style are appropriate to task, purpose, and audience.</td></tr>
<tr><td>5. Make strategic use of digital media and visual displays of data to express information and enhance understanding of presentations.</td></tr>
<tr><td>6. Adapt speech to a variety of contexts and communication tasks, demonstrating command of formal English when indicated or appropriate.</td></tr>
</table>

<table>
<tr><th colspan="4">CCSS: English Language Arts (ELA) "Language Strand"</th></tr>
<tr><th colspan="3">Grade-Specific Language Standards
(Grade-appropriate end-of-year expectations aligned to CCR Language anchor standards) →</th><th rowspan="2">Strand-Specific College & Career Readiness (CCR)
Anchor Standards for Language</th></tr>
<tr><th>K–8</th><th>9–10</th><th>11–12</th></tr>
<tr><td colspan="3" rowspan="9">❖ K–12 Language (L)

Key Features of the Language Standards:
• The ELA standards insist that instruction in reading, writing, speaking and listening, and language be a shared responsibility within the school.
• The standards expect that students will grow their vocabularies through a mix of conversations, direct instruction, and reading.
• The standards will help students determine word meanings, appreciate the nuances of words, and steadily expand their repertoire of words and phrases.
• The standards help prepare students for real-life experience at college and in 21st-century careers. The standards recognize that students must be able to use formal English in their writing and speaking but that they must also be able to make informed, skillful choices among the many ways to express themselves through language.
• Vocabulary and conventions are treated in their own strand not because skills in these areas should be handled in isolation but because their use extends across reading, writing, speaking, and listening.

Decoding the Numbering System for the Language Standards:

L.CCR3 = Language Strand, CCR Anchor, Standard 3
L.11–12.5b = Language Strand, Grade 11–12, Standard 5b</td><td>Conventions of Standard English</td></tr>
<tr><td>1. Demonstrate command of the conventions of standard English grammar and usage when writing or speaking.</td></tr>
<tr><td>2. Demonstrate command of the conventions of standard English capitalization, punctuation, and spelling when writing.</td></tr>
<tr><td>Knowledge of Language</td></tr>
<tr><td>3. Apply knowledge of language to understand how language functions in different contexts, to make effective choices for meaning or style, and to comprehend more fully when reading or listening.</td></tr>
<tr><td>Vocabulary Acquisition and Use</td></tr>
<tr><td>4. Determine or clarify the meaning of unknown and multiple–meaning words and phrases by using context clues, analyzing meaningful word parts, and consulting general and specialized reference materials, as appropriate.</td></tr>
<tr><td>5. Demonstrate understanding of figurative language, word relationships, and nuances in word meanings.</td></tr>
<tr><td>6. Acquire and use accurately a range of general academic and domain–specific words and phrases sufficient for reading, writing, speaking, and listening at the college and career readiness level; demonstrate independence in gathering vocabulary knowledge when encountering an unknown term important to comprehension or expression.</td></tr>
</table>

ELA Learning Progressions

PREPARED BY

Maryann D. Wiggs

Source: ***Common Core State Standards for English Language Arts & Literacy in History/Social Studies, Science, and Technical Subjects***, pp. 10–66. Retrieved from: www.corestandards.org.

Reading Foundations (RF) Standard 1 **Print Concepts**	
RF.1.1 **Grade 1 students:**	Demonstrate understanding of the organization and basic features of print. a. Recognize the distinguishing features of a sentence (e.g., first word capitalization, ending punctuation).
RF.K.1 **Kindergarten students:**	Demonstrate understanding of the organization and basic features of print. a. Follow words from left to right, top to bottom, and page by page. b. Recognize that spoken words are represented in written language by specific sequences of letters. c. Understand that words are separated by spaces in print. d. Recognize and name all upper- and lowercase letters of the alphabet.

Reading Foundations (RF) Standard 2 **Phonological Awareness**	
RF.1.2 **Grade 1 students:**	Demonstrate understanding of spoken words, syllables, and sounds (phonemes). a. Distinguish long from short vowel sounds in spoken single-syllable words. b. Orally produce single-syllable words by blending sounds (phonemes), including consonant blends. c. Isolate and pronounce initial, medial vowel, and final sounds (phonemes) in spoken single-syllable words. d. Segment spoken single-syllable words into their complete sequence of individual sounds (phonemes).
RF.K.2 **Kindergarten students:**	Demonstrate understanding of spoken words, syllables, and sounds (phonemes). a. Recognize and produce rhyming words. b. Count, pronounce, blend, and segment syllables in spoken words. c. Blend and segment onsets and rimes of single-syllable spoken words. d. Isolate and pronounce the initial, medial vowel, and final sounds (phonemes) in three-phoneme (consonant-vowel-consonant, or CVC) words.* (This does not include CVCs ending with /l/, /r/, or /x/.) e. Add or substitute individual sounds (phonemes) in simple, one-syllable words to make new words.

*Words, syllables, or phonemes written in /slashes/ refer to their pronunciation or phonology. Thus, /CVC/ is a word with three phonemes regardless of the number of letters in the spelling of the word.

Reading Foundations (RF) Standard 3 Phonics and Word Recognition	
RF.5.3 **Grade 5 students:**	Know and apply grade-level phonics and word analysis skills in decoding words. a. Use combined knowledge of all letter-sound correspondences, syllabication patterns, and morphology (e.g., roots and affixes) to read accurately unfamiliar multisyllabic words in context and out of context.
RF.4.3 **Grade 4 students:**	Know and apply grade-level phonics and word analysis skills in decoding words. a. Use combined knowledge of all letter-sound correspondences, syllabication patterns, and morphology (e.g., roots and affixes) to read accurately unfamiliar multisyllabic words in context and out of context.
RF.3.3 **Grade 3 students:**	Know and apply grade-level phonics and word analysis skills in decoding words. a. Identify and know the meaning of the most common prefixes and derivational suffixes. b. Decode words with common Latin suffixes. c. Decode multisyllable words. d. Read grade-appropriate irregularly spelled words.
RF.2.3 **Grade 2 students:**	Know and apply grade-level phonics and word analysis skills in decoding words. a. Distinguish long and short vowels when reading regularly spelled one-syllable words. b. Know spelling-sound correspondences for additional common vowel teams. c. Decode regularly spelled two-syllable words with long vowels. d. Decode words with common prefixes and suffixes. e. Identify words with inconsistent but common spelling-sound correspondences. f. Recognize and read grade-appropriate irregularly spelled words.
RF.1.3 **Grade 1 students:**	Know and apply grade-level phonics and word analysis skills in decoding words. a. Know the spelling-sound correspondences for common consonant digraphs. b. Decode regularly spelled one-syllable words. c. Know final *-e* and common vowel team conventions for representing long vowel sounds. d. Use knowledge that every syllable must have a vowel sound to determine the number of syllables in a printed word. e. Decode two-syllable words following basic patterns by breaking the words into syllables. f. Read words with inflectional endings. g. Recognize and read grade-appropriate irregularly spelled words.
RF.K.3 **Kindergarten students:**	Know and apply grade-level phonics and word analysis skills in decoding words. a. Demonstrate basic knowledge of one-to-one letter-sound correspondences by producing the primary or many of the most frequent sounds for each consonant. b. Associate the long and short sounds with common spellings (graphemes) for the five major vowels. c. Read common high-frequency words by sight (e.g., *the, of, to, you, she, my, is, are, do, does*). d. Distinguish between similarly spelled words by identifying the sounds of the letters that differ.

Reading Foundations (RF) Standard 4 Fluency	
RF.5.4 **Grade 5 students:**	Read with sufficient accuracy and fluency to support comprehension. a. Read on-level text with purpose and understanding. b. Read on-level prose and poetry orally with accuracy, appropriate rate, and expression on successive readings. c. Use context to confirm or self-correct word recognition and understanding, rereading as necessary.
RF.4.4 **Grade 4 students:**	Read with sufficient accuracy and fluency to support comprehension. a. Read on-level text with purpose and understanding. b. Read on-level prose and poetry orally with accuracy, appropriate rate, and expression on successive readings. c. Use context to confirm or self-correct word recognition and understanding, rereading as necessary.
RF.3.4 **Grade 3 students:**	Read with sufficient accuracy and fluency to support comprehension. a. Read on-level text with purpose and understanding. b. Read on-level prose and poetry orally with accuracy, appropriate rate, and expression on successive readings. c. Use context to confirm or self-correct word recognition and understanding, rereading as necessary.
RF.2.4 **Grade 2 students:**	Read with sufficient accuracy and fluency to support comprehension. a. Read on-level text with purpose and understanding. b. Read on-level text orally with accuracy, appropriate rate, and expression on successive readings. c. Use context to confirm or self-correct word recognition and understanding, rereading as necessary.
RF.1.4 **Grade 1 students:**	Read with sufficient accuracy and fluency to support comprehension. a. Read on-level text with purpose and understanding. b. Read on-level text orally with accuracy, appropriate rate, and expression on successive readings. c. Use context to confirm or self-correct word recognition and understanding, rereading as necessary.
RF.K.4 **Kindergarten students:**	Read emergent-reader texts with purpose and understanding.

R.CCR.1	**CCR Reading Anchor Standard 1:** **Read closely to determine what the text says explicitly and to make logical inferences from it; cite specific textual evidence when writing or speaking to support conclusions drawn from the text.**
RL.11–12.1 **Grade 11–12 students:**	Cite strong and thorough textual evidence to support analysis of what the text says explicitly as well as inferences drawn from the text, including determining where the text leaves matters uncertain.
RL.9–10.1 **Grade 9–10 students:**	Cite strong and thorough textual evidence to support analysis of what the text says explicitly as well as inferences drawn from the text.
RL.8.1 **Grade 8 students:**	Cite the textual evidence that most strongly supports an analysis of what the text says explicitly as well as inferences drawn from the text.
RL.7.1 **Grade 7 students:**	Cite several pieces of textual evidence to support analysis of what the text says explicitly as well as inferences drawn from the text.
RL.6.1 **Grade 6 students:**	Cite textual evidence to support analysis of what the text says explicitly as well as inferences drawn from the text.
RL.5.1 **Grade 5 students:**	Quote accurately from a text when explaining what the text says explicitly and when drawing inferences from the text.
RL.4.1 **Grade 4 students:**	Refer to details and examples in a text when explaining what the text says explicitly and when drawing inferences from the text.
RL.3.1 **Grade 3 students:**	Ask and answer questions to demonstrate understanding of a text, referring explicitly to the text as the basis for the answers.
RL.2.1 **Grade 2 students:**	Ask and answer such questions as *who*, *what*, *where*, *when*, *why*, and *how* to demonstrate understanding of key details in a text.
RL.1.1 **Grade 1 students:**	Ask and answer questions about key details in a text.
RL.K.1 **Kindergarten students:**	With prompting and support, ask and answer questions about key details in a text.

R.CCR.2	**CCR Reading Anchor Standard 2:** **Determine central ideas or themes of a text and analyze their development; summarize the key supporting details and ideas.**
RL.11–12.2 **Grade 11–12 students:**	Determine two or more themes or central ideas of a text and analyze their development over the course of the text, including how they interact and build on one another to produce a complex account; provide an objective summary of the text.
RL.9–10.2 **Grade 9–10 students:**	Determine a theme or central idea of a text and analyze in detail its development over the course of the text, including how it emerges and is shaped and refined by specific details; provide an objective summary of the text.
RL.8.2 **Grade 8 students:**	Determine a theme or central idea of a text and analyze its development over the course of the text, including its relationship to the characters, setting, and plot; provide an objective summary of the text.
RL.7.2 **Grade 7 students:**	Determine a theme or central idea of a text and analyze its development over the course of the text; provide an objective summary of the text.
RL.6.2 **Grade 6 students:**	Determine a theme or central idea of a text and how it is conveyed through particular details; provide a summary of the text distinct from personal opinions or judgments.
RL.5.2 **Grade 5 students:**	Determine a theme of a story, drama, or poem from details in the text, including how characters in a story or drama respond to challenges or how the speaker in a poem reflects upon a topic; summarize the text.
RL.4.2 **Grade 4 students:**	Determine a theme of a story, drama, or poem from details in the text; summarize the text.
RL.3.2 **Grade 3 students:**	Recount stories, including fables, folktales, and myths from diverse cultures; determine the central message, lesson, or moral and explain how it is conveyed through key details in the text.
RL.2.2 **Grade 2 students:**	Recount stories, including fables and folktales from diverse cultures, and determine their central message, lesson, or moral.
RL.1.2 **Grade 1 students:**	Retell stories, including key details, and demonstrate understanding of their central message or lesson.
RL.K.2 **Kindergarten students:**	With prompting and support, retell familiar stories, including key details.

R.CCR.3	**CCR Reading Anchor Standard 3:** **Analyze how and why individuals, events, and ideas develop and interact over the course of a text.**
RL.11–12.3 **Grade 11–12 students:**	Analyze the impact of the author's choices regarding how to develop and relate elements of a story or drama (e.g., where a story is set, how the action is ordered, how the characters are introduced and developed).
RL.9–10.3 **Grade 9–10 students:**	Analyze how complex characters (e.g., those with multiple or conflicting motivations) develop over the course of a text, interact with other characters, and advance the plot or develop the theme.
RL.8.3 **Grade 8 students:**	Analyze how particular lines of dialogue or incidents in a story or drama propel the action, reveal aspects of a character, or provoke a decision.
RL.7.3 **Grade 7 students:**	Analyze how particular elements of a story or drama interact (e.g., how setting shapes the characters or plot).
RL.6.3 **Grade 6 students:**	Describe how a particular story's or drama's plot unfolds in a series of episodes as well as how the characters respond or change as the plot moves toward a resolution.
RL.5.3 **Grade 5 students:**	Compare and contrast two or more characters, settings, or events in a story or drama, drawing on specific details in the text (e.g., how characters interact).
RL.4.3 **Grade 4 students:**	Describe in depth a character, setting, or event in a story or drama, drawing on specific details in the text (e.g., a character's thoughts, words, or actions).
RL.3.3 **Grade 3 students:**	Describe characters in a story (e.g., their traits, motivations, or feelings) and explain how their actions contribute to the sequence of events.
RL.2.3 **Grade 2 students:**	Describe how characters in a story respond to major events and challenges.
RL.1.3 **Grade 1 students:**	Describe characters, settings, and major events in a story, using key details.
RL.K.3 **Kindergarten students:**	With prompting and support, identify characters, settings, and major events in a story.

R.CCR.4	**CCR Reading Anchor Standard 4:** **Interpret words and phrases as they are used in a text, including determining technical, connotative, and figurative meanings, and analyze how specific word choices shape meaning or tone.**
RL.11–12.4 **Grade 11–12 students:**	Determine the meaning of words and phrases as they are used in the text, including figurative and connotative meanings; analyze the impact of specific word choices on meaning and tone, including words with multiple meanings or language that is particularly fresh, engaging, or beautiful. (Include Shakespeare as well as other authors.)
RL.9–10.4 **Grade 9–10 students:**	Determine the meaning of words and phrases as they are used in the text, including figurative and connotative meanings; analyze the cumulative impact of specific word choices on meaning and tone (e.g., how the language evokes a sense of time and place; how it sets a formal or informal tone).
RL.8.4 **Grade 8 students:**	Determine the meaning of words and phrases as they are used in a text, including figurative and connotative meanings; analyze the impact of specific word choices on meaning and tone, including analogies or allusions to other texts.
RL.7.4 **Grade 7 students:**	Determine the meaning of words and phrases as they are used in a text, including figurative and connotative meanings; analyze the impact of rhymes and other repetitions of sounds (e.g., alliteration) on a specific verse or stanza of a poem or section of a story or drama.
RL.6.4 **Grade 6 students:**	Determine the meaning of words and phrases as they are used in a text, including figurative and connotative meanings; analyze the impact of a specific word choice on meaning and tone.
RL.5.4 **Grade 5 students:**	Determine the meaning of words and phrases as they are used in a text, including figurative language such as metaphors and similes.
RL.4.4 **Grade 4 students:**	Determine the meaning of words and phrases as they are used in a text, including those that allude to significant characters found in mythology (e.g., *Herculean*).
RL.3.4 **Grade 3 students:**	Determine the meaning of words and phrases as they are used in a text, distinguishing literal from nonliteral language.
RL.2.4 **Grade 2 students:**	Describe how words and phrases (e.g., regular beats, alliteration, rhymes, repeated lines) supply rhythm and meaning in a story, poem, or song.
RL.1.4 **Grade 1 students:**	Identify words and phrases in stories or poems that suggest feelings or appeal to the senses.
RL.K.4 **Kindergarten students:**	Ask and answer questions about unknown words in a text.

R.CCR.5	**CCR Reading Anchor Standard 5:** **Analyze the structure of texts, including how specific sentences, paragraphs, and larger portions of the text (e.g., a section, chapter, scene, or stanza) relate to each other and the whole.**
RL.11–12.5 **Grade 11–12 students:**	Analyze how an author's choices concerning how to structure specific parts of a text (e.g., the choice of where to begin or end a story, the choice to provide a comedic or tragic resolution) contribute to its overall structure and meaning as well as its aesthetic impact.
RL.9–10.5 **Grade 9–10 students:**	Analyze how an author's choices concerning how to structure a text, order events within it (e.g., parallel plots), and manipulate time (e.g., pacing, flashbacks) create such effects as mystery, tension, or surprise.
RL.8.5 **Grade 8 students:**	Compare and contrast the structure of two or more texts and analyze how the differing structure of each text contributes to its meaning and style.
RL.7.5 **Grade 7 students:**	Analyze how a drama's or poem's form or structure (e.g., soliloquy, sonnet) contributes to its meaning.
RL.6.5 **Grade 6 students:**	Analyze how a particular sentence, chapter, scene, or stanza fits into the overall structure of a text and contributes to the development of the theme, setting, or plot.
RL.5.5 **Grade 5 students:**	Explain how a series of chapters, scenes, or stanzas fits together to provide the overall structure of a particular story, drama, or poem.
RL.4.5 **Grade 4 students:**	Explain major differences between poems, drama, and prose, and refer to the structural elements of poems (e.g., verse, rhythm, meter) and drama (e.g., casts of characters, settings, descriptions, dialogue, stage directions) when writing or speaking about a text.
RL.3.5 **Grade 3 students:**	Refer to parts of stories, dramas, and poems when writing or speaking about a text, using terms such as *chapter*, *scene*, and *stanza*; describe how each successive part builds on earlier sections.
RL.2.5 **Grade 2 students:**	Describe the overall structure of a story, including describing how the beginning introduces the story and the ending concludes the action.
RL.1.5 **Grade 1 students:**	Explain major differences between books that tell stories and books that give information, drawing on a wide reading of a range of text types.
RL.K.5 **Kindergarten students:**	Recognize common types of texts (e.g., storybooks, poems).

R.CCR.6	**CCR Reading Anchor Standard 6:** **Assess how point of view or purpose shapes the content and style of a text.**
RL.11–12.6 **Grade 11–12 students:**	Analyze a case in which grasping point of view requires distinguishing what is directly stated in a text from what is really meant (e.g., satire, sarcasm, irony, or understatement).
RL.9–10.6 **Grade 9–10 students:**	Analyze a particular point of view or cultural experience reflected in a work of literature from outside the United States, drawing on a wide reading of world literature.
RL.8.6 **Grade 8 students:**	Analyze how differences in the points of view of the characters and the audience or reader (e.g., created through the use of dramatic irony) create such effects as suspense or humor.
RL.7.6 **Grade 7 students:**	Analyze how an author develops and contrasts the points of view of different characters or narrators in a text.
RL.6.6 **Grade 6 students:**	Explain how an author develops the point of view of the narrator or speaker in a text.
RL.5.6 **Grade 5 students:**	Describe how a narrator's or speaker's point of view influences how events are described.
RL.4.6 **Grade 4 students:**	Compare and contrast the point of view from which different stories are narrated, including the difference between first- and third-person narrations.
RL.3.6 **Grade 3 students:**	Distinguish their own point of view from that of the narrator or those of the characters.
RL.2.6 **Grade 2 students:**	Acknowledge differences in the points of view of characters, including by speaking in a different voice for each character when reading dialogue aloud.
RL.1.6 **Grade 1 students:**	Identify who is telling the story at various points in a text.
RL.K.6 **Kindergarten students:**	With prompting and support, name the author and illustrator of a story and define the role of each in telling the story.

R.CCR.7	**CCR Reading Anchor Standard 7:** **Integrate and evaluate content presented in diverse formats and media, including visually and quantitatively, as well as in words.**
RL.11–12.7 **Grade 11–12 students:**	Analyze multiple interpretations of a story, drama, or poem (e.g., recorded or live production of a play or recorded novel or poetry), evaluating how each version interprets the source text. (Include at least one play by Shakespeare and one play by an American dramatist.)
RL.9–10.7 **Grade 9–10 students:**	Analyze the representation of a subject or a key scene in two different artistic mediums, including what is emphasized or absent in each treatment (e.g., Auden's "Musée des Beaux Arts" and Breughel's *Landscape with the Fall of Icarus*).
RL.8.7 **Grade 8 students:**	Analyze the extent to which a filmed or live production of a story or drama stays faithful to or departs from the text or script, evaluating the choices made by the director or actors.
RL.7.7 **Grade 7 students:**	Compare and contrast a written story, drama, or poem to its audio, filmed, staged, or multimedia version, analyzing the effects of techniques unique to each medium (e.g., lighting, sound, color, or camera focus and angles in a film).
RL.6.7 **Grade 6 students:**	Compare and contrast the experience of reading a story, drama, or poem to listening to or viewing an audio, video, or live version of the text, including contrasting what they "see" and "hear" when reading the text to what they perceive when they listen or watch.
RL.5.7 **Grade 5 students:**	Analyze how visual and multimedia elements contribute to the meaning, tone, or beauty of a text (e.g., graphic novel, multimedia presentation of fiction, folktale, myth, poem).
RL.4.7 **Grade 4 students:**	Make connections between the text of a story or drama and a visual or oral presentation of the text, identifying where each version reflects specific descriptions and directions in the text.
RL.3.7 **Grade 3 students:**	Explain how specific aspects of a text's illustrations contribute to what is conveyed by the words in a story (e.g., create mood, emphasize aspects of a character or setting).
RL.2.7 **Grade 2 students:**	Use information gained from the illustrations and words in a print or digital text to demonstrate understanding of its characters, setting, or plot.
RL.1.7 **Grade 1 students:**	Use illustrations and details in a story to describe its characters, setting, or events.
RL.K.7 **Kindergarten students:**	With prompting and support, describe the relationship between illustrations and the story in which they appear (e.g., what moment in a story an illustration depicts).

R.CCR.8	**CCR Reading Anchor Standard 8:** Delineate and evaluate the argument and specific claims in a text, including the validity of the reasoning as well as the relevance and sufficiency of the evidence.
RL.11–12.8 **Grade 11–12 students:**	(Not applicable to literature)
RL.9–10.8 **Grade 9–10 students:**	(Not applicable to literature)
RL.8.8 **Grade 8 students:**	(Not applicable to literature)
RL.7.8 **Grade 7 students:**	(Not applicable to literature)
RL.6.8 **Grade 6 students:**	(Not applicable to literature)
RL.5.8 **Grade 5 students:**	(Not applicable to literature)
RL.4.8 **Grade 4 students:**	(Not applicable to literature)
RL.3.8 **Grade 3 students:**	(Not applicable to literature)
RL.2.8 **Grade 2 students:**	(Not applicable to literature)
RL.1.8 **Grade 1 students:**	(Not applicable to literature)
RL.K.8 **Kindergarten students:**	(Not applicable to literature)

R.CCR.9	**CCR Reading Anchor Standard 9:** **Analyze how two or more texts address similar themes or topics in order to build knowledge or to compare the approaches the authors take.**
RL.11–12.9 **Grade 11–12 students:**	Demonstrate knowledge of eighteenth-, nineteenth- and early-twentieth-century foundational works of American literature, including how two or more texts from the same period treat similar themes or topics.
RL.9–10.9 **Grade 9–10 students:**	Analyze how an author draws on and transforms source material in a specific work (e.g., how Shakespeare treats a theme or topic from Ovid or the Bible or how a later author draws on a play by Shakespeare).
RL.8.9 **Grade 8 students:**	Analyze how a modern work of fiction draws on themes, patterns of events, or character types from myths, traditional stories, or religious works such as the Bible, including describing how the material is rendered new.
RL.7.9 **Grade 7 students:**	Compare and contrast a fictional portrayal of a time, place, or character and a historical account of the same period as a means of understanding how authors of fiction use or alter history.
RL.6.9 **Grade 6 students:**	Compare and contrast texts in different forms or genres (e.g., stories and poems; historical novels and fantasy stories) on their approaches to similar themes and topics.
RL.5.9 **Grade 5 students:**	Compare and contrast stories in the same genre (e.g., mysteries and adventure stories) on their approaches to similar themes and topics.
RL.4.9 **Grade 4 students:**	Compare and contrast the treatment of similar themes and topics (e.g., opposition of good and evil) and patterns of events (e.g., the quest) in stories, myths, and traditional literature from different cultures.
RL.3.9 **Grade 3 students:**	Compare and contrast the themes, settings, and plots of stories written by the same author about the same or similar characters (e.g., in books from a series).
RL.2.9 **Grade 2 students:**	Compare and contrast two or more versions of the same story (e.g., Cinderella stories) by different authors or from different cultures.
RL.1.9 **Grade 1 students:**	Compare and contrast the adventures and experiences of characters in stories.
RL.K.9 **Kindergarten students:**	With prompting and support, compare and contrast the adventures and experiences of characters in familiar stories.

R.CCR.10	**CCR Reading Anchor Standard 10:** **Read and comprehend complex literary and informational texts independently and proficiently.**
RL.11–12.10 **Grade 11–12 students:**	By the end of grade 11, read and comprehend literature, including stories, dramas, and poems, in the grades 11–CCR text complexity band proficiently, with scaffolding as needed at the high end of the range. By the end of grade 12, read and comprehend literature, including stories, dramas, and poems, at the high end of the grades 11–CCR text complexity band independently and proficiently.
RL.9–10.10 **Grade 9–10 students:**	By the end of grade 9, read and comprehend literature, including stories, dramas, and poems, in the grades 9–10 text complexity band proficiently, with scaffolding as needed at the high end of the range. By the end of grade 10, read and comprehend literature, including stories, dramas, and poems, at the high end of the grades 9–10 text complexity band independently and proficiently.
RL.8.10 **Grade 8 students:**	By the end of the year, read and comprehend literature, including stories, dramas, and poems, at the high end of the grades 6–8 text complexity band independently and proficiently.
RL.7.10 **Grade 7 students:**	By the end of the year, read and comprehend literature, including stories, dramas, and poems, in the grades 6–8 text complexity band proficiently, with scaffolding as needed at the high end of the range.
RL.6.10 **Grade 6 students:**	By the end of the year, read and comprehend literature, including stories, dramas, and poems, in the grades 6–8 text complexity band proficiently, with scaffolding as needed at the high end of the range.
RL.5.10 **Grade 5 students:**	By the end of the year, read and comprehend literature, including stories, dramas, and poetry, at the high end of the grades 4–5 text complexity band independently and proficiently.
RL.4.10 **Grade 4 students:**	By the end of the year, read and comprehend literature, including stories, dramas, and poetry, in the grades 4–5 text complexity band proficiently, with scaffolding as needed at the high end of the range.
RL.3.10 **Grade 3 students:**	By the end of the year, read and comprehend literature, including stories, dramas, and poetry, at the high end of the grades 2–3 text complexity band independently and proficiently.
RL.2.10 **Grade 2 students:**	By the end of the year, read and comprehend literature, including stories and poetry, in the grades 2–3 text complexity band proficiently, with scaffolding as needed at the high end of the range.
RL.1.10 **Grade 1 students:**	With prompting and support, read prose and poetry of appropriate complexity for grade 1.
RL.K.10 **Kindergarten students:**	Actively engage in group reading activities with purpose and understanding.

R.CCR.1	**CCR Reading Anchor Standard 1:** **Read closely to determine what the text says explicitly and to make logical inferences from it; cite specific textual evidence when writing or speaking to support conclusions drawn from the text.**
RI.11–12.1 **Grade 11–12 students:**	Cite strong and thorough textual evidence to support analysis of what the text says explicitly as well as inferences drawn from the text, including determining where the text leaves matters uncertain.
RI.9–10.1 **Grade 9–10 students:**	Cite strong and thorough textual evidence to support analysis of what the text says explicitly as well as inferences drawn from the text.
RI.8.1 **Grade 8 students:**	Cite the textual evidence that most strongly supports an analysis of what the text says explicitly as well as inferences drawn from the text.
RI.7.1 **Grade 7 students:**	Cite several pieces of textual evidence to support analysis of what the text says explicitly as well as inferences drawn from the text.
RI.6.1 **Grade 6 students:**	Cite textual evidence to support analysis of what the text says explicitly as well as inferences drawn from the text.
RI.5.1 **Grade 5 students:**	Quote accurately from a text when explaining what the text says explicitly and when drawing inferences from the text.
RI.4.1 **Grade 4 students:**	Refer to details and examples in a text when explaining what the text says explicitly and when drawing inferences from the text.
RI.3.1 **Grade 3 students:**	Ask and answer questions to demonstrate understanding of a text, referring explicitly to the text as the basis for the answers.
RI.2.1 **Grade 2 students:**	Ask and answer such questions as *who*, *what*, *where*, *when*, *why*, and *how* to demonstrate understanding of key details in a text.
RL.1.1 **Grade 1 students:**	Ask and answer questions about key details in a text.
RI.K.1 **Kindergarten students:**	With prompting and support, ask and answer questions about key details in a text.

R.CCR.2	**CCR Reading Anchor Standard 2:** **Determine central ideas or themes of a text and analyze their development; summarize the key supporting details and ideas.**
RI.11–12.2 **Grade 11–12 students:**	Determine two or more central ideas of a text and analyze their development over the course of the text, including how they interact and build on one another to provide a complex analysis; provide an objective summary of the text.
RI.9–10.2 **Grade 9–10 students:**	Determine a central idea of a text and analyze its development over the course of the text, including how it emerges and is shaped and refined by specific details; provide an objective summary of the text.
RI.8.2 **Grade 8 students:**	Determine a central idea of a text and analyze its development over the course of the text, including its relationship to supporting ideas; provide an objective summary of the text.
RI.7.2 **Grade 7 students:**	Determine two or more central ideas in a text and analyze their development over the course of the text; provide an objective summary of the text.
RI.6.2 **Grade 6 students:**	Determine a central idea of a text and how it is conveyed through particular details; provide a summary of the text distinct from personal opinions or judgments.
RI.5.2 **Grade 5 students:**	Determine two or more main ideas of a text and explain how they are supported by key details; summarize the text.
RI.4.2 **Grade 4 students:**	Determine the main idea of a text and explain how it is supported by key details; summarize the text.
RI.3.2 **Grade 3 students:**	Determine the main idea of a text; recount the key details and explain how they support the main idea.
RI.2.2 **Grade 2 students:**	Identify the main topic of a multiparagraph text as well as the focus of specific paragraphs within the text.
RI.1.2 **Grade 1 students:**	Identify the main topic and retell key details of a text.
RI.K.2 **Kindergarten students:**	With prompting and support, identify the main topic and retell key details of a text.

R.CCR.3	**CCR Reading Anchor Standard 3:** **Analyze how and why individuals, events, and ideas develop and interact over the course of a text.**
RI.11–12.3 **Grade 11–12 students:**	Analyze a complex set of ideas or sequence of events and explain how specific individuals, ideas, or events interact and develop over the course of the text.
RI.9–10.3 **Grade 9–10 students:**	Analyze how the author unfolds an analysis or series of ideas or events, including the order in which the points are made, how they are introduced and developed, and the connections that are drawn between them.
RI.8.3 **Grade 8 students:**	Analyze how a text makes connections among and distinctions between individuals, ideas, or events (e.g., through comparisons, analogies, or categories).
RI.7.3 **Grade 7 students:**	Analyze the interactions between individuals, events, and ideas in a text (e.g., how ideas influence individuals or events, or how individuals influence ideas or events).
RI.6.3 **Grade 6 students:**	Analyze in detail how a key individual, event, or idea is introduced, illustrated, and elaborated in a text (e.g., through examples or anecdotes).
RI.5.3 **Grade 5 students:**	Explain the relationships or interactions between two or more individuals, events, ideas, or concepts in a historical, scientific, or technical text based on specific information in the text.
RI.4.3 **Grade 4 students:**	Explain events, procedures, ideas, or concepts in a historical, scientific, or technical text, including what happened and why, based on specific information in the text.
RI.3.3 **Grade 3 students:**	Describe the relationship between a series of historical events, scientific ideas or concepts, or steps in technical procedures in a text, using language that pertains to time, sequence, and cause/effect.
RI.2.3 **Grade 2 students:**	Describe the connection between a series of historical events, scientific ideas or concepts, or steps in technical procedures in a text.
RI.1.3 **Grade 1 students:**	Describe the connection between two individuals, events, ideas, or pieces of information in a text.
RI.K.3 **Kindergarten students:**	With prompting and support, describe the connection between two individuals, events, ideas, or pieces of information in a text.

R.CCR.4	**CCR Reading Anchor Standard 4:** **Interpret words and phrases as they are used in a text, including determining technical, connotative, and figurative meanings, and analyze how specific word choices shape meaning or tone.**
RI.11–12.4 **Grade 11–12 students:**	Determine the meaning of words and phrases as they are used in a text, including figurative, connotative, and technical meanings; analyze how an author uses and refines the meaning of a key term or terms over the course of a text (e.g., how Madison defines *faction* in *Federalist* No. 10).
RI.9–10.4 **Grade 9–10 students:**	Determine the meaning of words and phrases as they are used in a text, including figurative, connotative, and technical meanings; analyze the cumulative impact of specific word choices on meaning and tone (e.g., how the language of a court opinion differs from that of a newspaper).
RI.8.4 **Grade 8 students:**	Determine the meaning of words and phrases as they are used in a text, including figurative, connotative, and technical meanings; analyze the impact of specific word choices on meaning and tone, including analogies or allusions to other texts.
RI.7.4 **Grade 7 students:**	Determine the meaning of words and phrases as they are used in a text, including figurative, connotative, and technical meanings; analyze the impact of a specific word choice on meaning and tone.
RI.6.4 **Grade 6 students:**	Determine the meaning of words and phrases as they are used in a text, including figurative, connotative, and technical meanings.
RI.5.4 **Grade 5 students:**	Determine the meaning of general academic and domain-specific words and phrases in a text relevant to a *grade 5 topic or subject area.*
RI.4.4 **Grade 4 students:**	Determine the meaning of general academic and domain-specific words or phrases in a text relevant to a *grade 4 topic or subject area.*
RI.3.4 **Grade 3 students:**	Determine the meaning of general academic and domain-specific words and phrases in a text relevant to a *grade 3 topic or subject area.*
RI.2.4 **Grade 2 students:**	Determine the meaning of words and phrases in a text relevant to a *grade 2 topic or subject area.*
RI.1.4 **Grade 1 students:**	Ask and answer questions to help determine or clarify the meaning of words and phrases in a text.
RI.K.4 **Kindergarten students:**	With prompting and support, ask and answer questions about unknown words in a text.

R.CCR.5	**CCR Reading Anchor Standard 5:** **Analyze the structure of texts, including how specific sentences, paragraphs, and larger portions of the text (e.g., a section, chapter, scene, or stanza) relate to each other and the whole.**
RI.11–12.5 **Grade 11–12 students:**	Analyze and evaluate the effectiveness of the structure an author uses in his or her exposition or argument, including whether the structure makes points clear, convincing, and engaging.
RI.9–10.5 **Grade 9–10 students:**	Analyze in detail how an author's ideas or claims are developed and refined by particular sentences, paragraphs, or larger portions of a text (e.g., a section or chapter).
RI.8.5 **Grade 8 students:**	Analyze in detail the structure of a specific paragraph in a text, including the role of particular sentences in developing and refining a key concept.
RI.7.5 **Grade 7 students:**	Analyze the structure an author uses to organize a text, including how the major sections contribute to the whole and to the development of the ideas.
RI.6.5 **Grade 6 students:**	Analyze how a particular sentence, paragraph, chapter, or section fits into the overall structure of a text and contributes to the development of the ideas.
RI.5.5 **Grade 5 students:**	Compare and contrast the overall structure (e.g., chronology, comparison, cause/effect, problem/solution) of events, ideas, concepts, or information in two or more texts.
RI.4.5 **Grade 4 students:**	Describe the overall structure (e.g., chronology, comparison, cause/effect, problem/solution) of events, ideas, concepts, or information in a text or part of a text.
RI.3.5 **Grade 3 students:**	Use text features and search tools (e.g., key words, sidebars, hyperlinks) to locate information relevant to a given topic efficiently.
RI.2.5 **Grade 2 students:**	Know and use various text features (e.g., captions, bold print, subheadings, glossaries, indexes, electronic menus, icons) to locate key facts or information in a text efficiently.
RI.1.5 **Grade 1 students:**	Know and use various text features (e.g., headings, tables of contents, glossaries, electronic menus, icons) to locate key facts or information in a text.
RI.K.5 **Kindergarten students:**	Identify the front cover, back cover, and title page of a book.

R.CCR.6	**CCR Reading Anchor Standard 6:** **Assess how point of view or purpose shapes the content and style of text.**
RI.11–12.6 **Grade 11–12 students:**	Determine an author's point of view or purpose in a text in which the rhetoric is particularly effective, analyzing how style and content contribute to the power, persuasiveness, or beauty of the text.
RI.9–10.6 **Grade 9–10 students:**	Determine an author's point of view or purpose in a text and analyze how an author uses rhetoric to advance that point of view or purpose.
RI.8.6 **Grade 8 students:**	Determine an author's point of view or purpose in a text and analyze how the author acknowledges and responds to conflicting evidence or viewpoints.
RI.7.6 **Grade 7 students:**	Determine an author's point of view or purpose in a text and analyze how the author distinguishes his or her position from that of others.
RI.6.6 **Grade 6 students:**	Determine an author's point of view or purpose in a text and explain how it is conveyed in the text.
RI.5.6 **Grade 5 students:**	Analyze multiple accounts of the same event or topic, noting important similarities and differences in the point of view they represent.
RI.4.6 **Grade 4 students:**	Compare and contrast a firsthand and secondhand account of the same event or topic; describe the differences in focus and the information provided.
RI.3.6 **Grade 3 students:**	Distinguish their own point of view from that of the author of a text.
RI.2.6 **Grade 2 students:**	Identify the main purpose of a text, including what the author wants to answer, explain, or describe.
RI.1.6 **Grade 1 students:**	Distinguish between information provided by pictures or other illustrations and information provided by the words in a text.
RI.K.6 **Kindergarten students:**	Name the author and illustrator of a text and define the role of each in presenting the ideas or information in a text.

R.CCR.7	**CCR Reading Anchor Standard 7:** **Integrate and evaluate content presented in diverse formats and media, including visually and quantitatively, as well as in words.**
RI.11–12.7 **Grade 11–12 students:**	Integrate and evaluate multiple sources of information presented in different media or formats (e.g., visually, quantitatively) as well as in words in order to address a question or solve a problem.
RI.9–10.7 **Grade 9–10 students:**	Analyze various accounts of a subject told in different media (e.g., a person's life story in both print and multimedia), determining which details are emphasized in each account.
RI.8.7 **Grade 8 students:**	Evaluate the advantages and disadvantages of using different mediums (e.g., print or digital text, video, multimedia) to present a particular topic or idea.
RI.7.7 **Grade 7 students:**	Compare and contrast a text to an audio, video, or multimedia version of the text, analyzing each medium's portrayal of the subject (e.g., how the delivery of a speech affects the impact of the words).
RI.6.7 **Grade 6 students:**	Integrate information presented in different media or formats (e.g., visually, quantitatively) as well as in words to develop a coherent understanding of a topic or issue.
RI.5.7 **Grade 5 students:**	Draw on information from multiple print or digital sources, demonstrating the ability to locate an answer to a question quickly or to solve a problem efficiently.
RI.4.7 **Grade 4 students:**	Interpret information presented visually, orally, or quantitatively (e.g., in charts, graphs, diagrams, time lines, animations, or interactive elements on Web pages) and explain how the information contributes to an understanding of the text in which it appears.
RI.3.7 **Grade 3 students:**	Use information gained from illustrations (e.g., maps, photographs) and the words in a text to demonstrate understanding of the text (e.g., where, when, why, and how key events occur).
RI.2.7 **Grade 2 students:**	Explain how specific images (e.g., a diagram showing how a machine works) contribute to and clarify a text.
RI.1.7 **Grade 1 students:**	Use the illustrations and details in a text to describe its key ideas.
RI.K.7 **Kindergarten students:**	With prompting and support, describe the relationship between illustrations and the text in which they appear (e.g., what person, place, thing, or idea in the text an illustration depicts).

R.CCR.8	**CCR Reading Anchor Standard 8:** **Delineate and evaluate the argument and specific claims in a text, including the validity of the reasoning as well as the relevance and sufficiency of the evidence.**
RI.11–12.8 **Grade 11–12 students:**	Delineate and evaluate the reasoning in seminal U.S. texts, including the application of constitutional principles and use of legal reasoning (e.g., in U.S. Supreme Court majority opinions and dissents) and the premises, purposes, and arguments in works of public advocacy (e.g., *The Federalist*, presidential addresses).
RI.9–10.8 **Grade 9–10 students:**	Delineate and evaluate the argument and specific claims in a text, assessing whether the reasoning is valid and the evidence is relevant and sufficient; identify false statements and fallacious reasoning.
RI.8.8 **Grade 8 students:**	Delineate and evaluate the argument and specific claims in a text, assessing whether the reasoning is sound and the evidence is relevant and sufficient; recognize when irrelevant evidence is introduced.
RI.7.8 **Grade 7 students:**	Trace and evaluate the argument and specific claims in a text, assessing whether the reasoning is sound and the evidence is relevant and sufficient to support the claims.
RI.6.8 **Grade 6 students:**	Trace and evaluate the argument and specific claims in a text, distinguishing claims that are supported by reasons and evidence from claims that are not.
RI.5.8 **Grade 5 students:**	Explain how an author uses reasons and evidence to support particular points in a text, identifying which reasons and evidence support which point(s).
RI.4.8 **Grade 4 students:**	Explain how an author uses reasons and evidence to support particular points in a text.
RI.3.8 **Grade 3 students:**	Describe the logical connection between particular sentences and paragraphs in a text (e.g., comparison, cause/effect, first/second/third in a sequence).
RI.2.8 **Grade 2 students:**	Describe how reasons support specific points the author makes in a text.
RI.1.8 **Grade 1 students:**	Identify the reasons an author gives to support points in a text.
RI.K.8 **Kindergarten students:**	With prompting and support, identify the reasons an author gives to support points in a text.

R.CCR.9	**CCR Reading Anchor Standard 9:** **Analyze how two or more texts address similar themes or topics in order to build knowledge or to compare the approaches the authors take.**
RI.11–12.9 **Grade 11–12 students:**	Analyze seventeenth-, eighteenth-, and nineteenth-century foundational U.S. documents of historical and literary significance (including The Declaration of Independence, the Preamble to the Constitution, the Bill of Rights, and Lincoln's Second Inaugural Address) for their themes, purposes, and rhetorical features.
RI.9–10.9 **Grade 9–10 students:**	Analyze seminal U.S. documents of historical and literary significance (e.g., Washington's Farewell Address, the Gettysburg Address, Roosevelt's Four Freedoms Speech, King's "Letter from Birmingham Jail"), including how they address related themes and concepts.
RI.8.9 **Grade 8 students:**	Analyze a case in which two or more texts provide conflicting information on the same topic and identify where the texts disagree on matters of fact or interpretation.
RI.7.9 **Grade 7 students:**	Analyze how two or more authors writing about the same topic shape their presentations of key information by emphasizing different evidence or advancing different interpretations of facts.
RI.6.9 **Grade 6 students:**	Compare and contrast one author's presentation of events with that of another (e.g., a memoir written by and a biography on the same person).
RI.5.9 **Grade 5 students:**	Integrate information from several texts on the same topic in order to write or speak about the subject knowledgeably.
RI.4.9 **Grade 4 students:**	Integrate information from two texts on the same topic in order to write or speak about the subject knowledgeably.
RI.3.9 **Grade 3 students:**	Compare and contrast the most important points and key details presented in two texts on the same topic.
RI.2.9 **Grade 2 students:**	Compare and contrast the most important points presented by two texts on the same topic.
RI.1.9 **Grade 1 students:**	Identify basic similarities in and differences between two texts on the same topic (e.g., in illustrations, descriptions, or procedures).
RI.K.9 **Kindergarten students:**	With prompting and support, identify basic similarities in and differences between two texts on the same topic (e.g., in illustrations, descriptions, or procedures).

R.CCR.10	**CCR Reading Anchor Standard 10:** **Read and comprehend complex literary and informational texts independently and proficiently.**
RI.11–12.10 **Grade 11–12 students:**	By the end of grade 11, read and comprehend literary nonfiction in the grades 11–CCR text complexity band proficiently, with scaffolding as needed at the high end of the range. By the end of grade 12, read and comprehend literary nonfiction at the high end of the grades 11–CCR text complexity band independently and proficiently.
RI.9–10.10 **Grade 9–10 students:**	By the end of grade 9, read and comprehend literary nonfiction in the grades 9–10 text complexity band proficiently, with scaffolding as needed at the high end of the range. By the end of grade 10, read and comprehend literary nonfiction at the high end of the grades 9–10 text complexity band independently and proficiently.
RI.8.10 **Grade 8 students:**	By the end of the year, read and comprehend literary nonfiction at the high end of the grades 6–8 text complexity band independently and proficiently.
RI.7.10 **Grade 7 students:**	By the end of the year, read and comprehend literary nonfiction in the grades 6–8 text complexity band proficiently, with scaffolding as needed at the high end of the range.
RI.6.10 **Grade 6 students:**	By the end of the year, read and comprehend literary nonfiction in the grades 6–8 text complexity band proficiently, with scaffolding as needed at the high end of the range.
RI.5.10 **Grade 5 students:**	By the end of the year, read and comprehend informational texts, including history/social studies, science, and technical texts, at the high end of the grades 4–5 text complexity band independently and proficiently.
RI.4.10 **Grade 4 students:**	By the end of the year, read and comprehend informational texts, including history/social studies, science, and technical texts, in the grades 4–5 text complexity band proficiently, with scaffolding as needed at the high end of the range.
RI.3.10 **Grade 3 students:**	By the end of the year, read and comprehend informational texts, including history/social studies, science, and technical texts, at the high end of the grades 2–3 text complexity band independently and proficiently.
RI.2.10 **Grade 2 students:**	By the end of the year, read and comprehend informational texts, including history/social studies, science, and technical texts, in the grades 2–3 text complexity band proficiently, with scaffolding as needed at the high end of the range.
RI.1.10 **Grade 1 students:**	With prompting and support, read informational texts appropriately complex for grade 1.
RI.K.10 **Kindergarten students:**	Actively engage in group reading activities with purpose and understanding.

W.CCR.1	**CCR Writing Anchor Standard 1:** **Write arguments to support claims in an analysis of substantive topics or texts, using valid reasoning and relevant and sufficient evidence.**
W.11–12.1 **Grade 11–12 students:**	Write arguments to support claims in an analysis of substantive topics or texts, using valid reasoning and relevant and sufficient evidence. a. Introduce precise, knowledgeable claim(s), establish the significance of the claim(s), distinguish the claim(s) from alternate or opposing claims, and create an organization that logically sequences claim(s), counterclaims, reasons, and evidence. b. Develop claim(s) and counterclaims fairly and thoroughly, supplying the most relevant evidence for each while pointing out the strengths and limitations of both in a manner that anticipates the audience's knowledge level, concerns, values, and possible biases. c. Use words, phrases, and clauses as well as varied syntax to link the major sections of the text, create cohesion, and clarify the relationships between claim(s) and reasons, between reasons and evidence, and between claim(s) and counterclaims. d. Establish and maintain a formal style and objective tone while attending to the norms and conventions of the discipline in which they are writing. e. Provide a concluding statement or section that follows from and supports the argument presented.
W.9–10.1 **Grade 9–10 students:**	Write arguments to support claims in an analysis of substantive topics or texts, using valid reasoning and relevant and sufficient evidence. a. Introduce precise claim(s), distinguish the claim(s) from alternate or opposing claims, and create an organization that establishes clear relationships among claim(s), counterclaims, reasons, and evidence. b. Develop claim(s) and counterclaims fairly, supplying evidence for each while pointing out the strengths and limitations of both in a manner that anticipates the audience's knowledge level and concerns. c. Use words, phrases, and clauses to link the major sections of the text, create cohesion, and clarify the relationships between claim(s) and reasons, between reasons and evidence, and between claim(s) and counterclaims. d. Establish and maintain a formal style and objective tone while attending to the norms and conventions of the discipline in which they are writing. e. Provide a concluding statement or section that follows from and supports the argument presented.
W.8.1 **Grade 8 students:**	Write arguments to support claims with clear reasons and relevant evidence. a. Introduce claim(s), acknowledge and distinguish the claim(s) from alternate or opposing claims, and organize the reasons and evidence logically. b. Support claim(s) with logical reasoning and relevant evidence, using accurate, credible sources and demonstrating an understanding of the topic or text. c. Use words, phrases, and clauses to create cohesion and clarify the relationships among claim(s), counterclaims, reasons, and evidence. d. Establish and maintain a formal style. e. Provide a concluding statement or section that follows from and supports the argument presented.
W.7.1 **Grade 7 students:**	Write arguments to support claims with clear reasons and relevant evidence. a. Introduce claim(s), acknowledge alternative or opposing claims, and organize reasons and evidence logically. b. Support claim(s) with logical reasoning and relevant evidence, using accurate, credible sources and demonstrating an understanding of the topic or text. c. Use words, phrases, and clauses to create cohesion and clarify the relationships among claim(s), reasons, and evidence. d. Establish and maintain a formal style. e. Provide a concluding statement or section that follows from and supports the argument presented.

(Continued on next page)

W.6.1 **Grade 6 students:**	Write arguments to support claims with clear reasons and relevant evidence. a. Introduce claims(s) and organize the reasons and evidence clearly. b. Support claim(s) with clear reasons and relevant evidence, using credible sources and demonstrating an understanding of the topic or text. c. Use words, phrases, and clauses to clarify the relationships among claim(s) and reasons. d. Establish and maintain a formal style. e. Provide a concluding statement or section that follows from the argument presented.
W.5.1 **Grade 5 students:**	Write opinion pieces on topics or texts, supporting a point of view with reasons and information. a. Introduce a topic or text clearly, state an opinion, and create an organizational structure in which ideas are logically grouped to support the writer's purpose. b. Provide logically ordered reasons that are supported by facts and details. c. Link opinion and reasons using words, phrases, and clauses (e.g., *consequently, specifically*). d. Provide a concluding statement or section related to the opinion presented.
W.4.1 **Grade 4 students:**	Write opinion pieces on topics or texts, supporting a point of view with reasons and information. a. Introduce a topic or text clearly, state an opinion, and create an organizational structure in which related ideas are grouped to support the writer's purpose. b. Provide reasons that are supported by facts and details. c. Link opinion and reasons using words and phrases (e.g., *for instance, in order to, in addition*). d. Provide a concluding statement or section related to the opinion presented.
W.3.1 **Grade 3 students:**	Write opinion pieces on topics or texts, supporting a point of view with reasons. a. Introduce the topic or text they are writing about, state an opinion, and create an organizational structure that lists reasons. b. Provide reasons that support the opinion. c. Use linking words and phrases (e.g., *because, therefore, since, for example*) to connect opinion and reasons. d. Provide a concluding statement or section.
W.2.1 **Grade 2 students:**	Write opinion pieces in which they introduce the topic or book they are writing about, state an opinion, supply reasons that support the opinion, use linking words (e.g., *because, and, also*) to connect opinion and reasons, and provide a concluding statement or section.
W.1.1 **Grade 1 students:**	Write opinion pieces in which they introduce the topic or name the book they are writing about, state an opinion, supply a reason for the opinion, and provide some sense of closure.
W.K.1 **Kindergarten students:**	Use a combination of drawing, dictating, and writing to compose opinion pieces in which they tell a reader the topic or the name of the book they are writing about and state an opinion or preference about the topic or book (e.g., *My favorite book is* ...).

W.CCR.2	**CCR Writing Anchor Standard 2:** **Write informative/explanatory texts to examine and convey complex ideas and information clearly and accurately through the effective selection, organization, and analysis of content.**
W.11–12.2 **Grade 11–12 students:**	Write informative/explanatory texts to examine and convey complex ideas, concepts, and information clearly and accurately through the effective selection, organization, and analysis of content. a. Introduce a topic; organize complex ideas, concepts, and information so that each new element builds on that which precedes it to create a unified whole; include formatting (e.g., headings), graphics (e.g., figures, tables), and multimedia when useful to aiding comprehension. b. Develop the topic thoroughly by selecting the most significant and relevant facts, extended definitions, concrete details, quotations, or other information and examples appropriate to the audience's knowledge of the topic. c. Use appropriate and varied transitions and syntax to link the major sections of the text, create cohesion, and clarify the relationships among complex ideas and concepts. d. Use precise language, domain-specific vocabulary, and techniques such as metaphor, simile, and analogy to manage the complexity of the topic. e. Establish and maintain a formal style and objective tone while attending to the norms and conventions of the discipline in which they are writing. f. Provide a concluding statement or section that follows from and supports the information or explanation presented (e.g., articulating implications or the significance of the topic).
W.9–10.2 **Grade 9–10 students:**	Write informative/explanatory texts to examine and convey complex ideas, concepts, and information clearly and accurately through the effective selection, organization, and analysis of content. a. Introduce a topic; organize complex ideas, concepts, and information to make important connections and distinctions; include formatting (e.g., headings), graphics (e.g., figures, tables), and multimedia when useful to aiding comprehension. b. Develop the topic with well-chosen, relevant, and sufficient facts, extended definitions, concrete details, quotations, or other information and examples appropriate to the audience's knowledge of the topic. c. Use appropriate and varied transitions to link the major sections of the text, create cohesion, and clarify the relationships among complex ideas and concepts. d. Use precise language and domain-specific vocabulary to manage the complexity of the topic. e. Establish and maintain a formal style and objective tone while attending to the norms and conventions of the discipline in which they are writing. f. Provide a concluding statement or section that follows from and supports the information or explanation presented (e.g., articulating implications or the significance of the topic).
W.8.2 **Grade 8 students:**	Write informative/explanatory texts to examine a topic and convey ideas, concepts, and information through the selection, organization, and analysis of relevant content. a. Introduce a topic clearly, previewing what is to follow; organize ideas, concepts, and information into broader categories; include formatting (e.g., headings), graphics (e.g., charts, tables), and multimedia when useful to aiding comprehension b. Develop the topic with relevant, well-chosen facts, definitions, concrete details, quotations, or other information and examples. c. Use appropriate and varied transitions to create cohesion and clarify the relationships among ideas and concepts. d. Use precise language and domain-specific vocabulary to inform about or explain the topic. e. Establish and maintain a formal style. f. Provide a concluding statement or section that follows from and supports the information or explanation presented.

(Continued on next page)

W.7.2 **Grade 7 students:**	Write informative/explanatory texts to examine a topic and convey ideas, concepts, and information through the selection, organization, and analysis of relevant content. a. Introduce a topic clearly, previewing what is to follow; organize ideas, concepts, and information, using strategies such as definition, classification, comparison/contrast, and cause/effect; include formatting (e.g., headings), graphics (e.g., charts, tables), and multimedia when useful to aiding comprehension. b. Develop the topic with relevant facts, definitions, concrete details, quotations, or other information and examples. c. Use appropriate transitions to create cohesion and clarify the relationships among ideas and concepts. d. Use precise language and domain-specific vocabulary to inform about or explain the topic. e. Establish and maintain a formal style. f. Provide a concluding statement or section that follows from and supports the information or explanation presented.
W.6.2 **Grade 6 students:**	Write informative/explanatory texts to examine a topic and convey ideas, concepts, and information through the selection, organization, and analysis of relevant content. a. Introduce a topic; organize ideas, concepts, and information, using strategies such as definition, classification, comparison/contrast, and cause/effect; include formatting (e.g., headings), graphics (e.g., charts, tables), and multimedia when useful to aiding comprehension. b. Develop the topic with relevant facts, definitions, concrete details, quotations, or other information and examples. c. Use appropriate transitions to clarify the relationships among ideas and concepts. d. Use precise language and domain-specific vocabulary to inform about or explain the topic. e. Establish and maintain a formal style. f. Provide a concluding statement or section that follows from and supports the information or explanation presented.
W.5.2 **Grade 5 students:**	Write informative/explanatory texts to examine a topic and convey ideas and information clearly. a. Introduce a topic clearly, provide a general observation and focus, and group related information logically; include formatting (e.g., headings), illustrations, and multimedia when useful to aiding comprehension. b. Develop the topic with facts, definitions, concrete details, quotations, or other information and examples related to the topic. c. Link ideas within and across categories of information using words, phrases, and clauses (e.g., *in contrast, especially*). d. Use precise language and domain-specific vocabulary to inform about or explain the topic. e. Provide a concluding statement or section related to the information or explanation presented.
W.4.2 **Grade 4 students:**	Write informative/explanatory texts to examine a topic and convey ideas and information clearly. a. Introduce a topic clearly and group related information in paragraphs and sections; include formatting (e.g., headings), illustrations, and multimedia when useful to aiding comprehension. b. Develop the topic with facts, definitions, concrete details, quotations, or other information and examples related to the topic. c. Link ideas within categories of information using words and phrases (e.g., *another, for example, also, because*). d. Use precise language and domain-specific vocabulary to inform about or explain the topic. e. Provide a concluding statement or section related to the information or explanation.

(Continued on next page)

W.3.2 **Grade 3 students:**	Write informative/explanatory texts to examine a topic and convey ideas and information clearly. a. Introduce a topic and group related information together; include illustrations when useful to aiding comprehension. b. Develop the topic with facts, definitions, and details. c. Use linking words and phrases (e.g., *also, another, and, more, but*) to connect ideas within categories of information. d. Provide a concluding statement or section.
W.2.2 **Grade 2 students:**	Write informative/explanatory texts in which they introduce a topic, use facts and definitions to develop points, and provide a concluding statement or section.
W.1.2 **Grade 1 students:**	Write informative/explanatory texts in which they name a topic, supply some facts about the topic, and provide some sense of closure.
W.K.2 **Kindergarten students:**	Use a combination of drawing, dictating, and writing to compose informative/explanatory texts in which they name what they are writing about and supply some information about the topic.

W.CCR.3	**CCR Writing Anchor Standard 3:** **Write narratives to develop real or imagined experiences or events using effective technique, well-chosen details, and well-structured event sequences.**
W.11–12.3 **Grade 11–12 students:**	Write narratives to develop real or imagined experiences or events using effective technique, well-chosen details, and well-structured event sequences. a. Engage and orient the reader by setting out a problem, situation, or observation and its significance, establishing one or multiple point(s) of view, and introducing a narrator and/or characters; create a smooth progression of experiences or events. b. Use narrative techniques, such as dialogue, pacing, description, reflection, and multiple plot lines, to develop experiences, events, and/or characters. c. Use a variety of techniques to sequence events so that they build on one another to create a coherent whole and build toward a particular tone and outcome (e.g., a sense of mystery, suspense, growth, or resolution). d. Use precise words and phrases, telling details, and sensory language to convey a vivid picture of the experiences, events, setting, and/or characters. e. Provide a conclusion that follows from and reflects on what is experienced, observed, or resolved over the course of the narrative.
W.9–10.3 **Grade 9–10 students:**	Write narratives to develop real or imagined experiences or events using effective technique, well-chosen details, and well-structured event sequences. a. Engage and orient the reader by setting out a problem, situation, or observation, establishing one or multiple point(s) of view, and introducing a narrator and/or characters; create a smooth progression of experiences or events. b. Use narrative techniques, such as dialogue, pacing, description, reflection, and multiple plot lines, to develop experiences, events, and/or characters. c. Use a variety of techniques to sequence events so that they build on one another to create a coherent whole. d. Use precise words and phrases, telling details, and sensory language to convey a vivid picture of the experiences, events, setting, and/or characters. e. Provide a conclusion that follows from and reflects on what is experienced, observed, or resolved over the course of the narrative.
W.8.3 **Grade 8 students:**	Write narratives to develop real or imagined experiences or events using effective technique, relevant descriptive details, and well-structured event sequences. a. Engage and orient the reader by establishing a context and point of view and introducing a narrator and/or characters; organize an event sequence that unfolds naturally and logically. b. Use narrative techniques, such as dialogue, pacing, description, and reflection, to develop experiences, events, and/or characters. c. Use a variety of transition words, phrases, and clauses to convey sequence, signal shifts from one time frame or setting to another, and show the relationships among experiences and events. d. Use precise words and phrases, relevant descriptive details, and sensory language to capture the action and convey experiences and events. e. Provide a conclusion that follows from and reflects on the narrated experiences or events.

(Continued on next page)

W.7.3 **Grade 7 students:**	Write narratives to develop real or imagined experiences or events using effective technique, relevant descriptive details, and well-structured event sequences. a. Engage and orient the reader by establishing a context and point of view and introducing a narrator and/or characters; organize an event sequence that unfolds naturally and logically. b. Use narrative techniques, such as dialogue, pacing, and description, to develop experiences, events, and/or characters. c. Use a variety of transition words, phrases, and clauses to convey sequence and signal shifts from one time frame or setting to another. d. Use precise words and phrases, relevant descriptive details, and sensory language to capture the action and convey experiences and events. e. Provide a conclusion that follows from and reflects on the narrated experiences or events.
W.6.3 **Grade 6 students:**	Write narratives to develop real or imagined experiences or events using effective technique, relevant descriptive details, and well-structured event sequences. a. Engage and orient the reader by establishing a context and introducing a narrator and/or characters; organize an event sequence that unfolds naturally and logically. b. Use narrative techniques, such as dialogue, pacing, and description, to develop experiences, events, and/or characters. c. Use a variety of transition words, phrases, and clauses to convey sequence and signal shifts from one time frame or setting to another. d. Use precise words and phrases, relevant descriptive details, and sensory language to convey experiences and events. e. Provide a conclusion that follows from the narrated experiences or events.
W.5.3 **Grade 5 students:**	Write narratives to develop real or imagined experiences or events using effective technique, descriptive details, and clear event sequences. a. Orient the reader by establishing a situation and introducing a narrator and/or characters; organize an event sequence that unfolds naturally. b. Use narrative techniques, such as dialogue, description, and pacing, to develop experiences and events or show the responses of characters to situations. c. Use a variety of transitional words, phrases, and clauses to manage the sequence of events. d. Use concrete words and phrases and sensory details to convey experiences and events precisely. e. Provide a conclusion that follows from the narrated experiences or events.
W.4.3 **Grade 4 students:**	Write narratives to develop real or imagined experiences or events using effective technique, descriptive details, and clear event sequences. a. Orient the reader by establishing a situation and introducing a narrator and/or characters; organize an event sequence that unfolds naturally. b. Use dialogue and description to develop experiences and events or show the responses of characters to situations. c. Use a variety of transitional words and phrases to manage the sequence of events. d. Use concrete words and phrases and sensory details to convey experiences and events precisely. e. Provide a conclusion that follows from the narrated experiences or events.

(Continued on next page)

W.3.3 **Grade 3 students:**	Write narratives to develop real or imagined experiences or events using effective technique, descriptive details, and clear event sequences. a. Establish a situation and introduce a narrator and/or characters; organize an event sequence that unfolds naturally. b. Use dialogue and descriptions of actions, thoughts, and feelings to develop experiences and events or show the response of characters to situations. c. Use temporal words and phrases to signal event order. d. Provide a sense of closure.
W.2.3 **Grade 2 students:**	Write narratives in which they recount a well-elaborated event or short sequence of events, include details to describe actions, thoughts, and feelings, use temporal words to signal event order, and provide a sense of closure.
W.1.3 **Grade 1 students:**	Write narratives in which they recount two or more appropriately sequenced events, include some details regarding what happened, use temporal words to signal event order, and provide some sense of closure.
W.K.3 **Kindergarten students:**	Use a combination of drawing, dictating, and writing to narrate a single event or several loosely linked events, tell about the events in the order in which they occurred, and provide a reaction to what happened.

W.CCR.4	**CCR Writing Anchor Standard 4:** **Produce clear and coherent writing in which the development, organization, and style are appropriate to task, purpose, and audience.**
W.11–12.4 **Grade 11–12 students:**	Produce clear and coherent writing in which the development, organization, and style are appropriate to task, purpose, and audience. (Grade-specific expectations for writing types are defined in standards 1–3.)
W.9–10.4 **Grade 9–10 students:**	Produce clear and coherent writing in which the development, organization, and style are appropriate to task, purpose, and audience. (Grade-specific expectations for writing types are defined in standards 1–3.)
W.8.4 **Grade 8 students:**	Produce clear and coherent writing in which the development, organization, and style are appropriate to task, purpose, and audience. (Grade-specific expectations for writing types are defined in standards 1–3.)
W.7.4 **Grade 7 students:**	Produce clear and coherent writing in which the development, organization, and style are appropriate to task, purpose, and audience. (Grade-specific expectations for writing types are defined in standards 1–3.)
W.6.4 **Grade 6 students:**	Produce clear and coherent writing in which the development, organization, and style are appropriate to task, purpose, and audience. (Grade-specific expectations for writing types are defined in standards 1–3.)
W.5.4 **Grade 5 students:**	Produce clear and coherent writing in which the development and organization are appropriate to task, purpose, and audience. (Grade-specific expectations for writing types are defined in standards 1–3.)
W.4.4 **Grade 4 students:**	Produce clear and coherent writing in which the development and organization are appropriate to task, purpose, and audience. (Grade-specific expectations for writing types are defined in standards 1–3.)
W.3.4 **Grade 3 students:**	With guidance and support from adults, produce writing in which the development and organization are appropriate to task and purpose. (Grade-specific expectations for writing types are defined in standards 1–3.)
W.2.4 **Grade 2 students:**	(Begins in grade 3)
W.1.4 **Grade 1 students:**	(Begins in grade 3)
W.K.4 **Kindergarten students:**	(Begins in grade 3)

W.CCR.5	**CCR Writing Anchor Standard 5:** **Develop and strengthen writing as needed by planning, revising, editing, rewriting, or trying a new approach.**
W.11–12.5 **Grade 11–12 students:**	Develop and strengthen writing as needed by planning, revising, editing, rewriting, or trying a new approach, focusing on addressing what is most significant for a specific purpose and audience. (Editing for conventions should demonstrate command of Language standards 1–3, up to and including grades 11–12.)
W.9–10.5 **Grade 9–10 students:**	Develop and strengthen writing as needed by planning, revising, editing, rewriting, or trying a new approach, focusing on addressing what is most significant for a specific purpose and audience. (Editing for conventions should demonstrate command of Language standards 1–3, up to and including grades 9–10.)
W.8.5 **Grade 8 students:**	With some guidance and support from peers and adults, develop and strengthen writing as needed by planning, revising, editing, rewriting, or trying a new approach, focusing on how well purpose and audience have been addressed. (Editing for conventions should demonstrate command of Language standards 1–3, up to and including grade 8.)
W.7.5 **Grade 7 students:**	With some guidance and support from peers and adults, develop and strengthen writing as needed by planning, revising, editing, rewriting, or trying a new approach, focusing on how well purpose and audience have been addressed. (Editing for conventions should demonstrate command of Language standards 1–3, up to and including grade 7.)
W.6.5 **Grade 6 students:**	With some guidance and support from peers and adults, develop and strengthen writing as needed by planning, revising, editing, rewriting, or trying a new approach. (Editing for conventions should demonstrate command of Language standards 1–3, up to and including grade 6.)
W.5.5 **Grade 5 students:**	With guidance and support from peers and adults, develop and strengthen writing as needed by planning, revising, editing, rewriting, or trying a new approach. (Editing for conventions should demonstrate command of Language standards 1–3, up to and including grade 5.)
W.4.5 **Grade 4 students:**	With guidance and support from peers and adults, develop and strengthen writing as needed by planning, revising, and editing. (Editing for conventions should demonstrate command of Language standards 1–3, up to and including grade 4.)
W.3.5 **Grade 3 students:**	With guidance and support from peers and adults, develop and strengthen writing as needed by planning, revising, and editing. (Editing for conventions should demonstrate command of Language standards 1–3, up to and including grade 3.)
W.2.5 **Grade 2 students:**	With guidance and support from adults and peers, focus on a topic and strengthen writing as needed by revising and editing.
W.1.5 **Grade 1 students:**	With guidance and support from adults, focus on a topic, respond to questions and suggestions from peers, and add details to strengthen writing as needed.
W.K.5 **Kindergarten students:**	With guidance and support from adults, respond to questions and suggestions from peers and add details to strengthen writing as needed.

W.CCR.6	**CCR Writing Anchor Standard 6:** **Use technology, including the Internet, to produce and publish writing and to interact and collaborate with others.**
W.11–12.6 **Grade 11–12 students:**	Use technology, including the Internet, to produce, publish, and update individual or shared writing products in response to ongoing feedback, including new arguments or information.
W.9–10.6 **Grade 9–10 students:**	Use technology, including the Internet, to produce, publish, and update individual or shared writing products, taking advantage of technology's capacity to link to other information and to display information flexibly and dynamically.
W.8.6 **Grade 8 students:**	Use technology, including the Internet, to produce and publish writing and present the relationships between information and ideas efficiently as well as to interact and collaborate with others.
W.7.6 **Grade 7 students:**	Use technology, including the Internet, to produce and publish writing and link to and cite sources as well as to interact and collaborate with others, including linking to and citing sources.
W.6.6 **Grade 6 students:**	Use technology, including the Internet, to produce and publish writing as well as to interact and collaborate with others; demonstrate sufficient command of keyboarding skills to type a minimum of three pages in a single sitting.
W.5.6 **Grade 5 students:**	With some guidance and support from adults, use technology, including the Internet, to produce and publish writing as well as to interact and collaborate with others; demonstrate sufficient command of keyboarding skills to type a minimum of two pages in a single sitting.
W.4.6 **Grade 4 students:**	With some guidance and support from adults, use technology, including the Internet, to produce and publish writing as well as to interact and collaborate with others; demonstrate sufficient command of keyboarding skills to type a minimum of one page in a single sitting.
W.3.6 **Grade 3 students:**	With guidance and support from adults, use technology to produce and publish writing (using keyboarding skills) as well as to interact and collaborate with others.
W.2.6 **Grade 2 students:**	With guidance and support from adults, use a variety of digital tools to produce and publish writing, including in collaboration with peers.
W.1.6 **Grade 1 students:**	With guidance and support from adults, use a variety of digital tools to produce and publish writing, including in collaboration with peers.
W.K.6 **Kindergarten students:**	With guidance and support from adults, explore a variety of digital tools to produce and publish writing, including in collaboration with peers.

W.CCR.7	**CCR Writing Anchor Standard 7:** **Conduct short as well as more sustained research projects based on focused questions, demonstrating understanding of the subject under investigation.**
W.11–12.7 **Grade 11–12 students:**	Conduct short as well as more sustained research projects to answer a question (including a self-generated question) or solve a problem; narrow or broaden the inquiry when appropriate, synthesize multiple sources on the subject, demonstrating understanding of the subject under investigation.
W.9–10.7 **Grade 9–10 students:**	Conduct short as well as more sustained research projects to answer a question (including a self-generated question) or solve a problem; narrow or broaden the inquiry when appropriate; synthesize multiple sources on the subject, demonstrating understanding of the subject under investigation.
W.8.7 **Grade 8 students:**	Conduct short research projects to answer a question (including a self-generated question), drawing on several sources and generating additional related, focused questions that allow for multiple avenues of exploration.
W.7.7 **Grade 7 students:**	Conduct short research projects to answer a question, drawing on several sources and generating additional related, focused questions for further research and investigation.
W.6.7 **Grade 6 students:**	Conduct short research projects to answer a question, drawing on several sources and refocusing the inquiry when appropriate.
W.5.7 **Grade 5 students:**	Conduct short research projects that use several sources to build knowledge through investigation of different aspects of a topic.
W.4.7 **Grade 4 students:**	Conduct short research projects that build knowledge through investigation of different aspects of a topic.
W.3.7 **Grade 3 students:**	Conduct short research projects that build knowledge about a topic.
W.2.7 **Grade 2 students:**	Participate in shared research and writing projects (e.g., read a number of books on a single topic to produce a report; record science observations).
W.1.7 **Grade 1 students:**	Participate in shared research and writing projects (e.g., explore a number of "how-to" books on a given topic and use them to write a sequence of instructions).
W.K.7 **Kindergarten students:**	Participate in shared research and writing projects (e.g., explore a number of books by a favorite author and express opinions about them).

W.CCR.8	**CCR Writing Anchor Standard 8:** **Gather relevant information from multiple print and digital sources, assess the credibility and accuracy of each source, and integrate the information while avoiding plagiarism.**
W.11–12.8 **Grade 11–12 students:**	Gather relevant information from multiple authoritative print and digital sources, using advanced searches effectively; assess the strengths and limitations of each source in terms of the task, purpose, and audience; integrate information into the text selectively to maintain the flow of ideas, avoiding plagiarism and overreliance on any one source and following a standard format for citation.
W.9–10.8 **Grade 9–10 students:**	Gather relevant information from multiple authoritative print and digital sources, using advanced searches effectively; assess the usefulness of each source in answering the research question; integrate information into the text selectively to maintain the flow of ideas, avoiding plagiarism and following a standard format for citation.
W.8.8 **Grade 8 students:**	Gather relevant information from multiple print and digital sources, using search terms effectively; assess the credibility and accuracy of each source; and quote or paraphrase the data and conclusions of others while avoiding plagiarism and following a standard format for citation.
W.7.8 **Grade 7 students:**	Gather relevant information from multiple print and digital sources, using search terms effectively; assess the credibility and accuracy of each source; and quote or paraphrase the data and conclusions of others while avoiding plagiarism and following a standard format for citation.
W.6.8 **Grade 6 students:**	Gather relevant information from multiple print and digital sources; assess the credibility of each source; and quote or paraphrase the data and conclusions of others while avoiding plagiarism and providing basic bibliographic information for sources.
W.5.8 **Grade 5 students:**	Recall relevant information from experiences or gather relevant information from print and digital sources; summarize or paraphrase information in notes and finished work, and provide a list of sources.
W.4.8 **Grade 4 students:**	Recall relevant information from experiences or gather relevant information from print and digital sources; take notes and categorize information, and provide a list of sources.
W.3.8 **Grade 3 students:**	Recall information from experiences or gather information from print and digital sources; take brief notes on sources and sort evidence into provided categories.
W.2.8 **Grade 2 students:**	Recall information from experiences or gather information from provided sources to answer a question.
W.1.8 **Grade 1 students:**	With guidance and support from adults, recall information from experiences or gather information from provided sources to answer a question.
W.K.8 **Kindergarten students:**	With guidance and support from adults, recall information from experiences or gather information from provided sources to answer a question.

W.CCR.9	**CCR Writing Anchor Standard 9:** **Draw evidence from literary or informational texts to support analysis, reflection, and research.**
W.11–12.9 **Grade 11–12 students:**	Draw evidence from literary or informational texts to support analysis, reflection, and research. a. Apply *grades 11–12 Reading standards* to literature (e.g., "Demonstrate knowledge of eighteenth-, nineteenth- and early-twentieth-century foundational works of American literature, including how two or more texts from the same period treat similar themes or topics"). b. Apply *grades 11–12 Reading standards* to literary nonfiction (e.g., "Delineate and evaluate the reasoning in seminal U.S. texts, including the application of constitutional principles and use of legal reasoning [e.g., in U.S. Supreme Court Case majority opinions and dissents] and the premises, purposes, and arguments in works of public advocacy [e.g., *The Federalist*, presidential addresses]").
W.9–10.9 **Grade 9–10 students:**	Draw evidence from literary or informational texts to support analysis, reflection, and research. a. Apply *grades 9–10 Reading standards* to literature (e.g., "Analyze how an author draws on and transforms source material in a specific work [e.g., how Shakespeare treats a theme or topic from Ovid or the Bible or how a later author draws on a play by Shakespeare]"). b. Apply *grades 9–10 Reading standards* to literary nonfiction (e.g., "Delineate and evaluate the argument and specific claims in a text, assessing whether the reasoning is valid and the evidence is relevant and sufficient; identify false statements and fallacious reasoning").
W.8.9 **Grade 8 students:**	Draw evidence from literary or informational texts to support analysis, reflection, and research. a. Apply *grade 8 Reading standards* to literature (e.g., "Analyze how a modern work of fiction draws on themes, patterns of events, or character types from myths, traditional stories, or religious works such as the Bible, including describing how the material is rendered new"). b. Apply *grade 8 Reading standards* to literary nonfiction (e.g., "Delineate and evaluate the argument and specific claims in a text, assessing whether the reasoning is sound and the evidence is relevant and sufficient; recognize when irrelevant evidence is introduced").
W.7.9 **Grade 7 students:**	Draw evidence from literary or informational texts to support analysis, reflection, and research. a. Apply *grade 7 Reading standards* to literature (e.g., "Compare and contrast a fictional portrayal of a time, place, or character and a historical account of the same period as a means of understanding how authors of fiction use or alter history"). b. Apply *grade 7 Reading standards* to literary nonfiction (e.g. "Trace and evaluate the argument and specific claims in a text, assessing whether the reasoning is sound and the evidence is relevant and sufficient to support the claims").
W.6.9 **Grade 6 students:**	Draw evidence from literary or informational texts to support analysis, reflection, and research. a. Apply *grade 6 Reading standards* to literature (e.g., "Compare and contrast texts in different forms or genres [e.g., stories and poems; historical novels; and fantasy stories] in terms of their approaches to similar themes and topics"). b. Apply *grade 6 Reading standards* to literary nonfiction (e.g., "Trace and evaluate the argument and specific claims in a text, distinguishing claims that are supported by reasons and evidence from claims that are not").

(Continued on next page)

W.5.9 **Grade 5 students:**	Draw evidence from literary or informational texts to support analysis, reflection, and research. a. Apply *grade 5 Reading standards* to literature (e.g., "Compare and contrast two or more characters, settings, or events in a story or a drama, drawing on specific details in the text [e.g., how characters interact]"). b. Apply *grade 5 Reading standards* to informational texts (e.g., "Explain how an author uses reasons and evidence to support particular points in a text, identifying which reasons and evidence support which point[s]").
W.4.9 **Grade 4 students:**	Draw evidence from literary or informational texts to support analysis, reflection, and research. a. Apply *grade 4 Reading standards* to literature (e.g., "Describe in depth a character, setting, or event in a story or drama, drawing on specific details in the text [e.g., a character's thoughts, words, or actions]."). b. Apply *grade 4 Reading standards* to informational texts (e.g., "Explain how an author uses reasons and evidence to support particular points in a text").
W.3.9 **Grade 3 students:**	(Begins in grade 4)
W.2.9 **Grade 2 students:**	(Begins in grade 4)
W.1.9 **Grade 1 students:**	(Begins in grade 4)
W.K.9 **Kindergarten students:**	(Begins in grade 4)

W.CCR.10	**CCR Writing Anchor Standard 10:** **Write routinely over extended time frames (time for research, reflection, and revision) and shorter time frames (a single sitting or a day or two) for a range of tasks, purposes, and audiences.**
W.11–12.10 **Grade 11–12 students:**	Write routinely over extended time frames (time for research, reflection, and revision) and shorter time frames (a single sitting or a day or two) for a range of tasks, purposes, and audiences.
W.9–10.10 **Grade 9–10 students:**	Write routinely over extended time frames (time for research, reflection, and revision) and shorter time frames (a single sitting or a day or two) for a range of tasks, purposes, and audiences.
W.8.10 **Grade 8 students:**	Write routinely over extended time frames (time for research, reflection, and revision) and shorter time frames (a single sitting or a day or two) for a range of discipline-specific tasks, purposes, and audiences.
W.7.10 **Grade 7 students:**	Write routinely over extended time frames (time for research, reflection, and revision) and shorter time frames (a single sitting or a day or two) for a range of discipline-specific tasks, purposes, and audiences.
W.6.10 **Grade 6 students:**	Write routinely over extended time frames (time for research, reflection, and revision) and shorter time frames (a single sitting or a day or two) for a range of discipline-specific tasks, purposes, and audiences.
W.5.10 **Grade 5 students:**	Write routinely over extended time frames (time for research, reflection, and revision) and shorter time frames (a single sitting or a day or two) for a range of discipline-specific tasks, purposes, and audiences.
W.4.10 **Grade 4 students:**	Write routinely over extended time frames (time for research, reflection, and revision) and shorter time frames (a single sitting or a day or two) for a range of discipline-specific tasks, purposes, and audiences.
W.3.10 **Grade 3 students:**	Write routinely over extended time frames (time for research, reflection, and revision) and shorter time frames (a single sitting or a day or two) for a range of discipline-specific tasks, purposes, and audiences.
W.2.10 **Grade 2 students:**	(Begins in grade 3)
W.1.10 **Grade 1 students:**	(Begins in grade 3)
W.K.10 **Kindergarten students:**	(Begins in grade 3)

SL.CCR.1	**CCR Speaking and Listening Anchor Standard 1:** **Prepare for and participate effectively in a range of conversations and collaborations with diverse partners, building on others' ideas and expressing their own clearly and persuasively.**
SL.11–12.1 **Grade 11–12 students:**	Initiate and participate effectively in a range of collaborative discussions (one-on-one, in groups, and teacher-led) with diverse partners on *grades 11–12 topics, texts, and issues*, building on others' ideas and expressing their own clearly and persuasively. a. Come to discussions prepared, having read and researched material under study; explicitly draw on that preparation by referring to evidence from texts and other research on the topic or issue to stimulate a thoughtful, well-reasoned exchange of ideas. b. Work with peers to promote civil, democratic discussions and decision-making, set clear goals and deadlines, and establish individual roles as needed. c. Propel conversations by posing and responding to questions that probe reasoning and evidence; ensure a hearing for a full range of positions on a topic or issue; clarify, verify, or challenge ideas and conclusions; and promote divergent and creative perspectives. d. Respond thoughtfully to diverse perspectives; synthesize comments, claims, and evidence made on all sides of an issue; resolve contradictions when possible; and determine what additional information or research is required to deepen the investigation or complete the task.
SL.9–10.1 **Grade 9–10 students:**	Initiate and participate effectively in a range of collaborative discussions (one-on-one, in groups, and teacher-led) with diverse partners on *grades 9–10 topics, texts, and issues*, building on others' ideas and expressing their own clearly and persuasively. a. Come to discussions prepared, having read and researched material under study; explicitly draw on that preparation by referring to evidence from texts and other research on the topic or issue to stimulate a thoughtful, well-reasoned exchange of ideas. b. Work with peers to set rules for collegial discussions and decision-making (e.g., informal consensus, taking votes on key issues, presentation of alternate views), clear goals and deadlines, and individual roles as needed. c. Propel conversations by posing and responding to questions that relate the current discussion to broader themes or larger ideas; actively incorporate others into the discussion; and clarify, verify, or challenge ideas and conclusions. d. Respond thoughtfully to diverse perspectives, summarize points of agreement and disagreement, and, when warranted, qualify or justify their own views and understanding and make new connections in light of the evidence and reasoning presented.
SL.8.1 **Grade 8 students:**	Engage effectively in a range of collaborative discussions (one-on-one, in groups, and teacher-led) with diverse partners on *grade 8 topics, texts, and issues*, building on others' ideas and expressing their own clearly. a. Come to discussions prepared, having read or researched material under study; explicitly draw on that preparation by referring to evidence on the topic, text, or issue to probe and reflect on ideas under discussion. b. Follow rules for collegial discussions and decision-making, track progress toward specific goals and deadlines, and define individual roles as needed. c. Pose questions that connect the ideas of several speakers and respond to others' questions and comments with relevant evidence, observations, and ideas. d. Acknowledge new information expressed by others, and, when warranted, qualify or justify their own views in light of the evidence presented.

(Continued on next page)

SL.7.1 **Grade 7 students:**	Engage effectively in a range of collaborative discussions (one-on-one, in groups, and teacher-led) with diverse partners on *grade 7 topics, texts, and issues*, building on others' ideas and expressing their own clearly. a. Come to discussions prepared, having read or researched material under study; explicitly draw on that preparation by referring to evidence on the topic, text, or issue to probe and reflect on ideas under discussion. b. Follow rules for collegial discussions, track progress toward specific goals and deadlines, and define individual roles as needed. c. Pose questions that elicit elaboration and respond to others' questions and comments with relevant observations and ideas that bring the discussion back on topic as needed. d. Acknowledge new information expressed by others and, when warranted, modify their own views.
SL.6.1 **Grade 6 students:**	Engage effectively in a range of collaborative discussions (one-on-one, in groups, and teacher-led) with diverse partners on *grade 6 topics, texts, and issues*, building on others' ideas and expressing their own clearly. a. Come to discussions prepared, having read or studied required material; explicitly draw on that preparation by referring to evidence on the topic, text, or issue to probe and reflect on ideas under discussion. b. Follow rules for collegial discussions, set specific goals and deadlines, and define individual roles as needed. c. Pose and respond to specific questions with elaboration and detail by making comments that contribute to the topic, text, or issue under discussion. d. Review the key ideas expressed and demonstrate understanding of multiple perspectives through reflection and paraphrasing.
SL.5.1 **Grade 5 students:**	Engage effectively in a range of collaborative discussions (one-on-one, in groups, and teacher-led) with diverse partners on *grade 5 topics and texts*, building on others' ideas and expressing their own clearly. a. Come to discussions prepared, having read or studied required material; explicitly draw on that preparation and other information known about the topic to explore ideas under discussion. b. Follow agreed-upon rules for discussions and carry out assigned roles. c. Pose and respond to specific questions by making comments that contribute to the discussion and elaborate on the remarks of others. d. Review the key ideas expressed and draw conclusions in light of information and knowledge gained from the discussions.
SL.4.1 **Grade 4 students:**	Engage effectively in a range of collaborative discussions (one-on-one, in groups, and teacher-led) with diverse partners on *grade 4 topics and texts*, building on others' ideas and expressing their own clearly. a. Come to discussions prepared, having read or studied required material; explicitly draw on that preparation and other information known about the topic to explore ideas under discussion. b. Follow agreed-upon rules for discussions and carry out assigned roles. c. Pose and respond to specific questions to clarify or follow up on information, and make comments that contribute to the discussion and link to the remarks of others. d. Review the key ideas expressed and explain their own ideas and understanding in light of the discussion.

(Continued on next page)

SL.3.1 **Grade 3 students:**	Engage effectively in a range of collaborative discussions (one-on-one, in groups, and teacher-led) with diverse partners on *grade 3 topics and texts*, building on others' ideas and expressing their own clearly. a. Come to discussions prepared, having read or studied required material; explicitly draw on that preparation and other information known about the topic to explore ideas under discussion. b. Follow agreed-upon rules for discussions (e.g., gaining the floor in respectful ways, listening to others with care, speaking one at a time about the topics and texts under discussion). c. Ask questions to check understanding of information presented, stay on topic, and link their comments to the remarks of others. d. Explain their own ideas and understanding in light of the discussion.
SL.2.1 **Grade 2 students:**	Participate in collaborative conversations with diverse partners about *grade 2 topics and texts* with peers and adults in small and larger groups. a. Follow agreed-upon rules for discussions (e.g., gaining the floor in respectful ways, listening to others with care, speaking one at a time about the topics and texts under discussion). b. Build on others' talk in conversations by linking their comments to the remarks of others. c. Ask for clarification and further explanation as needed about the topics and texts under discussion.
SL.1.1 **Grade 1 students:**	Participate in collaborative conversations with diverse partners about *grade 1 topics and texts* with peers and adults in small and larger groups. a. Follow agreed-upon rules for discussions (e.g., listening to others with care, speaking one at a time about the topics and texts under discussion). b. Build on others' talk in conversations by responding to the comments of others through multiple exchanges. c. Ask questions to clear up any confusion about the topics and texts under discussion.
SL.K.1 **Kindergarten students:**	Participate in collaborative conversations with diverse partners about *kindergarten topics and texts* with peers and adults in small and larger groups. a. Follow agreed-upon rules for discussions (e.g., listening to others and taking turns speaking about the topics and texts under discussion). b. Continue a conversation through multiple exchanges.

SL.CCR.2	**CCR Speaking and Listening Anchor Standard 2:** **Integrate and evaluate information presented in diverse media and formats, including visually, quantitatively, and orally.**
SL.11–12.2 **Grade 11–12 students:**	Integrate multiple sources of information presented in diverse formats and media (e.g., visually, quantitatively, orally) in order to make informed decisions and solve problems, evaluating the credibility and accuracy of each source and noting any discrepancies among the data.
SL.9–10.2 **Grade 9–10 students:**	Integrate multiple sources of information presented in diverse media or formats (e.g., visually, quantitatively, orally) evaluating the credibility and accuracy of each source.
SL.8.2 **Grade 8 students:**	Analyze the purpose of information presented in diverse media and formats (e.g., visually, quantitatively, orally) and evaluate the motives (e.g., social, commercial, political) behind its presentation.
SL.7.2 **Grade 7 students:**	Analyze the main ideas and supporting details presented in diverse media and formats (e.g., visually, quantitatively, orally) and explain how the ideas clarify a topic, text, or issue under study.
SL.6.2 **Grade 6 students:**	Interpret information presented in diverse media and formats (e.g., visually, quantitatively, orally) and explain how it contributes to a topic, text, or issue under study.
SL.5.2 **Grade 5 students:**	Summarize a written text read aloud or information presented in diverse media and formats, including visually, quantitatively, and orally.
SL.4.2 **Grade 4 students:**	Paraphrase portions of a text read aloud or information presented in diverse media and formats, including visually, quantitatively, and orally.
SL.3.2 **Grade 3 students:**	Determine the main ideas and supporting details of a text read aloud or information presented in diverse media and formats, including visually, quantitatively, and orally.
SL.2.2 **Grade 2 students:**	Recount or describe key ideas or details from a text read aloud or information presented orally or through other media.
SL.1.2 **Grade 1 students:**	Ask and answer questions about key details in a text read aloud or information presented orally or through other media.
SL.K.2 **Kindergarten students:**	Confirm understanding of a text read aloud or information presented orally or through other media by asking and answering questions about key details and requesting clarification if something is not understood.

SL.CCR.3	**CCR Speaking and Listening Anchor Standard 3:** **Evaluate a speaker's point of view, reasoning, and use of evidence and rhetoric.**
SL.11–12.3 **Grade 11–12 students:**	Evaluate a speaker's point of view, reasoning, and use of evidence and rhetoric, assessing the stance, premises, links among ideas, word choice, points of emphasis, and tone used.
SL.9–10.3 **Grade 9–10 students:**	Evaluate a speaker's point of view, reasoning, and use of evidence and rhetoric, identifying any fallacious reasoning or exaggerated or distorted evidence.
SL.8.3 **Grade 8 students:**	Delineate a speaker's argument and specific claims, evaluating the soundness of the reasoning and relevance and sufficiency of the evidence and identifying when irrelevant evidence is introduced.
SL.7.3 **Grade 7 students:**	Delineate a speaker's argument and specific claims, evaluating the soundness of the reasoning and the relevance and sufficiency of the evidence.
SL.6.3 **Grade 6 students:**	Delineate a speaker's argument and specific claims, distinguishing claims that are supported by reasons and evidence from claims that are not.
SL.5.3 **Grade 5 students:**	Summarize the points a speaker makes and explain how each claim is supported by reasons and evidence.
SL.4.3 **Grade 4 students:**	Identify the reasons and evidence a speaker provides to support particular points.
SL.3.3 **Grade 3 students:**	Ask and answer questions about information from a speaker, offering appropriate elaboration and detail.
SL.2.3 **Grade 2 students:**	Ask and answer questions about what a speaker says in order to clarify comprehension, gather additional information, or deepen understanding of a topic or issue.
SL.1.3 **Grade 1 students:**	Ask and answer questions about what a speaker says in order to gather additional information or clarify something that is not understood.
SL.K.3 **Kindergarten students:**	Ask and answer questions in order to seek help, get information, or clarify something that is not understood.

SL.CCR.4	**CCR Speaking and Listening Anchor Standard 4:** **Present information, findings, and supporting evidence such that listeners can follow the line of reasoning and the organization, development, and style are appropriate to task, purpose, and audience.**
SL.11–12.4 **Grade 11–12 students:**	Present information, findings, and supporting evidence, conveying a clear and distinct perspective, such that listeners can follow the line of reasoning, alternative or opposing perspectives are addressed, and the organization, development, substance, and style are appropriate to purpose, audience, and a range of formal and informal tasks.
SL.9–10.4 **Grade 9–10 students:**	Present information, findings, and supporting evidence clearly, concisely, and logically such that listeners can follow the line of reasoning and the organization, development, substance, and style are appropriate to purpose, audience, and task.
SL.8.4 **Grade 8 students:**	Present claims and findings, emphasizing salient points in a focused, coherent manner with relevant evidence, sound valid reasoning, and well-chosen details; use appropriate eye contact, adequate volume, and clear pronunciation.
SL.7.4 **Grade 7 students:**	Present claims and findings, emphasizing salient points in a focused, coherent manner with pertinent descriptions, facts, details, and examples; use appropriate eye contact, adequate volume, and clear pronunciation.
SL.6.4 **Grade 6 students:**	Present claims and findings, sequencing ideas logically and using pertinent descriptions, facts, and details to accentuate main ideas or themes; use appropriate eye contact, adequate volume, and clear pronunciation.
SL.5.4 **Grade 5 students:**	Report on a topic or text or present an opinion, sequencing ideas logically and using appropriate facts and relevant, descriptive details to support main ideas or themes; speak clearly at an understandable pace.
SL.4.4 **Grade 4 students:**	Report on a topic or text, tell a story, or recount an experience in an organized manner, using appropriate facts and relevant, descriptive details to support main ideas or themes; speak clearly at an understandable pace.
SL.3.4 **Grade 3 students:**	Report on a topic or text, tell a story, or recount an experience with appropriate facts and relevant, descriptive details, speaking clearly at an understandable pace.
SL.2.4 **Grade 2 students:**	Tell a story or recount an experience with appropriate facts and relevant, descriptive details, speaking audibly in coherent sentences.
SL.1.4 **Grade 1 students:**	Describe people, places, things, and events with relevant details, expressing ideas and feelings clearly.
SL.K.4 **Kindergarten students:**	Describe familiar people, places, things, and events and, with prompting and support, provide additional detail.

SL.CCR.5	**CCR Speaking and Listening Anchor Standard 5:** **Make strategic use of digital media and visual displays of data to express information and enhance understanding of presentations.**
SL.11–12.5 **Grade 11–12 students:**	Make strategic use of digital media (e.g., textual, graphical, audio, visual, and interactive elements) in presentations to enhance understanding of findings, reasoning, and evidence and to add interest.
SL.9–10.5 **Grade 9–10 students:**	Make strategic use of digital media (e.g., textual, graphical, audio, visual, and interactive elements) in presentations to enhance understanding of findings, reasoning, and evidence and to add interest.
SL.8.5 **Grade 8 students:**	Integrate multimedia and visual displays into presentations to clarify information, strengthen claims and evidence, and add interest.
SL.7.5 **Grade 7 students:**	Include multimedia components and visual displays in presentations to clarify claims and findings and emphasize salient points.
SL.6.5 **Grade 6 students:**	Include multimedia components (e.g., graphics, images, music, sound) and visual displays in presentations to clarify information.
SL.5.5 **Grade 5 students:**	Include multimedia components (e.g., graphics, sound) and visual displays in presentations when appropriate to enhance the development of main ideas or themes.
SL.4.5 **Grade 4 students:**	Add audio recordings and visual displays to presentations when appropriate to enhance the development of main ideas or themes.
SL.3.5 **Grade 3 students:**	Create engaging audio recordings of stories or poems that demonstrate fluid reading at an understandable pace; add visual displays when appropriate to emphasize or enhance certain facts or details.
SL.2.5 **Grade 2 students:**	Create audio recordings of stories or poems; add drawings or other visual displays to stories or recountals of experiences when appropriate to clarify ideas, thoughts, and feelings.
SL.1.5 **Grade 1 students:**	Add drawings or other visual displays to descriptions when appropriate to clarify ideas, thoughts, and feelings.
SL.K.5 **Kindergarten students:**	Add drawings or other visual displays to descriptions as desired to provide additional detail.

SL.CCR.6	**CCR Speaking and Listening Anchor Standard 6:** **Adapt speech to a variety of contexts and communicative tasks, demonstrating command of formal English when indicated or appropriate.**
SL.11–12.6 **Grade 11–12 students:**	Adapt speech to a variety of contexts and tasks, demonstrating a command of formal English when indicated or appropriate. (See grades 11–12 Language standards 1 and 3 for specific expectations.)
SL.9–10.6 **Grade 9–10 students:**	Adapt speech to a variety of contexts and tasks, demonstrating command of formal English when indicated or appropriate. (See grades 9–10 Language standards 1 and 3 for specific expectations.)
SL.8.6 **Grade 8 students:**	Adapt speech to a variety of contexts and tasks, demonstrating command of formal English when indicated or appropriate. (See grade 8 Language standards 1 and 3 for specific expectations.)
SL.7.6 **Grade 7 students:**	Adapt speech to a variety of contexts and tasks, demonstrating command of formal English when indicated or appropriate. (See grade 7 Language standards 1 and 3 for specific expectations.)
SL.6.6 **Grade 6 students:**	Adapt speech to a variety of contexts and tasks, demonstrating command of formal English when indicated or appropriate. (See grade 6 Language standards 1 and 3 for specific expectations.)
SL.5.6 **Grade 5 students:**	Adapt speech to a variety of contexts and tasks, using formal English when appropriate to task and situation. (See grade 5 Language standards 1 and 3 for specific expectations.)
SL.4.6 **Grade 4 students:**	Differentiate between contexts that call for formal English (e.g., presenting ideas) and situations where informal discourse is appropriate (e.g., small-group discussion); use formal English when appropriate to task and situation. (See grade 4 Language standards 1 and 3 for specific expectations.)
SL.3.6 **Grade 3 students:**	Speak in complete sentences when appropriate to task and situation in order to provide requested detail or clarification. (See grade 3 Language standards 1 and 3 for specific expectations.)
SL.2.6 **Grade 2 students:**	Produce complete sentences when appropriate to task and situation in order to provide requested detail or clarification. (See grade 2 Language standards 1 and 3 for specific expectations.)
SL.1.6 **Grade 1 students:**	Produce complete sentences when appropriate to task and situation. (See grade 1 Language standards 1 and 3 for specific expectations.)
SL.K.6 **Kindergarten students:**	Speak audibly and express thoughts, feelings, and ideas clearly

L.CCR.1	**CCR Language Anchor Standard 1:** **Demonstrate command of the conventions of standard English grammar and usage when writing or speaking.**
L.11–12.1 **Grade 11–12 students:**	Demonstrate command of the conventions of standard English grammar and usage when writing or speaking. a. Apply the understanding that usage is a matter of convention, can change over time, and is sometimes contested. b. Resolve issues of complex or contested usage, consulting references (e.g., *Merriam-Webster's Dictionary of English Usage, Garner's Modern American Usage*) as needed.
L.9–10.1 **Grade 9–10 students:**	Demonstrate command of the conventions of standard English grammar and usage when writing or speaking. a. Use parallel structure.* b. Use various types of phrases (noun, verb, adjectival, adverbial, participial, prepositional, absolute) and clauses (independent, dependent; noun, relative, adverbial) to convey specific meanings and add variety and interest to writing or presentations.
L.8.1 **Grade 8 students:**	Demonstrate command of the conventions of standard English grammar and usage when writing or speaking. a. Explain the function of verbals (gerunds, participles, infinitives) in general and their function in particular sentences. b. Form and use verbs in the active and passive voice. c. Form and use verbs in the indicative, imperative, interrogative, conditional, and subjunctive mood. d. Recognize and correct inappropriate shifts in verb voice and mood.*
L.7.1 **Grade 7 students:**	Demonstrate command of the conventions of standard English grammar and usage when writing or speaking. a. Explain the function of phrases and clauses in general and their function in specific sentences. b. Choose among simple, compound, complex, and compound-complex sentences to signal differing relationships among ideas. c. Place phrases and clauses within a sentence, recognizing and correcting misplaced and dangling modifiers.*
L.6.1 **Grade 6 students:**	Demonstrate command of the conventions of standard English grammar and usage when writing or speaking. a. Ensure that pronouns are in the proper case (subjective, objective, possessive). b. Use intensive pronouns (e.g., *myself, ourselves*). c. Recognize and correct inappropriate shifts in pronoun number and person.* d. Recognize and correct vague pronouns (i.e., ones with unclear or ambiguous antecedents).* e. Recognize variations from standard English in their own and others' writing and speaking, and identify and use strategies to improve expression in conventional language.*
L.5.1 **Grade 5 students:**	Demonstrate command of the conventions of standard English grammar and usage when writing or speaking. a. Explain the function of conjunctions, prepositions, and interjections in general and their function in particular sentences. b. Form and use the perfect verb tenses (e.g., *I had walked*; *I have walked*; *I will have walked*). c. Use verb tense to convey various times, sequences, states, and conditions. d. Recognize and correct inappropriate shifts in verb tense.* e. Use correlative conjunctions (e.g., either/or, neither/nor).

*Skills marked with an asterisk (*) in Language standards 1–3 are particularly likely to require continued attention in higher grades as they are applied to increasingly sophisticated writing and speaking.

(Continued on next page)

L.4.1 **Grade 4 students:**	Demonstrate command of the conventions of standard English grammar and usage when writing or speaking. a. Use relative pronouns (*who, whose, whom, which, that*) and relative adverbs (*where, when, why*). b. Form and use the progressive verb tenses (e.g., *I was walking*; *I am walking*; *I will be walking*). c. Use modal auxiliaries (e.g., *can, may, must*) to convey various conditions. d. Order adjectives within sentences according to conventional patterns (e.g., *a small red bag* rather than *a red small bag*). e. Form and use prepositional phrases. f. Produce complete sentences, recognizing and correcting inappropriate fragments and run-ons.* g. Correctly use frequently confused words (e.g., *to, too, two*; *there, their*).*
L.3.1 **Grade 3 students:**	Demonstrate command of the conventions of standard English grammar and usage when writing or speaking. a. Explain the function of nouns, pronouns, verbs, adjectives, and adverbs in general and their functions in particular sentences. b. Form and use regular and irregular plural nouns. c. Use abstract nouns (e.g., *childhood*). d. Form and use regular and irregular verbs. e. Form and use the simple verb tenses (e.g., *I walked*; *I walk*; *I will walk*). f. Ensure subject-verb and pronoun-antecedent agreement.* g. Form and use comparative and superlative adjectives and adverbs, and choose between them depending on what is to be modified. h. Use coordinating and subordinating conjunctions. i. Produce simple, compound, and complex sentences.
L.2.1 **Grade 2 students:**	Demonstrate command of the conventions of standard English grammar and usage when writing or speaking. a. Use collective nouns (e.g., *group*). b. Form and use frequently occurring irregular plural nouns (e.g., *feet, children, teeth, mice, fish*). c. Use reflexive pronouns (e.g., *myself, ourselves*). d. Form and use the past tense of frequently occurring irregular verbs (e.g., *sat, hid, told*). e. Use adjectives and adverbs, and choose between them depending on what is to be modified. f. Produce, expand, and rearrange complete simple and compound sentences (e.g., *The boy watched the movie*; *The little boy watched the movie*; *The action movie was watched by the little boy*).

*Skills marked with an asterisk (*) in Language standards 1–3 are particularly likely to require continued attention in higher grades as they are applied to increasingly sophisticated writing and speaking.

(Continued on next page)

L.1.1 **Grade 1 students:**	Demonstrate command of the conventions of standard English grammar and usage when writing or speaking. a. Print all upper- and lowercase letters. b. Use common, proper, and possessive nouns. c. Use singular and plural nouns with matching verbs in basic sentences (e.g., *He hops*; *We hop*). d. Use personal, possessive, and indefinite pronouns (e.g., *I, me, my*; *they, them, their*; *anyone, everything*). e. Use verbs to convey a sense of past, present, and future (e.g., *Yesterday I walked home*; *Today I walk home*; *Tomorrow I will walk home*). f. Use frequently occurring adjectives. g. Use frequently occurring conjunctions (e.g., *and, but, or, so, because*). h. Use determiners (e.g., articles, demonstratives). i. Use frequently occurring prepositions (e.g., *during, beyond, toward*). j. Produce and expand complete simple and compound declarative, interrogative, imperative, and exclamatory sentences in response to prompts.
L.K.1 **Kindergarten students:**	Demonstrate command of the conventions of standard English grammar and usage when writing or speaking. a. Print many upper- and lowercase letters. b. Use frequently occurring nouns and verbs. c. Form regular plural nouns orally by adding /s/ or /es/ (e.g., *dog, dogs*; *wish, wishes*). d. Understand and use question words (interrogatives) (e.g., *who, what, where, when, why, how*). e. Use the most frequently occurring prepositions (e.g., *to, from, in, out, on, off, for, of, by, with*). f. Produce and expand complete sentences in shared language activities.

* Skills marked with an asterisk (*) in Language standards 1–3 are particularly likely to require continued attention in higher grades as they are applied to increasingly sophisticated writing and speaking.

L.CCR.2	**CCR Language Anchor Standard 2:** **Demonstrate command of the conventions of standard English capitalization, punctuation, and spelling when writing.**
L.11–12.2 **Grade 11–12 students:**	Demonstrate command of the conventions of standard English capitalization, punctuation, and spelling when writing. a. Observe hyphenation conventions. b. Spell correctly.
L.9–10.2 **Grade 9–10 students:**	Demonstrate command of the conventions of standard English capitalization, punctuation, and spelling when writing. a. Use a semicolon (and perhaps a conjunctive adverb) to link two or more closely related independent clauses. b. Use a colon to introduce a list or quotation. c. Spell correctly.
L.8.2 **Grade 8 students:**	Demonstrate command of the conventions of standard English capitalization, punctuation, and spelling when writing. a. Use punctuation (comma, ellipsis, dash) to indicate a pause or break. b. Use an ellipsis to indicate an omission. c. Spell correctly.
L.7.2 **Grade 7 students:**	Demonstrate command of the conventions of standard English capitalization, punctuation, and spelling when writing. a. Use a comma to separate coordinate adjectives (e.g., *It was a fascinating, enjoyable movie* but not *He wore an old[,] green shirt*). b. Spell correctly.
L.6.2 **Grade 6 students:**	Demonstrate command of the conventions of standard English capitalization, punctuation, and spelling when writing. a. Use punctuation (commas, parentheses, dashes) to set off nonrestrictive/parenthetical elements.* b. Spell correctly.
L.5.2 **Grade 5 students:**	Demonstrate command of the conventions of standard English capitalization, punctuation, and spelling when writing. a. Use punctuation to separate items in a series.* b. Use a comma to separate an introductory element from the rest of the sentence. c. Use a comma to set off the words *yes* and *no* (e.g., *Yes, thank you*), to set off a tag question from the rest of the sentence (e.g., *It's true, isn't it?*), and to indicate direct address (e.g., *Is that you, Steve?*). d. Use underlining, quotation marks, or italics to indicate titles of works. e. Spell grade-appropriate words correctly, consulting references as needed.
L.4.2 **Grade 4 students:**	Demonstrate command of the conventions of standard English capitalization, punctuation, and spelling when writing. a. Use correct capitalization. b. Use commas and quotation marks to mark direct speech and quotations from a text. c. Use a comma before a coordinating conjunction in a compound sentence. d. Spell grade-appropriate words correctly, consulting references as needed.

* Skills marked with an asterisk (*) in Language standards 1–3 are particularly likely to require continued attention in higher grades as they are applied to increasingly sophisticated writing and speaking.

(Continued on next page)

L.3.2 **Grade 3 students:**	Demonstrate command of the conventions of standard English capitalization, punctuation, and spelling when writing. a. Capitalize appropriate words in titles. b. Use commas in addresses. c. Use commas and quotation marks in dialogue. d. Form and use possessives. e. Use conventional spelling for high-frequency and other studied words and for adding suffixes to base words (e.g., *sitting, smiled, cries, happiness*). f. Use spelling patterns and generalizations (e.g., word families, position-based spellings, syllable patterns, ending rules, meaningful word parts) in writing words. g. Consult reference materials, including beginning dictionaries, as needed to check and correct spellings.
L.2.2 **Grade 2 students:**	Demonstrate command of the conventions of standard English capitalization, punctuation, and spelling when writing. a. Capitalize holidays, product names, and geographic names. b. Use commas in greetings and closings of letters. c. Use an apostrophe to form contractions and frequently occurring possessives. d. Generalize learned spelling patterns when writing words (e.g., *cage* → *badge*; *boy* → *boil*). e. Consult reference materials, including beginning dictionaries, as needed to check and correct spellings.
L.1.2 **Grade 1 students:**	Demonstrate command of the conventions of standard English capitalization, punctuation, and spelling when writing. a. Capitalize dates and names of people. b. Use end punctuation for sentences. c. Use commas in dates and to separate single words in a series. d. Use conventional spelling for words with common spelling patterns and for frequently occurring irregular words. e. Spell untaught words phonetically, drawing on phonemic awareness and spelling conventions.
L.K.2 **Kindergarten students:**	Demonstrate command of the conventions of standard English capitalization, punctuation, and spelling when writing. a. Capitalize the first word in a sentence and the pronoun *I*. b. Recognize and name end punctuation. c. Write a letter or letters for most consonant and short-vowel sounds (phonemes). d. Spell simple words phonetically, drawing on knowledge of sound-letter relationships.

*Skills marked with an asterisk (*) in Language standards 1–3 are particularly likely to require continued attention in higher grades as they are applied to increasingly sophisticated writing and speaking.

L.CCR.3	**CCR Language Anchor Standard 3:** **Apply knowledge of language to understand how language functions in different contexts, to make effective choices for meaning or style, and to comprehend more fully when reading or listening.**
L.11–12.3 **Grade 11–12 students:**	Apply knowledge of language to understand how language functions in different contexts, to make effective choices for meaning or style, and to comprehend more fully when reading or listening. a. Vary syntax for effect, consulting references (e.g., Tufte's *Artful Sentences*) for guidance as needed; apply an understanding of syntax to the study of complex texts when reading.
L.9–10.3 **Grade 9–10 students:**	Apply knowledge of language to understand how language functions in different contexts, to make effective choices for meaning or style, and to comprehend more fully when reading or listening. a. Write and edit work so that it conforms to the guidelines in a style manual (e.g., *MLA Handbook*, Turabian's *Manual for Writers*) appropriate for the discipline and writing type.
L.8.3 **Grade 8 students:**	Use knowledge of language and its conventions when writing, speaking, reading, or listening. a. Use verbs in the active and passive voice and in the conditional and subjunctive mood to achieve particular effects (e.g., emphasizing the actor or the action; expressing uncertainty; or describing a state contrary to fact).
L.7.3 **Grade 7 students:**	Use knowledge of language and its conventions when writing, speaking, reading, or listening. a. Choose language that expresses ideas precisely and concisely, recognizing and eliminating wordiness and redundancy.*
L.6.3 **Grade 6 students:**	Use knowledge of language and its conventions when writing, speaking, reading, or listening. a. Vary sentence patterns for meaning, reader/listener interest, and style.* b. Maintain consistency in style and tone.*
L.5.3 **Grade 5 students:**	Use knowledge of language and its conventions when writing, speaking, reading, or listening. a. Expand, combine, and reduce sentences for meaning, reader/listener interest, and style. b. Compare and contrast the varieties of English (e.g., dialects, registers) used in stories, dramas, or poems.
L.4.3 **Grade 4 students:**	Use knowledge of language and its conventions when writing, speaking, reading, or listening. a. Choose words and phrases to convey ideas precisely.* b. Choose punctuation for effect.* c. Differentiate between contexts that call for formal English (e.g., presenting ideas) and situations where informal discourse is appropriate (e.g., small-group discussion).
L.3.3 **Grade 3 students:**	Use knowledge of language and its conventions when writing, speaking, reading, or listening. a. Choose words and phrases for effect.* b. Recognize and observe differences between the conventions of spoken and written standard English.
L.2.3 **Grade 2 students:**	Use knowledge of language and its conventions when writing, speaking, reading, or listening. a. Compare formal and informal uses of English.
L.1.3 **Grade 1 students:**	(Begins in grade 2)
L.K.3 **Kindergarten students:**	(Begins in grade 2)

*Skills marked with an asterisk (*) in Language standards 1–3 are particularly likely to require continued attention in higher grades as they are applied to increasingly sophisticated writing and speaking.

L.CCR.4	**CCR Language Anchor Standard 4:** **Determine or clarify the meaning of unknown and multiple-meaning words and phrases by using context clues, analyzing meaningful word parts, and consulting general and specialized reference materials, as appropriate.**
L.11–12.4 **Grade 11–12 students:**	Determine or clarify the meaning of unknown and multiple-meaning words and phrases based on *grades 11–12 reading and content*, choosing flexibly from a range of strategies. a. Use context (e.g., the overall meaning of a sentence, paragraph, or text; a word's position or function in a sentence) as a clue to the meaning of a word or phrase. b. Identify and correctly use patterns of word changes that indicate different meanings or parts of speech (e.g., *conceive, conception, conceivable*). c. Consult general and specialized reference materials (e.g., dictionaries, glossaries, thesauruses), both print and digital, to find the pronunciation of a word or determine or clarify its precise meaning, its part of speech, its etymology, or its standard usage. d. Verify the preliminary determination of the meaning of a word or phrase (e.g., by checking the inferred meaning in context or in a dictionary).
L.9–10.4 **Grade 9–10 students:**	Determine or clarify the meaning of unknown and multiple-meaning words and phrases based on *grades 9–10 reading and content*, choosing flexibly from a range of strategies. a. Use context (e.g., the overall meaning of a sentence, paragraph, or text; a word's position or function in a sentence) as a clue to the meaning of a word or phrase. b. Identify and correctly use patterns of word changes that indicate different meanings or parts of speech (e.g., *analyze, analysis, analytical*; *advocate, advocacy*). c. Consult general and specialized reference materials (e.g., dictionaries, glossaries, thesauruses), both print and digital, to find the pronunciation of a word or determine or clarify its precise meaning, its part of speech, or its etymology. d. Verify the preliminary determination of the meaning of a word or phrase (e.g., by checking the inferred meaning in context or in a dictionary).
L.8.4 **Grade 8 students:**	Determine or clarify the meaning of unknown and multiple-meaning words or phrases based on *grade 8 reading and content*, choosing flexibly from a range of strategies. a. Use context (e.g., the overall meaning of a sentence or paragraph; a word's position or function in a sentence) as a clue to the meaning of a word or phrase. b. Use common, grade-appropriate Greek or Latin affixes and roots as clues to the meaning of a word (e.g., *precede, recede, secede*). c. Consult general and specialized reference materials (e.g., dictionaries, glossaries, thesauruses), both print and digital, to find the pronunciation of a word or determine or clarify its precise meaning or its part of speech. d. Verify the preliminary determination of the meaning of a word or phrase (e.g., by checking the inferred meaning in context or in a dictionary).

(Continued on next page)

L.7.4 **Grade 7 students:**	Determine or clarify the meaning of unknown and multiple-meaning words and phrases based on *grade 7 reading and content*, choosing flexibly from a range of strategies. a. Use context (e.g., the overall meaning of a sentence or paragraph; a word's position or function in a sentence) as a clue to the meaning of a word or phrase. b. Use common, grade-appropriate Greek or Latin affixes and roots as clues to the meaning of a word (e.g., *belligerent, bellicose, rebel*). c. Consult general and specialized reference materials (e.g., dictionaries, glossaries, thesauruses), both print and digital, to find the pronunciation of a word or determine or clarify its precise meaning or its part of speech. d. Verify the preliminary determination of the meaning of a word or phrase (e.g., by checking the inferred meaning in context or in a dictionary).
L.6.4 **Grade 6 students:**	Determine or clarify the meaning of unknown and multiple-meaning words and phrases based on *grade 6 reading and content*, choosing flexibly from a range of strategies. a. Use context (e.g., the overall meaning of a sentence or paragraph; a word's position or function in a sentence) as a clue to the meaning of a word or phrase. b. Use common, grade-appropriate Greek or Latin affixes and roots as clues to the meaning of a word (e.g., *audience, auditory, audible*). c. Consult reference materials (e.g., dictionaries, glossaries, thesauruses), both print and digital, to find the pronunciation of a word or determine or clarify its precise meaning or its part of speech. d. Verify the preliminary determination of the meaning of a word or phrase (e.g., by checking the inferred meaning in context or in a dictionary).
L.5.4 **Grade 5 students:**	Determine or clarify the meaning of unknown and multiple-meaning words and phrases based on *grade 5 reading and content*, choosing flexibly from a range of strategies. a. Use context (e.g., cause/effect relationships and comparisons in text) as a clue to the meaning of a word or phrase. b. Use common, grade-appropriate Greek and Latin affixes and roots as clues to the meaning of a word (e.g., *photograph, photosynthesis*). c. Consult reference materials (e.g., dictionaries, glossaries, thesauruses), both print and digital, to find the pronunciation and determine or clarify the precise meaning of key words and phrases.
L.4.4 **Grade 4 students:**	Determine or clarify the meaning of unknown and multiple-meaning words and phrases based on *grade 4 reading and content*, choosing flexibly from a range of strategies. a. Use context (e.g., definitions, examples, or restatements in text) as a clue to the meaning of a word or phrase. b. Use common, grade-appropriate Greek and Latin affixes and roots as clues to the meaning of a word (e.g., *telegraph, photograph, autograph*). c. Consult reference materials (e.g., dictionaries, glossaries, thesauruses), both print and digital, to find the pronunciation and determine or clarify the precise meaning of key words and phrases.

(Continued on next page)

L.3.4 **Grade 3 students:**	Determine or clarify the meaning of unknown and multiple-meaning words and phrases based on *grade 3 reading and content*, choosing flexibly from a range of strategies. a. Use sentence-level context as a clue to the meaning of a word or phrase. b. Determine the meaning of the new word formed when a known affix is added to a known word (e.g., *agreeable/disagreeable, comfortable/uncomfortable, care/careless, heat/preheat*). c. Use a known root word as a clue to the meaning of an unknown word with the same root (e.g., *company, companion*). d. Use glossaries or beginning dictionaries, both print and digital, to determine or clarify the precise meaning of key words and phrases.
L.2.4 **Grade 2 students:**	Determine or clarify the meaning of unknown and multiple-meaning words and phrases based on *grade 2 reading and content*, choosing flexibly from an array of strategies. a. Use sentence-level context as a clue to the meaning of a word or phrase. b. Determine the meaning of the new word formed when a known prefix is added to a known word (e.g., *happy/unhappy, tell/retell*). c. Use a known root word as a clue to the meaning of an unknown word with the same root (e.g., *addition, additional*). d. Use knowledge of the meaning of individual words to predict the meaning of compound words (e.g., *birdhouse, lighthouse, housefly*; *bookshelf, notebook, bookmark*). e. Use glossaries and beginning dictionaries, both print and digital, to determine or clarify the meaning of words and phrases.
L.1.4 **Grade 1 students:**	Determine or clarify the meaning of unknown and multiple-meaning words and phrases based on *grade 1 reading and content*, choosing flexibly from an array of strategies. a. Use sentence-level context as a clue to the meaning of a word or phrase. b. Use frequently occurring affixes as a clue to the meaning of a word. c. Identify frequently occurring root words (e.g., *look*) and their inflectional forms (e.g., *looks, looked, looking*).
L.K.4 **Kindergarten students:**	Determine or clarify the meaning of unknown and multiple-meaning words and phrases based on *kindergarten reading and content*. a. Identify new meanings for familiar words and apply them accurately (e.g., knowing *duck* is a bird and learning the verb *to duck*). b. Use the most frequently occurring inflections and affixes (e.g., *-ed, -s, re-, un-, pre-, -ful, -less*) as a clue to the meaning of an unknown word.

L.CCR.5	**CCR Language Anchor Standard 5:** **Demonstrate understanding of figurative language, word relationships, and nuances in word meanings.**
L.11–12.5 **Grade 11–12 students:**	Demonstrate understanding of figurative language, word relationships, and nuances in word meanings. a. Interpret figures of speech (e.g., hyperbole, paradox) in context and analyze their role in the text. b. Analyze nuances in the meaning of words with similar denotations.
L.9–10.5 **Grade 9–10 students:**	Demonstrate understanding of figurative language, word relationships, and nuances in word meanings. a. Interpret figures of speech (e.g., euphemism, oxymoron) in context and analyze their role in the text. b. Analyze nuances in the meaning of words with similar denotations.
L.8.5 **Grade 8 students:**	Demonstrate understanding of figurative language, word relationships, and nuances in word meanings. a. Interpret figures of speech (e.g. verbal irony, puns) in context. b. Use the relationship between particular words to better understand each of the words. c. Distinguish among the connotations (associations) of words with similar denotations (definitions) (e.g., *bullheaded, willful, firm, persistent, resolute*).
L.7.5 **Grade 7 students:**	Demonstrate understanding of figurative language, word relationships, and nuances in word meanings. a. Interpret figures of speech (e.g., literary, biblical, and mythological allusions) in context. b. Use the relationship between particular words (e.g., synonym/antonym, analogy) to better understand each of the words. c. Distinguish among the connotations (associations) of words with similar denotations (definitions) (e.g., *refined, respectful, polite, diplomatic, condescending*).
L.6.5 **Grade 6 students:**	Demonstrate understanding of figurative language, word relationships, and nuances in word meanings. a. Interpret figures of speech (e.g., personification) in context. b. Use the relationship between particular words (e.g., cause/effect, part/whole, item/category) to better understand each of the words. c. Distinguish among the connotations (associations) of words with similar denotations (definitions) (e.g., *stingy, scrimping, economical, unwasteful, thrifty*).
L.5.5 **Grade 5 students:**	Demonstrate understanding of figurative language, word relationships, and nuances in word meanings. a. Interpret figurative language, including similes and metaphors, in context. b. Recognize and explain the meaning of common idioms, adages, and proverbs. c. Use the relationship between particular words (e.g., synonyms, antonyms, homographs) to better understand each of the words.

(Continued on next page)

L.4.5 **Grade 4 students:**	Demonstrate understanding of figurative language, word relationships, and nuances in word meanings. a. Explain the meaning of simple similes and metaphors (e.g., *as pretty as a picture*) in context. b. Recognize and explain the meaning of common idioms, adages, and proverbs. c. Demonstrate understanding of words by relating them to their opposites (antonyms) and to words with similar but not identical meanings (synonyms).
L.3.5 **Grade 3 students:**	Demonstrate understanding of word relationships and nuances in word meanings. a. Distinguish the literal and nonliteral meanings of words and phrases in context (e.g., *take steps*). b. Identify real-life connections between words and their use (e.g., describe people who are *friendly* or *helpful*). c. Distinguish shades of meaning among related words that describe states of mind or degrees of certainty (e.g., *knew, believed, suspected, heard, wondered*).
L.2.5 **Grade 2 students:**	Demonstrate understanding of word relationships and nuances in word meanings. a. Identify real-life connections between words and their use (e.g., describe foods that are *spicy* or *juicy*). b. Distinguish shades of meaning among closely related verbs (e.g., *toss, throw, hurl*) and closely related adjectives (e.g., *thin, slender, skinny, scrawny*).
L.1.5 **Grade 1 students:**	With guidance and support from adults, demonstrate understanding of word relationships and nuances in word meanings. a. Sort words into categories (e.g., colors, clothing) to gain a sense of the concepts the categories represent. b. Define words by category and by one or more key attributes (e.g., a *duck* is a bird that swims; a *tiger* is a large cat with stripes). c. Identify real-life connections between words and their use (e.g., note places at home that are *cozy*). d. Distinguish shades of meaning among verbs differing in manner (e.g., *look, peek, glance, stare, glare, scowl*) and adjectives differing in intensity (e.g., *large, gigantic*) by defining or choosing them or by acting out the meanings.
L.K.5 **Kindergarten students:**	With guidance and support from adults, explore word relationships and nuances in word meanings. a. Sort common objects into categories (e.g., shapes, foods) to gain a sense of the concepts the categories represent. b. Demonstrate understanding of frequently occurring verbs and adjectives by relating them to their opposites (antonyms). c. Identify real-life connections between words and their use (e.g., note places at school that are *colorful*). d. Distinguish shades of meaning among verbs describing the same general action (e.g., *walk, march, strut, prance*) by acting out the meanings.

L.CCR.6	**CCR Language Anchor Standard 6:** **Acquire and use accurately grade-appropriate conversational, general academic, and domain-specific words and phrases, including those that signal spatial and temporal relationships (e.g., *After dinner that night we went looking for them*).**
L.11–12.6 **Grade 11–12 students:**	Acquire and use accurately general academic and domain-specific words and phrases sufficient for reading, writing, speaking, and listening at the college and career readiness level; demonstrate independence in gathering vocabulary knowledge when considering a word or phrase important to comprehension or expression.
L.9–10.6 **Grade 9–10 students:**	Acquire and use accurately general academic and domain-specific words and phrases sufficient for reading, writing, speaking, and listening at the college and career readiness level; demonstrate independence in gathering vocabulary knowledge when considering a word or phrase important to comprehension or expression.
L.8.6 **Grade 8 students:**	Acquire and use accurately grade-appropriate general academic and domain-specific words and phrases; gather vocabulary knowledge when considering a word or phrase important to comprehension or expression.
L.7.6 **Grade 7 students:**	Acquire and use accurately grade-appropriate general academic and domain-specific words and phrases; gather vocabulary knowledge when considering a word or phrase important to comprehension or expression.
L.6.6 **Grade 6 students:**	Acquire and use accurately grade-appropriate general academic and domain-specific words and phrases; gather vocabulary knowledge when considering a word or phrase important to comprehension or expression.
L.5.6 **Grade 5 students:**	Acquire and use accurately grade-appropriate general academic and domain-specific words and phrases, including those that signal contrast, addition, and other logical relationships (e.g., *however, although, nevertheless, similarly, moreover, in addition*).
L.4.6 **Grade 4 students:**	Acquire and use accurately grade-appropriate general academic and domain-specific words and phrases, including those that signal precise actions, emotions, or states of being (e.g., *quizzed, whined, stammered*) and that are basic to a particular topic (e.g., *wildlife, conservation*, and *endangered* when discussing animal preservation).
L.3.6 **Grade 3 students:**	Use words and phrases acquired through conversations, reading and being read to, and responding to texts, including using adjectives and adverbs to describe (e.g., *After dinner that night we went looking for them*).
L.2.6 **Grade 2 students:**	Use words and phrases acquired through conversations, reading and being read to, and responding to texts, including using adjectives and adverbs to describe (e.g., *When other kids are happy that makes me happy*).
L.1.6 **Grade 1 students:**	Use words and phrases acquired through conversations, reading and being read to, and responding to texts, including using frequently occurring conjunctions to signal simple relationships (e.g., *because*).
L.K.6 **Kindergarten students:**	Use words and phrases acquired through conversations, reading and being read to, and responding to texts.

R.CCR.1	**CCR Reading Anchor Standard 1:** **Read closely to determine what the text says explicitly and to make logical inferences from it; cite specific textual evidence when writing or speaking to support conclusions drawn from the text.**
RH.11–12.1 Grade 11–12 Students:	Cite specific textual evidence to support analysis of primary and secondary sources, connecting insights gained from specific details to an understanding of the text as a whole.
RH.9–10.1 Grade 9–10 Students:	Cite specific textual evidence to support analysis of primary and secondary sources, attending to such features as the date and origin of the information.
RH.6–8.1 Grade 6–8 Students:	Cite specific textual evidence to support analysis of primary and secondary sources.

R.CCR.2	**CCR Reading Anchor Standard 2:** **Determine central ideas or themes of a text and analyze their development; summarize the key supporting details and ideas.**
RH.11–12.2 Grade 11–12 Students:	Determine the central ideas or information of a primary or secondary source; provide an accurate summary that makes clear the relationships among the key details and ideas.
RH.9–10.2 Grade 9–10 Students:	Determine the central ideas or information of a primary or secondary source; provide an accurate summary of how key events or ideas develop over the course of the text.
RH.6–8.2 Grade 6–8 Students:	Determine the central ideas or information of a primary or secondary source; provide an accurate summary of the source distinct from prior knowledge or opinions.

R.CCR.3	**CCR Reading Anchor Standard 3:** **Analyze how and why individuals, events, or ideas develop and interact over the course of a text.**
RH.11–12.3 **Grade 11–12 students:**	Evaluate various explanations for actions or events and determine which explanation best accords with textual evidence, acknowledging where the text leaves matters uncertain.
RH.9–10.3 **Grade 9–10 students:**	Analyze in detail a series of events described in a text; determine whether earlier events caused later ones or simply preceded them.
RH.6–8.3 **Grade 6–8 students:**	Identify key steps in a text's description of a process related to history/social studies (e.g., how a bill becomes law, how interest rates are raised or lowered).

R.CCR.4	**CCR Reading Anchor Standard 4:** **Interpret words and phrases as they are used in a text, including determining technical, connotative, and figurative meanings, and analyze how specific word choices shape meaning or tone.**
RH.11–12.4 **Grade 11–12 students:**	Determine the meaning of words and phrases as they are used in a text, including analyzing how an author uses and refines the meaning of a key term over the course of a text (e.g., how Madison defines *faction* in *Federalist* No. 10).
RH.9–10.4 **Grade 9–10 students:**	Determine the meaning of words and phrases as they are used in a text, including vocabulary describing political, social, or economic aspects of history/social studies.
RH.6–8.4 **Grade 6–8 students:**	Determine the meaning of words and phrases as they are used in a text, including vocabulary specific to domains related to history/social studies.

R.CCR.5	**CCR Reading Anchor Standard 5:** **Analyze the structure of texts, including how specific sentences, paragraphs, and larger portions of the text (e.g., a section, chapter, scene, or stanza) relate to each other and the whole.**
RH.11–12.5 **Grade 11–12 students:**	Analyze in detail how a complex primary source is structured, including how key sentences, paragraphs, and larger portions of the text contribute to the whole.
RH.9–10.5 **Grade 9–10 students:**	Analyze how a text uses structure to emphasize key points or advance an explanation or analysis.
RH.6–8.5 **Grade 6–8 students:**	Describe how a text presents information (e.g., sequentially, comparatively, causally).

R.CCR.6	**CCR Reading Anchor Standard 6:** **Assess how point of view or purpose shapes the content and style of a text.**
RH.11–12.6 **Grade 11–12 students:**	Evaluate authors' differing points of view on the same historical event or issue by assessing the authors' claims, reasoning, and evidence.
RH.9–10.6 **Grade 9–10 students:**	Compare the point of view of two or more authors for how they treat the same or similar topics, including which details they include and emphasize in their respective accounts.
RH.6–8.6 **Grade 6–8 students:**	Identify aspects of a text that reveal an author's point of view or purpose (e.g., loaded language, inclusion or avoidance of particular facts).

R.CCR.7	**CCR Reading Anchor Standard 7:** **Integrate and evaluate content presented in diverse formats and media, including visually and quantitatively, as well as in words.**
RH.11–12.7 **Grade 11–12 students:**	Integrate and evaluate multiple sources of information presented in diverse formats and media (e.g., visually, quantitatively, as well as in words) in order to address a question or solve a problem.
RH.9–10.7 **Grade 9–10 students:**	Integrate quantitative or technical analysis (e.g., charts, research data) with qualitative analysis in print or digital text.
RH.6–8.7 **Grade 6–8 students:**	Integrate visual information (e.g., in charts, graphs, photographs, videos, or maps) with other information in print and digital texts.

R.CCR.8	**CCR Reading Anchor Standard 8:** **Delineate and evaluate the argument and specific claims in a text, including the validity of the reasoning as well as the relevance and sufficiency of the evidence.**
RH.11–12.8 **Grade 11–12 students:**	Evaluate an author's premises, claims, and evidence by corroborating or challenging them with other information.
RH.9–10.8 **Grade 9–10 students:**	Assess the extent to which the reasoning and evidence in a text support the author's claims.
RH.6–8.8 **Grade 6–8 students:**	Distinguish among fact, opinion, and reasoned judgment in a text.

R.CCR.9	**CCR Reading Anchor Standard 9:** **Analyze how two or more texts address similar themes or topics in order to build knowledge or to compare the approaches the authors take.**
RH.11–12.9 **Grade 11–12 students:**	Integrate information from diverse sources, both primary and secondary, into a coherent understanding of an idea or event, noting discrepancies among sources.
RH.9–10.9 **Grade 9–10 students:**	Compare and contrast treatments of the same topic in several primary and secondary sources.
RH.6–8.9 **Grade 6–8 students:**	Analyze the relationship between a primary and secondary source on the same topic.

R.CCR.10	**CCR Reading Anchor Standard 10:** **Read and comprehend complex literary and informational texts independently and proficiently.**
RH.11–12.10 **Grade 11–12 students:**	By the end of grade 12, read and comprehend history/social studies texts in the grades 11–CCR text complexity band independently and proficiently.
RH.9–10.10 **Grade 9–10 students:**	By the end of grade 10, read and comprehend history/social studies texts in the grades 9–10 text complexity band independently and proficiently.
RH.6–8.10 **Grade 6–8 students:**	By the end of grade 8, read and comprehend history/social studies texts in the grades 6–8 text complexity band independently and proficiently.

R.CCR.1	**CCR Reading Anchor Standard 1:** **Read closely to determine what the text says explicitly and to make logical inferences from it; cite specific textual evidence when writing or speaking to support conclusions drawn from the text.**
RST.11–12.1 **Grade 11–12 students:**	Cite specific textual evidence to support analysis of science and technical texts, attending to important distinctions the author makes and to any gaps or inconsistencies in the account.
RST.9–10.1 **Grade 9–10 students:**	Cite specific textual evidence to support analysis of science and technical texts, attending to the precise details of explanations or descriptions.
RST.6–8.1 **Grade 6–8 students:**	Cite specific textual evidence to support analysis of science and technical texts.

R.CCR.2	**CCR Reading Anchor Standard 2:** **Determine central ideas or themes of a text and analyze their development; summarize the key supporting details and ideas.**
RST.11–12.2 **Grade 11–12 students:**	Determine the central ideas or conclusions of a text; summarize complex concepts, processes, or information presented in a text by paraphrasing them in simpler but still accurate terms.
RST.9–10.2 **Grade 9–10 students:**	Determine the central ideas or conclusions of a text; trace the text's explanation or depiction of a complex process, phenomenon, or concept; provide an accurate summary of the text.
RST.6–8.2 **Grade 6–8 students:**	Determine the central ideas or conclusions of a text; provide an accurate summary of the text distinct from prior knowledge or opinions.

R.CCR.3	**CCR Reading Anchor Standard 3:** **Analyze how and why individuals, events, or ideas develop and interact over the course of a text.**
RST.11–12.3 **Grade 11–12 students:**	Follow precisely a complex multistep procedure when carrying out experiments, taking measurements, or performing technical tasks; analyze the specific results based on explanations in the text.
RST.9–10.3 **Grade 9–10 students:**	Follow precisely a complex multistep procedure when carrying out experiments, taking measurements, or performing technical tasks, attending to special cases or exceptions defined in the text.
RST.6–8.3 **Grade 6–8 students:**	Follow precisely a multistep procedure when carrying out experiments, taking measurements, or performing technical tasks.

R.CCR.4	**CCR Reading Anchor Standard 4:** **Interpret words and phrases as they are used in a text, including determining technical, connotative, and figurative meanings, and analyze how specific word choices shape meaning or tone.**
RST.11–12.4 **Grade 11–12 students:**	Determine the meaning of symbols, key terms, and other domain-specific words and phrases as they are used in a specific scientific or technical context relevant to *grades 11–12 texts and topics*.
RST.9–10.4 **Grade 9–10 students:**	Determine the meaning of symbols, key terms, and other domain-specific words and phrases as they are used in a specific scientific or technical context relevant to *grades 9–10 texts and topics*.
RST.6–8.4 **Grade 6–8 students:**	Determine the meaning of symbols, key terms, and other domain-specific words and phrases as they are used in a specific scientific or technical context relevant to *grades 6–8 texts and topics*.

R.CCR.5	**CCR Reading Anchor Standard 5:** **Analyze the structure of texts, including how specific sentences, paragraphs, and larger portions of the text (e.g., a section, chapter, scene, or stanza) relate to each other and the whole.**
RST.11–12.5 **Grade 11–12 students:**	Analyze how the text structures information or ideas into categories or hierarchies, demonstrating understanding of the information or ideas.
RST.9–10.5 **Grade 9–10 students:**	Analyze the structure of the relationships among concepts in a text, including relationships among key terms (e.g., *force, friction, reaction force, energy*).
RST.6–8.5 **Grade 6–8 students:**	Analyze the structure an author uses to organize a text, including how the major sections contribute to the whole and to an understanding of the topic.

R.CCR.6	**CCR Reading Anchor Standard 6:** **Assess how point of view or purpose shapes the content and style of a text.**
RST.11–12.6 **Grade 11–12 students:**	Analyze the author's purpose in providing an explanation, describing a procedure, or discussing an experiment in a text, identifying important issues that remain unresolved.
RST.9–10.6 **Grade 9–10 students:**	Analyze the author's purpose in providing an explanation, describing a procedure, or discussing an experiment in a text, defining the question the author seeks to address.
RST.6–8.6 **Grade 6–8 students:**	Analyze the author's purpose in providing an explanation, describing a procedure, or discussing an experiment in a text.

R.CCR.7	**CCR Reading Anchor Standard 7:** **Integrate and evaluate content presented in diverse formats and media, including visually and quantitatively, as well as in words.**
RST.11–12.7 **Grade 11–12 students:**	Integrate and evaluate multiple sources of information presented in diverse formats and media (e.g., quantitative data, video, multimedia) in order to address a question or solve a problem.
RST.9–10.7 **Grade 9–10 students:**	Translate quantitative or technical information expressed in words in a text into visual form (e.g., a table or chart) and translate information expressed visually or mathematically (e.g., in an equation) into words.
RST.6–8.7 **Grade 6–8 students:**	Integrate quantitative or technical information expressed in words in a text with a version of that information expressed visually (e.g., in a flowchart, diagram, model, graph, or table).

R.CCR.8	**CCR Reading Anchor Standard 8:** **Delineate and evaluate the argument and specific claims in a text, including the validity of the reasoning as well as the relevance and sufficiency of the evidence.**
RST.11–12.8 **Grade 11–12 students:**	Evaluate the hypotheses, data, analysis, and conclusions in a science or technical text, verifying the data when possible and corroborating or challenging conclusions with other sources of information.
RST.9–10.8 **Grade 9–10 students:**	Assess the extent to which the reasoning and evidence in a text support the author's claim or a recommendation for solving a scientific or technical problem.
RST.6–8.8 **Grade 6–8 students:**	Distinguish among facts, reasoned judgment based on research findings, and speculation in a text.

R.CCR.9	**CCR Reading Anchor Standard 9:** **Analyze how two or more texts address similar themes or topics in order to build knowledge or to compare the approaches the authors take.**
RST.11–12.9 **Grade 11–12 students:**	Synthesize information from a range of sources (e.g., texts, experiments, simulations) into a coherent understanding of a process, phenomenon, or concept, resolving conflicting information when possible.
RST.9–10.9 **Grade 9–10 students:**	Compare and contrast findings presented in a text to those from other sources (including their own experiments), noting when the findings support or contradict previous explanations or accounts.
RST.6–8.9 **Grade 6–8 students:**	Compare and contrast the information gained from experiments, simulations, video, or multimedia sources with that gained from reading a text on the same topic.

R.CCR.10	**CCR Reading Anchor Standard 10:** **Read and comprehend complex literary and informational texts independently and proficiently.**
RST.11–12.10 **Grade 11–12 students:**	By the end of grade 12, read and comprehend science/technical texts in the grades 11–CCR text complexity band independently and proficiently.
RST.9–10.10 **Grade 9–10 students:**	By the end of grade 10, read and comprehend science/technical texts in the grades 9–10 text complexity band independently and proficiently.
RST.6–8.10 **Grade 6–8 students:**	By the end of grade 8, read and comprehend science/technical texts in the grades 6–8 text complexity band independently and proficiently.

W.CCR.1	**CCR Writing Anchor Standard 1:** **Write arguments to support claims in an analysis of substantive topics or texts using valid reasoning and relevant and sufficient evidence.**
WHST.11–12.1 **Grade 11–12 students:**	Write arguments focused on *discipline-specific content.* a. Introduce precise, knowledgeable claim(s), establish the significance of the claim(s), distinguish the claim(s) from alternate or opposing claims, and create an organization that logically sequences the claim(s), counterclaims, reasons, and evidence. b. Develop claim(s) and counterclaims fairly and thoroughly, supplying the most relevant data and evidence for each while pointing out the strengths and limitations of both claim(s) and counterclaims in a discipline-appropriate form that anticipates the audience's knowledge level, concerns, values, and possible biases. c. Use words, phrases, and clauses as well as varied syntax to link the major sections of the text, create cohesion, and clarify the relationships between claim(s) and reasons, between reasons and evidence, and between claim(s) and counterclaims. d. Establish and maintain a formal style and objective tone while attending to the norms and conventions of the discipline in which they are writing. e. Provide a concluding statement or section that follows from or supports the argument presented.
WHST.9–10.1 **Grade 9–10 students:**	Write arguments focused on *discipline-specific content.* a. Introduce precise claim(s), distinguish the claim(s) from alternate or opposing claims, and create an organization that establishes clear relationships among the claim(s), counterclaims, reasons, and evidence. b. Develop claim(s) and counterclaims fairly, supplying data and evidence for each while pointing out the strengths and limitations of both claim(s) and counterclaims in a discipline-appropriate form and in a manner that anticipates the audience's knowledge level and concerns. c. Use words, phrases, and clauses to link the major sections of the text, create cohesion, and clarify the relationships between claim(s) and reasons, between reasons and evidence, and between claim(s) and counterclaims. d. Establish and maintain a formal style and objective tone while attending to the norms and conventions of the discipline in which they are writing. e. Provide a concluding statement or section that follows from or supports the argument presented.
WHST.6–8.1 **Grade 6–8 students:**	Write arguments focused on *discipline-specific content.* a. Introduce claim(s) about a topic or issue, acknowledge and distinguish the claim(s) from alternate or opposing claims, and organize the reasons and evidence logically. b. Support claim(s) with logical reasoning and relevant, accurate data and evidence that demonstrate an understanding of the topic or text, using credible sources. c. Use words, phrases, and clauses to create cohesion and clarify the relationships among claim(s), counterclaims, reasons, and evidence. d. Establish and maintain a formal style. e. Provide a concluding statement or section that follows from and supports the argument presented.

W.CCR.2	**CCR Writing Anchor Standard 2:** **Write informative/explanatory texts to examine and convey complex ideas and information clearly and accurately through the effective selection, organization, and analysis of content.**
WHST.11–12.2 **Grade 11–12 students:**	Write informative/explanatory texts, including the narration of historical events, scientific procedures/ experiments, or technical processes. a. Introduce a topic and organize complex ideas, concepts, and information so that each new element builds on that which precedes it to create a unified whole; include formatting (e.g., headings), graphics (e.g., figures, tables), and multimedia when useful to aiding comprehension. b. Develop the topic thoroughly by selecting the most significant and relevant facts, extended definitions, concrete details, quotations, or other information and examples appropriate to the audience's knowledge of the topic. c. Use varied transitions and sentence structures to link the major sections of the text, create cohesion, and clarify the relationships among complex ideas and concepts. d. Use precise language, domain-specific vocabulary and techniques such as metaphor, simile, and analogy to manage the complexity of the topic; convey a knowledgeable stance in a style that responds to the discipline and context as well as to the expertise of likely readers. e. Provide a concluding statement or section that follows from and supports the information or explanation provided (e.g., articulating implications or the significance of the topic).
WHST.9–10.2 **Grade 9–10 students:**	Write informative/explanatory texts, including the narration of historical events, scientific procedures/ experiments, or technical processes. a. Introduce a topic and organize ideas, concepts, and information to make important connections and distinctions; include formatting (e.g., headings), graphics (e.g., figures, tables), and multimedia when useful to aiding comprehension. b. Develop the topic with well-chosen, relevant, and sufficient facts, extended definitions, concrete details, quotations, or other information and examples appropriate to the audience's knowledge of the topic. c. Use varied transitions and sentence structures to link the major sections of the text, create cohesion, and clarify the relationships among ideas and concepts. d. Use precise language and domain-specific vocabulary to manage the complexity of the topic and convey a style appropriate to the discipline and context as well as to the expertise of likely readers. e. Establish and maintain a formal style and objective tone while attending to the norms and conventions of the discipline in which they are writing. f. Provide a concluding statement or section that follows from and supports the information or explanation presented (e.g., articulating implications or the significance of the topic).
WHST.6–8.2 **Grade 6–8 students:**	Write informative/explanatory texts, including the narration of historical events, scientific procedures/ experiments, or technical processes. a. Introduce a topic clearly, previewing what is to follow; organize ideas, concepts, and information into broader categories as appropriate to achieving purpose; include formatting (e.g., headings), graphics (e.g., charts, tables), and multimedia when useful to aiding comprehension. b. Develop the topic with relevant, well-chosen facts, definitions, concrete details, quotations, or other information and examples. c. Use appropriate and varied transitions to create cohesion and clarify the relationships among ideas and concepts. d. Use precise language and domain-specific vocabulary to inform about or explain the topic. e. Establish and maintain a formal style and objective tone. f. Provide a concluding statement or section that follows from and supports the information or explanation presented.

W.CCR.3	**CCR Writing Anchor Standard 3:** **Write narratives to develop real or imagined experiences or events using effective technique, well-chosen details, and well-structured event sequences.**
WHST.11–12.3 **Grade 11–12 students:**	(See note; not applicable as a separate requirement)
WHST.9–10.3 **Grade 9–10 students:**	(See note; not applicable as a separate requirement)
WHST.6–8.3 **Grade 6–8 students:**	(See note; not applicable as a separate requirement)

Note: Students' narrative skills continue to grow in these grades. The standards require that students be able to incorporate narrative elements effectively into arguments and informative/explanatory texts. In history/social studies, students must be able to incorporate narrative accounts into their analyses of individuals or events of historical import. In science and technical subjects, students must be able to write precise enough descriptions of the step-by-step procedures they use in their investigations or technical work that others can replicate them and (possibly) reach the same results.

W.CCR.4	**CCR Writing Anchor Standard 4:** **Produce clear and coherent writing in which the development, organization, and style are appropriate to task, purpose, and audience.**
WHST.11–12.4 **Grade 11–12 students:**	Produce clear and coherent writing in which the development, organization, and style are appropriate to task, purpose, and audience.
WHST.9–10.4 **Grade 9–10 students:**	Produce clear and coherent writing in which the development, organization, and style are appropriate to task, purpose, and audience.
WHST.6–8.4 **Grade 6–8 students:**	Produce clear and coherent writing in which the development, organization, and style are appropriate to task, purpose, and audience.

W.CCR.5	**CCR Writing Anchor Standard 5:** **Develop and strengthen writing as needed by planning, revising, editing, rewriting, or trying a new approach.**
WHST.11–12.5 **Grade 11–12 students:**	Develop and strengthen writing as needed by planning, revising, editing, rewriting, or trying a new approach, focusing on addressing what is most significant for a specific purpose and audience.
WHST.9–10.5 **Grade 9–10 students:**	Develop and strengthen writing as needed by planning, revising, editing, rewriting, or trying a new approach, focusing on addressing what is most significant for a specific purpose and audience.
WHST.6–8.5 **Grade 6–8 students:**	With some guidance and support from peers and adults, develop and strengthen writing as needed by planning, revising, editing, rewriting, or trying a new approach, focusing on how well purpose and audience have been addressed.

W.CCR.6	**CCR Writing Anchor Standard 6:** **Use technology, including the Internet, to produce and publish writing and to interact and collaborate with others.**
WHST.11–12.6 **Grade 11–12 students:**	Use technology, including the Internet, to produce, publish, and update individual or shared writing products in response to ongoing feedback, including new arguments or information.
WHST.9–10.6 **Grade 9–10 students:**	Use technology, including the Internet, to produce, publish, and update individual or shared writing products, taking advantage of technology's capacity to link to other information and to display information flexibly and dynamically.
WHST.6–8.6 **Grade 6–8 students:**	Use technology, including the Internet, to produce and publish writing and present the relationships between information and ideas clearly and efficiently

W.CCR.7	**CCR Writing Anchor Standard 7:** **Conduct short as well as more sustained research projects based on focused questions, demonstrating understanding of the subject under investigation.**
WHST.11–12.7 **Grade 11–12 students:**	Conduct short as well as more sustained research projects to answer a question (including a self-generated question) or solve a problem; narrow or broaden the inquiry when appropriate; synthesize multiple sources on the subject, demonstrating understanding of the subject under investigation.
WHST.9–10.7 **Grade 9–10 students:**	Conduct short as well as more sustained research projects to answer a question (including a self-generated question) or solve a problem; narrow or broaden the inquiry when appropriate; synthesize multiple sources on the subject, demonstrating understanding of the subject under investigation.
WHST.6–8.7 **Grade 6–8 students:**	Conduct short research projects to answer a question (including a self-generated question), drawing on several sources and generating additional related, focused questions that allow for multiple avenues of exploration.

W.CCR.8	**CCR Writing Anchor Standard 8:** **Gather relevant information from multiple print and digital sources, assess the credibility and accuracy of each source, and integrate the information while avoiding plagiarism.**
WHST.11–12.8 **Grade 11–12 students:**	Gather relevant information from multiple authoritative print and digital sources, using advanced searches effectively; assess the strengths and limitations of each source in terms of the specific task, purpose, and audience; integrate information into the text selectively to maintain the flow of ideas, avoiding plagiarism and overreliance on any one source and following a standard format for citation.
WHST.9–10.8 **Grade 9–10 students:**	Gather relevant information from multiple authoritative print and digital sources, using advanced searches effectively; assess the usefulness of each source in answering the research question; integrate information into the text selectively to maintain the flow of ideas, avoiding plagiarism and following a standard format for citation.
WHST.6–8.8 **Grade 6–8 students:**	Gather relevant information from multiple print and digital sources, using search terms effectively; assess the credibility and accuracy of each source; and quote or paraphrase the data and conclusions of others while avoiding plagiarism and following a standard format for citation.

W.CCR.9	**CCR Writing Anchor Standard 9:** **Draw evidence from literary or informational texts to support analysis, reflection, and research.**
WHST.11–12.9 **Grade 11–12 students:**	Draw evidence from informational texts to support analysis, reflection, and research.
WHST.9–10.9 **Grade 9–10 students:**	Draw evidence from informational texts to support analysis, reflection, and research.
WHST.6–8.9 **Grade 6–8 students:**	Draw evidence from informational texts to support analysis, reflection, and research.

W.CCR.10	**CCR Writing Anchor Standard 10:** **Write routinely over extended time frames (time for research, reflection, and revision) and shorter time frames (a single setting or a day or two) for a range of tasks, purposes, and audiences.**
WHST.11–12.10 **Grade 11–12 students:**	Write routinely over extended time frames (time for reflection and revision) and shorter time frames (a single sitting or a day or two) for a range of discipline-specific tasks, purposes, and audiences.
WHST.9–10.10 **Grade 9–10 students:**	Write routinely over extended time frames (time for reflection and revision) and shorter time frames (a single sitting or a day or two) for a range of discipline-specific tasks, purposes, and audiences.
WHST.6–8.10 **Grade 6–8 students:**	Write routinely over extended time frames (time for reflection and revision) and shorter time frames (a single sitting or a day or two) for a range of discipline-specific tasks, purposes, and audiences.

Index